GLOBAL
SOUTH
ASIA

Padma Kaimal
K. Sivaramakrishnan
Anand A. Yang
SERIES EDITORS

High-Tech Housewives

Indian IT Workers, Gendered Labor, and Transmigration

AMY BHATT

UNIVERSITY OF WASHINGTON PRESS

Seattle

Portions of chapter 4 were published previously as Amy Bhatt, Madhavi Murty, and Priti Ramamurthy, "Hegemonic Developments: The New Indian Middle Class, Gendered Subalterns, and Diasporic Returnees in the Event of Neoliberalism," *Signs: A Journal of Women in Culture and Society* 36, no. 1 (2010): 127–52, www.journals.uchicago.edu/journals/signs; and Amy Bhatt, "Resident 'Non-resident' Indians: Gender, Labor and the Return to India," in *Transnational Migration to Asia: The Question of Return,* ed. Michiel Baas, 55–72 (Amsterdam: Amsterdam University Press, 2015), reprinted with permission of Amsterdam University Press.

University of Washington Press
www.washington.edu/uwpress

Library of Congress Cataloging-in-Publication Data on file

ISBN 978-0-295-74354-7 (Hardcover)
ISBN 978-0-295-74355-4 (Paperback)
ISBN 978-0-295-74356-1 (Ebook)

To my favorites, Kevin Bromer and Anika Bromer

To my eternal supporters, Ranjana and Pradip Bhatt

Contents

Acknowledgments

When I first moved to Seattle in 2004, I became involved with Chaya Seattle (now API Chaya), an advocacy organization aimed at ending family-based violence and creating community among South Asian women in the region. As the tech industries in the Pacific Northwest exploded, so too did the South Asian population. In particular, the arrival of new temporary workers from India, along with women coming on family reunification visas, were a vital part of this IT boom. Some of these women came to the attention of Chaya staff as they faced isolation and sometimes violence in their home lives. Although not all H-4 holders experienced abuse, many were stuck in remote suburbs and were largely absent from the larger South Asian community institutions in the area. I began volunteering on a small project aimed at reaching out to those women, which ultimately brought me into contact with some of the participants of this study. While the issue of H-4 vulnerability was still my foremost concern, I grew interested in a larger question: what role does the family play in sustaining and promoting transnational migration and how do women fare as a result of that movement?

To answer that question and others, I tapped into a rich network of Indian information technology (IT) workers, thanks to introductions from colleagues such as Tapoja Chaudhuri, Sharmistha Ghosh, and Bill Nordwall. Through those introductions, I met nearly a hundred current and former H-1B and H-4 visa holders who were willing to share their stories and experiences with me. It is their stories that drive this study; they are the embodied subjects of transnationalism whose labor is a major force in the IT industry globally. While my focus was predominantly on the Pacific Northwest, it quickly became clear to me that their stories did not end with their arrival to the United States. Instead, their initial migration on the H-1B or H-4 visa was a stepping-stone along a circuitous journey that often included moving back and forth between India and the United States. In order to trace the consequences of these repeated migrations, I traveled to Bangalore and Hyderabad, India, to visit some of the former H-1B and H-4 visa holders I had met in Seattle and to meet others like them who had moved back after living in the United States for long stretches. Even though living in India was not always their final goal, the "R2I" (return to India) proved to be an important key to understanding how families were practicing a form of transnationalism that was tied to their immediate and future aspirations, but also constrained by the global job market, immigration restrictions in the United States, and family concerns. My time in India was considerably aided by Madhu Chawla, my gracious hostess in Delhi; the Murty family, who treated me like a family member during my time in Hyderabad; and Carol Upadhya and the National Institute of Advanced Studies in Bangalore. Special thanks goes to the Bhatt and Pancholi families in Mumbai and Pune, who not only helped me navigate the transportation, hotel, and visa logistics required of ethnographic fieldwork abroad, but also taught me the true value of transnational family life.

This book and the years of research it encompasses would not have been possible without the many sources of financial and intellectual support that I received along the way. At the University of Washington, I am thankful for the resources provided by the Department of Gender, Women and Sexuality Studies, a UW presidential writing fellowship, the Chester Fritz Fellowship for International Study and Exchange, five Foreign Language and Area Studies Fellowships from the South Asia Center at the Jackson School of International Studies, the Society of Scholars Fellowship at the Simpson Center for the Humanities, and the Project in Interdisciplinary Pedagogy Fellowship from UW Bothell. The mentorship of Priti Ramamurthy, David Allen, Chandan Reddy, Sareeta Amrute, Judith Howard, Amanda Swarr, Shirley Yee, Tani Barlow, Rachel Chapman, Michael Shapiro, Heidi Pauwels, Nikhil Singh, Bruce Burgett, Julie Shayne, and S. Charusheela pushed and refined my thinking and writing. The comrades-in-writing and thinking that I met during my time in Seattle provided inspiration and much-needed company, laughs, and happy hours during the hard, lonely years of work: Thank you, Michelle McGowen, Teresa Mares, Madhavi Murthy, Juned Shaikh, Nalini Iyer, Sarah Burnett, Abel Kerevel, Matt Bunt, Dave Citrin, Uma Rao, Gita Mehrotra, and Shiwani Srivastava (who, in particular, taught me a great deal about finding my voice and writing for a broader audience).

I have also had the good fortune to be surrounded by supportive colleagues at the University of Maryland, Baltimore County, who have helped me to refine this project. The resources from a Summer Faculty Fellowship from the College of Arts, Humanities and Social Sciences and a Summer Faculty Research Fellowship and a Scholarly Completion Fund Award from the Dresher Center for the Humanities allowed me to expand my data collection in India and Seattle and to provide a longitudinal view of Indian IT transmigration. I have benefited greatly from the rich intellectual community at UMBC, where I have shared and workshopped my writing among colleagues in Gender and Women's Studies, Asian Studies, Language Literacy and Culture, Media and Communication Studies, and American Studies. In particular, I thank Carole McCann, Scott Casper, Constantine Vaporis, Anna Shields, Theo Gonzalves, Jason Loviglio, Fan Yang, Rebecca Adelman, Susan McDonough, Jessica Berman, Dawn Biehler, Nicole King, Tamara Bhalla, Viviana McManus, Mejdulene Shomali, and Christine Mair. I also thank Elle Trusz, Kimberley Hardaway, and Elle Everhart for the outstanding administrative support they provided, and the graduate and undergraduate assistants with whom I have had the pleasure of working: Richa Sabu, Saba Ghulamali, Emerald Christopher, and most importantly, Sherella Cupid, whose responsiveness and attention to detail helped me better my writing and teaching. Kate Drabinski and Christine Mallinson deserve special recognition for acting as vital sounding boards and because they are simply awesome and brilliant. Baltimore would not be home without you.

My work has also benefited from critical feedback from the Yale Modern South Asia Workshop, the University of Maryland, College Park Transnational South Asia Colloquium, the Dresher Center for the Humanities Brownbag Series, and the American Institute for Indian Studies Workshop at the Conference on South Asia at Madison, Wisconsin.

This book is also the product of the hard work of the excellent team at the University of Washington Press. I have had the privilege of working with the smart and exceedingly patient Larin McLaughlin, editor-in-chief. I thank Mike Baccam, Julie Van Pelt, Rachael Levay, Sue Carter, Eileen Allen, and other members of press and production team, as well as Ranjit Arab, who first encouraged me to submit this manuscript. I would also like to express my gratitude to the esteemed editors of the Global South Asia series: Padma Kaimal, Kalyanakrishnan (Shivi) Sivaramakrishnan, and Anand A. Yang. I am honored to have my book included among such excellent examples of scholarship related to contemporary and historic South Asian issues. Lastly, the book has been much improved thanks to the careful reading of two anonymous readers. I am humbled by their thoughtful feedback and support for the project.

On a personal note, I am grateful for the unflagging support of my family: my father, Pradip Bhatt, whose migration set in motion my own trajectory, and who is missed every day; my mother, Ranjana Bhatt, who was once a bride traveling across oceans to start a new life in the United States, and who is the backbone of our family; Rekha Bhatt, Mike Bales, and my sweet-est little niece, Dahlia, whose residence in Seattle means that I always will have a home in the Pacific Northwest; my brother, Ajay Bhatt; and the Bromer-Frey family—Denise, Craig, Elise, Chris, and Alex—whose love and support I have enjoyed for more than twenty years. I must also thank my "chosen family," who are always with me, no matter the distance: Sarah Childers, Phelps Feeley, Neha Chawla, Nishima Chudasama, Megan McCann, Tim Jones, Greg Reaume, Seema and Saul Clifasefi, April Wilkin-son, Ryan Pederson, Connie Okada, Bernard Kelley, and Jared and Amy Mass. I am truly lucky to have you as part of my community.

At its core, this book is about how the social reproductive work of the household makes paid labor possible. I cannot thank the following people enough for the ways in which their caring work (both remunerated and gifted) has allowed me to pursue my own aspirations: Zanele Nxumalo, for her loving care of my daughter during her early life; the teachers at the Baltimore Montessori School who tend to her each day; Ellen Krouss, Chris Leonard, Josh Birenbaum, and the other families in Baltimore who have provided much-appreciated playdates and other breaks from parenting so that I might write uninterrupted. Finally, my work could not happen with-out the care I receive daily from the loves of my life: Kevin Bromer, whose devotion to the life we have built and belief in my abilities keep me focused and forward moving, and Anika Bromer, who pushes me to work harder and faster, so that I might spend as much time as possible with her.

High-Tech Housewives

Gender, Transmigration, and Citizenship

SITTING AT A PICNIC TABLE AT CROSSROADS PARK IN BELLEVUE, Washington, Sarika and I blend into the multi-ethnic crowd while enjoying the last vestiges of the Seattle summer. We are meeting outside with the hope of catching some of the late afternoon sunshine. The park is thirteen miles from Seattle's downtown waterfront, two and half miles from Microsoft's headquarters, and just across the street from the Crossroads Mall shopping complex. A native of Mumbai and now a local resident, Sarika relishes the uncharacteristic warmth of the day. It is a stark contrast to her arrival during the gray and damp Seattle winter six years earlier, after her wedding in February 2004: "I thought it was pretty grim, when I first came. No sun, nothing. Just rain, rain, rain all the time," Sarika laments.

Sarika met her husband, Dilip, while they attended college in Mumbai. After graduation, she began working for a small information technology (IT) company, where she put her newly earned degree in computer engineering to the test. Dilip had come on a student visa to the United States, hoping to complete a master's degree in computer science. Upon finishing his degree, he was hired by a contracting company on a temporary H-1B guest worker visa. The company then placed him on a two-year project at Microsoft, and Dilip settled into a shared apartment with three other Indian men. Soon after, Dilip proposed to Sarika, who was still in India and establishing herself as a software developer. Over the winter holidays, Dilip reunited with Sarika for two weeks of celebrations in their home city. As soon as the couple completed their nuptials and the requisite visits to their relatives' homes, they set about the task of filing the mountain of paperwork that would allow Sarika to come to the US on an H-4 family reunification visa. A month later, the application was approved, and Sarika boarded a flight to join Dilip in Seattle.

Prior to attending college, Sarika had not considered moving abroad, but once she selected engineering as a major, she began to recognize the inevitability of migration: "It's what we all do. If you are really serious and want to get good, you must go. It's all about America." Sarika was not unlike many other young IT professionals in India who assume that time abroad is the best way to develop new skills and work experience. As Sarika watched Dilip progress in his career, she hoped that after getting married, she would be able to find work in the US. Even though she knew the H-4 visa had work restrictions and she was apprehensive about moving so far from away her personal and professional networks, Sarika had hoped that she would quickly find a job that would sponsor her own H-1B visa. At worst, she anticipated that she could apply for work authorization while going through the green card process with her husband. She was sure that moving would allow her to advance her career in the heart of the software industry, alongside Dilip.

But, once Sarika arrived, things were quite different. As a dependent spouse on an H-4 visa, she found that IT employers were reluctant to sponsor her for an H-1B, even though she was an experienced developer. Initially regretting her decision, Sarika recalled, "You start thinking that you've made a big mistake and it's all a big mistake. For those girls whose husbands are not supportive, it can get really, really bad." Although Sarika was well qualified to work as a programmer, her H-4 visa barred her from pursuing formal job opportunities. Consequently, instead of jetting off to work in one of the glittering office parks that dot the western Washington landscape, Sarika is now a suburban housewife whose day revolves around chores and shopping.

Since arriving in Seattle, Sarika has been in career purgatory for more than half a decade. Dilip has applied for permanent residency, but delays in processing mean that the couple will likely have to wait several more years before their application is approved. For Sarika, this means she will continue to wait for work authorization. In the meantime, Dilip hopes that his contracting agency will renew his assignment as they simultaneously move through the immigration process. Rather than settle into a comfortable life in the US, as she once hoped, Sarika is readying herself for another long period of uncertainty. Quite possibly, if Dilip loses his job or his H-1B is not renewed, they will be forced to leave the country altogether. And yet, as a couple, they have decided to endure their liminal status in the hope that they will someday hold the coveted "green card"—or even more valuable, US citizenship. Stretching out her legs, Sarika turns in the direction of the mall, her eyes lingering on a Microsoft employee shuttle, which has stopped at the cross light. "This was not what I expected," she sighs.

Sarika and Dilip's story is a common one among their peers. They are part of a growing class of technically trained Indians who do not seek settlement abroad, necessarily, but who tend to view migration as an instrumental factor for advancing their professional and personal lives.[1] At first glance, it seems as though Sarika and Dilip's decision was financially motivated, since he was the first to secure a foothold in a US-based technology company. Sarika moved as a trailing, or "dependent," spouse, and her choice could be read as a calculated decision that prioritized her partner's earning potential in the US over her own career. The consequences and reasons for her migration, however, are more complex: Sarika's own career aspirations, along with cultural and familial expectations, shaped her educational trajectory, as well as her decision to marry and immigrate with Dilip. While she maintains hope that temporary migration will lead to more permanent national affiliations that will give her better social and economic opportunities in the future, for now she has assumed a caregiving role that has allowed Dilip to focus on and progress in his career.

This book is an ethnographic examination of the limits, opportunities, experiences, and politics that characterize the lives of transnational migrants such as Sarika and Dilip. It explores how an alphabet soup of visas, immigration policies, and citizenship requirements shape their life cycle, intimate decision-making, and long-term planning as they move between their home and host countries. It also emphasizes the role that the unpaid and undervalued labor of women plays in creating the conditions that allow knowledge workers to circulate between global technology centers.[2] While migration literature related to middle-class or professional migrants overwhelmingly focuses on the experiences of men as workers, women are vital to migration and settlement as educated and trained workers, and more commonly, as wives.[3] Today, women represent nearly half of all global migrants. Often moving as part of family reunification programs, women make up 52 percent of the Global North's migrant population.[4] If we do not seriously consider the work that women do in both formal and informal economies, our understanding of professional forms of transmigration is woefully incomplete.

It is no coincidence that Sarika and Dilip are from India; the circulation of workers between India and the US has a long history that dates back to the turn of the nineteenth century.[5] Several excellent historical accounts have detailed the multiple pathways that transported Indians abroad during the pre- and postcolonial periods,[6] as well as the ways in which Indian leaders and international universities cultivated relationships to develop new generations of technically trained national workers who set their sights abroad.[7] As a result of heavy state-led investment in technology-centered education programs after Independence in 1947, India has emerged as a leading producer of engineers, information technology professionals, and software developers globally. After the US immigration system was over-hauled in 1965 to prioritize skills, labor needs, and family reunification, Indian emigration accelerated as many sought to move to the United States.[8] Since 1990, US companies have recruited Indians through the H-1B tem-porary guest worker program, which brings in foreign workers who possess specialized skills in fields such as information technology, education, finance, and health care.[9] The visa is issued for three years with the possibil-ity for an extension to six years. Within that time, the employer must decide whether to sponsor the temporary employee. Otherwise, the visa holder is required to find a new job or obtain a different category of visa. In the worst-case scenario, the person must leave the country.

Today, Indians are the second fastest growing immigrant group in the US, thanks in part to the H-1B program, and they have established multi-generational communities across the nation.[10] English-educated and techni-cally trained, Indian workers are regarded as important liaisons between offshore contractors and parent tech industry companies, where the major-ity of H-1B visa holders are concentrated.[11] Each year, tens of thousands of (primarily) young, heterosexual Indian men come to work on H-1B visas.[12] Many more apply but do not obtain visas.[13] Even more striking than the annual influx of Indian H-1B visa holders is the flow of spouses and children who immigrate through the H-4 family reunification visa.[14] While H-1B visas are capped annually, H-4 visas are not. Thus, the number of spouses and children migrating annually is even higher than the numbers of H-1B visas issued, which creates a surplus population of family members who are also part of "temporary worker" migration. These family members are considered dependents and, as a result, tens of thousands of women find themselves in the same position as Sarika: they are legally permitted to stay in the US, but they are unable to work, file for permanent residency, or, in some cases, even open a bank account or library card in their own name.[15]

High-Tech Housewives examines how these transnational migrants—or transmigrants—create lives that are not geographically bound, but are shaped by the politics, policies, and imaginaries of migration and settlement. More specifically, it is a consideration of how migration intersects with the gendered work of social reproduction as it affects intimate family relation-ships, as well as claims to citizenship and belonging. As precarious subjects of globalization, transmigrants must grapple with their liminal positioning. As "nonresident Indians," or NRIs, they occupy different positions at various points in time: students, temporary workers, dependent spouses, permanent residents, citizens, returnees, and re-migrants. Their circulation between and across these categories and geographic locations informs how they sustain families and build communities. Some decide to return to India, while others are forced to leave upon losing their jobs; others spend some time in India but then decide to migrate back to the United States. As such, they cannot be classified easily as migrants, immigrants, or returnees. Rather, their categorization is dependent on their visa or naturalization status, family network, company affiliation, and personal identification at any given moment.[16] As Deborah Boehm argues in her study of Mexican transnational migration, "Place matters even as it is transcended"; to that end, this study shows how transmigration is as much about navigating borders as it is about creating homes that can move, adapt, and shift across locations.[17]

In this book, I ask three key questions: First, how do transmigrants adapt to the precariousness created by the collusion of state and industry desires to maintain an easily expandable and retractable flow of labor through temporary worker programs? Without a doubt, transmigrants occupy a contested space in debates over the changing nature of work, economic growth, and immigration.[18] As David Harvey has argued, corporate-state alliances that are motivated by profit, just-in-time production, and efficiency over the rights of labor or needs of human capital have become ordinary in an era in which neoliberalism is no longer viewed as one ideology among many, but has become widely accepted as foundational to economic prosperity and social progress.[19] Indian technology transmigrants in particular have been valorized as ideal subjects of neoliberalism and as "circulating brains" by some advocates of high-skilled immigration and looser migration restrictions. At the same time, critics of temporary worker programs paint them as weak winners of globalization, indentured servants, or "techno-braceros" who are caught in unequal circuits of labor exchange and exploitation.[20] *High-Tech Housewives* is an attempt to moderate across these perspectives by demonstrating both the disadvantage and opportunity that temporary migrant worker programs levy, particularly for women and other "non-economic" actors who are part of the same migration flows. For that reason, I center the role that women play in supporting and sustaining such forms of movements.

Second, how do notions of gender, culture, class, and family inform transmigration through household dynamics and intimate relationships?

While many accounts of migration focus on formal economic and political rationalities and drivers, I aim to show how the gendered and informal work of the household operates as a vital domain through which mobility and circulation are sustained. Moreover, the transmigrant household is a stratified space in which cultural and gender norms, along with constraints created by immigration policies, are consolidated to produce what I call the *transnational housewife*. I theorize this term to signal the social roles played by non-wage-earning actors whose place-making and caretaking activities underpin workers' ability to be ideal global employees. The women in this study classify as "high-tech" transnational housewives; they are closely aligned with the global technology industries. However, the term *transnational housewife* is intended to showcase the caregiving work that women do more broadly to allow cross-border migration, even at the expense of their own careers or well-being. While this study can be read as reflective of old narratives about cultural patriarchy that place women's ambitions as secondary to those of men, examining the intimate lives inside transmigrant households reveals how decision-making around migration and settlement is structured by a complex set of factors, such as cultural norms, kinship obligations, friendship networks, gendered and racialized discrimination in the workplace, and disciplining visa regimes that create worker vulnerability. These factors shape how migrants position themselves in the US and India as flexible and mobile, even though such positioning can also lead to loss in terms of community formation, belonging and emplacement, and gender equality within the household and workplace.

Finally, how do transmigrants navigate their career opportunities and personal aspirations alongside increasing immigration restrictions and regulations? Scholars of transnationalism have argued that in a world of increasing mobility and market logics, multidirectional flows of people, goods, finance, and ideas have reduced the regulatory function of national boundaries. As part of global knowledge economies that rely on dispersed and virtual networks of production, Indian IT workers are emblematic of globalization as companies rely on their labor to ensure a twenty-four-hour cycle of work and service, regardless of location. However, they are also subject to job and immigration insecurity when they migrate abroad as guest workers. One way that transmigrants resolve this tension between the demands of the global economy and the material barriers to settlement posed by the host state is to spend years working toward obtaining permanent residency or citizenship. Even if they do not plan on settling in the United States long-term, citizenship becomes an important juridical tool for facilitating movement. It also operates as a way for transmigrants to reconcile the physical and psychic displacement created by migration and helps them circulate as valuable economic and social agents whose labors bridge multiple national locations.

TRANSNATIONAL HOUSEWIVES

In considering these questions, this book intervenes into debates over the role of gender in transmigration and how global movement impacts ideas about citizenship and belonging. Often framed as a decision driven by push and pull factors, transnational migration is viewed as a choice made by individuals who move abroad to pursue better opportunities than those available in their home countries. Viewing transnational migration as primarily about self-determination or economic rationalities eclipses the extra-economic factors that are vital to migration and the resulting life worlds they create, as well as the role the state plays in creating the conditions for emigration or immigration. Moreover, studies of transmigration have generally focused on men's experiences when they migrate for work, while women are presumed to remain in home countries to care for children and family networks.[21] In the cases examined in this book, transmigration is more often a family process, as spouses and children also move along with primary workers. Women's roles in the household as transnational housewives are crucial to maintaining the kind of circulating lifestyle that allows men to pursue job opportunities across borders, even as their own employment prospects are limited or undermined. Moreover, their positioning as housewives is juridically enforced through family reunification policies that create patriarchal family models in which men are breadwinners and women are dependents who are prohibited from working while living in the US.

The acceptance of this division is partly, though by no means exclusively, cultural. As Smitha Radhakrishnan argues in her sociological study of transnational Indian IT workers, many retain traditional attitudes about gender and family roles even as they cultivate culturally appropriate notions of difference grounded in ideas about individualism, development, and modernity.[22] Like the "new Indian woman," who is typically urban, educated, global in her outlook, but aligned with Indian family norms, transnational housewives are expected to prioritize the "pure" space of the home.[23] By devoting themselves to the home, where cultural and ethnic identities are safeguarded from the potentially alien values of the host society, women perform the social reproductive work that is vital to maintaining connections to life in India and creating homes abroad. They bring together friends, host religious and cultural celebrations, keep up with far-flung relatives, and participate in informal economic activities such as cooking, sewing, and childcare as well as teaching arts, language, music, and dance. They also manage the household and are responsible for creating networks that can be transported back to India if or when the family returns.

However, cultural explanations obscure how the true cost of transmigrant labor is externalized or offset by the dependent housewife's labor. My use of the term *housewife* is derived from Marxist feminist articulations of the unpaid and gendered work done in the household to produce workers who are able to meet the needs of late capitalism. As feminist economist Gillian J. Hewitson writes, this devalued and non-wage work is an "essential component of the development of future citizens, workers, and taxpayers."[24] Though Marx and Engels acknowledged the need for women's labor in the home, this work is systematically characterized as existing outside of the economic realm and viewed as an extension of women's "natural" biosocial role as caretakers, rather than as foundational to capitalism itself. Examining the subordination of women historically, sociologist Maria Mies famously argued that this rendering of women's work as "non-economic" leads to a gendered division of labor that places women below men economically and socially.[25] Through the "housewifization" of labor, which requires a structural separation of the sexes into different domains, men are able to accumulate capital as they occupy the social role of the "breadwinner" who is free to sell his labor precisely because women, as housewives, are not free to do the same. Though few legal provisions prohibit women from working or mandate that they remain in the home in the majority of contemporary societies, housewifization is functionally enacted through US immigration policies that allow transmigrant men to earn wages, while the women who accompany them cannot. Reducing women's unremunerated care work to affect or a "natural" manifestation of their biological capacities systematically devalues gendered labor and obscures the true cost of labor power.

Examining the Indian transnational household through the lens of the housewife reveals how masculine mobility is predicated on feminine dependency as women give up their careers or put them on hold in order to support labor migration. While some women certainly choose to disengage from formal workplaces to facilitate migration, others are forced into such situations because of structural and juridical factors. Regardless of choice, culture and nature become the alibi for state policies that keep certain women out of the workforce and further minimize the threat of competition from foreign workers by limiting which migrants can and cannot work. Moreover, for industries reliant on temporary workers, spousal migration (and subsequent dependency) actually stabilizes the workforce, as workers are less likely to seek other positions or better opportunities if they have obligations at home. To that end, the transnational household supports the needs of some workers who seek career advancement through migration, but primarily in patriarchal gendered terms and to the benefit of capital. Housewifization has significant consequences; as my study shows, women who occupy these dependent roles experience a material loss of financial stability and personal autonomy as they are reduced from workers to primary caregivers, wives, and mothers. The term *housewife* thus indicates the social location that women occupy and how it is shaped by structural factors, rather than a diminutive identity category.

CIRCULATING CITIZENSHIP

While transmigration may be partly predicated on gendered divisions of labor, it is also tied to migrants' ability to navigate complex immigration and naturalization processes. Studies of transnationalism tend to emphasize the porousness of borders, particularly as migrants seek out ways to circumvent formal state immigration mechanisms. In such accounts, the value of citizenship has been deemphasized amid the growing acceptance of globalization and the decreasing regulatory functions of governments that control flows across borders. My study eschews that perception and instead starts with the important role that borders, visas, immigration policies, and temporary and permanent residency programs play in the ability for some to become transmigrants at all. The H-1B program is an example of one such bureaucratic mechanism: it renders workers as "temporary" but allows them to apply for a change in immigration status, thereby enabling them to apply for permanent residency and even citizenship.[26] Because of this malleability, workers do not necessarily resist their liminal classification, as their flexible status makes them valuable as knowledge workers. Instead, they use the H-1B to pursue a pathway to permanent residency and/or citizenship, and, along with matrimonial and reproductive strategies, seek to claim belonging in the US, even while knowing that they may not be successful or even want to settle permanently in the US. The idea of citizenship is therefore mobilized to ensure a foothold in their host nation, even if workers decide to repatriate or continue to circulate between India and the US.

While citizenship has been conceptualized as a conduit to claiming rights in a polity, as a social category, as a process, and as a juridical formation, I underscore the ways in which it is mobilized to create circuits of movement that have repercussions for future generations.[27] As Aihwa Ong argued in her classic elucidation of flexible citizenship among wealthy migrants from Hong Kong, it is also a tool to be deployed in order to propel certain forms of migration and relocation.[28] Though the transmigrants in my study are less elite than those in Ong's sample and instead are part of a professional migrating middle class, they nonetheless seek US citizenship in order to claim better opportunities in the global labor market, facilitate travel and future movement, and ensure their children's ability to study or work in the US.[29] For those who return to India, US citizenship also helps transmigrants negotiate higher ex-patriot salaries and maintain links to employment opportunities abroad. The long path to citizenship, however, leaves many in a transitory state.[30] Taking a historical approach, Lisong Liu has profiled a similar trend among Chinese professionals who seek to create transnational ties through family and citizenship strategies.[31] Chinese migrants pursue a "one family, two systems" strategy, where men retain their natal citizenship and return to the homeland regularly in order to maintain residency, while women remain in the US, where they apply for citizenship and care for children born abroad. Among the Indian transmigrants profiled here, the household is rarely divided in such a manner; instead, women opt to move to the US as dependent spouses with the hope of moving into the formal labor market. Rather than engage in divided or staged migration, Indian transmigrants use temporary worker programs to facilitate the movement of additional family members, which has the effect of turning the entire household into a migratory unit.

At the same time, citizenship allows transmigrants to recode their insecure positions vis-à-vis racial and national hierarchies in the global IT industry and their displacement from the Indian national context as a benefit. Scholars have argued that the desire of migrants to maintain links with the home nation-state creates new hybrid, transcultural, or hyphenated identities and underscores the dualistic nature of migrant identity.[32] My analysis challenges such dualism and is instead informed by the ways in which transmigration, as Julie Chu argues, is indicative of "a world where neither locality nor home could be assumed to be stable objects and points of anchorage."[33] I show how transmigrants move beyond a dyadic focus on going abroad and returning, and are driven by aspirations for mobility and circulation. I argue that transmigrants act as bridge builders who view their time abroad as a way to develop skills that will translate into better career opportunities personally, and also as a way to "give back" to the Indian state's development and modernization efforts.[34] This sensibility travels with some transmigrants when they shift into the role of the "returnee" who decides to move back to India. I trace how these practices of bridge building help transmigrants position themselves across multiple locations as ideal citizen-subjects through the logics of neoliberalism, self-governance, and entrepreneurialism.

CIRCUITS OF ETHNOGRAPHY

This book begins in King County, Washington, where many technology transmigrants work and reside. King County encompasses Seattle and its suburbs (a region colloquially called the "Eastside"). Historically, Indians have concentrated on the Eastern Seaboard, in Southern California, and in midwestern metropolises, but the growing opportunities in the technology sectors in Northern California and Washington State have drawn many westward. Though the Pacific Northwest is home to an established and multigenerational South Asian population that began with the settlement of Punjabi migrants in the 1890s and expanded after 1965, the region is relatively understudied in accounts of Indian immigration and the US technology industry. In contrast, the influence of Indian IT workers in Santa Clara County, which includes the infamous "Silicon Valley," has been well documented.[35] Between 2000 and 2010, the Indian population grew there by 68 percent. In Cupertino alone, which is host to Apple and over sixty other high-tech firms, Indians make up 22.6 percent of the population, compared to 0.9 percent nationally.[36]

Though industry growth was historically less prolific in the Pacific Northwest, the region has become a major technology hub in the past thirty years. Long associated with the aviation industry, thanks to the Boeing Company, Seattle and its suburbs were transformed from an ancillary to a major technology player after the founding of the Microsoft Corporation in 1975 in Redmond, Washington. Early on, Microsoft began recruiting students from Indian universities who were skilled in engineering, computer science, and information technology.[37] Today, Boeing and Microsoft are the top two largest employers in the county, and both continue to draw Indian workers to the region.[38] King County also hosts several other major high-tech firms, such as Amazon, and branch offices of Indian-owned contract firms, such as Infosys, Tata Consultancy Services, and Aditi, all of which supply Indian workers directly to American companies.

So who are these new Indian transmigrants? For the most part, this temporary labor force is made up of young men between twenty and forty years old: it is estimated that almost 85 percent of all H-1B visas go to men in this age bracket.[39] When traveling through the Eastside, one is immediately struck by the groups of Indian men walking to bus stops from which they will be shuttled to various technology campuses. Many proudly display plastic-encased lanyards with dark badges that designate full-time employee status, while others wear brightly colored badges that reflect their work as contractors. The Indian men who dominate the IT landscape are ubiquitous along the roadways and commercial centers. So, too, are young kurta- and jeans-clad women who shuffle up and down the wide suburban sidewalks, with some displaying badges and others pushing strollers or carrying grocery bags.

From April 2008 to June 2010, and then again for two months in the summer of 2015, I conducted official open-ended interviews with fifty-five such transmigrants (thirty-six women and nineteen men).[40] These individuals came to the United States initially as (1) students enrolled in undergraduate or graduate programs; (2) workers who were directly issued temporary work permits; or (3) as spouses on H-4 visas. At the time of our meetings, study participants had been living in the US anywhere between six months to ten years. All participants had at least a bachelor's degree in a technical field, and many also held master's or doctoral degrees, as well as other certifications and diplomas. The majority of my informants hailed from the southern Indian cities of Chennai, Bangalore, and Hyderabad, as well as Delhi, Mumbai, and Pune. The South Indian arrivals spoke Tamil, Kannada, and Telegu and were considered relatively new among the North India–dominated Seattle community. Though there was regional diversity among my participants, almost all came from upper-caste Hindu, English-medium educated, and middle-class backgrounds and were already part of networks of friends and family members that had traveled abroad for school or work.[41] Each participant in my study had successfully navigated the US immigration system, and many had shifted from holding H-1B/H-4 visas to acquiring green cards, while some had even become citizens. Undoubtedly, the voices of individuals who lack such clear class and caste advantage are missing in this account and remain a vital area for future consideration.

In addition to formal interviews, I spent time participating in various community functions, such as cultural, activist, and arts events, informal dinner parties at private homes, and smaller gatherings at coffee shops, restaurants, or pubs. I conducted many of my interviews on the campuses of Microsoft, Amazon, or other technology companies, as well. These corporate spaces were key locations for connecting to H-1B workers as almost all host internal company Listservs for temporary workers and also regularly sponsor Indian concerts, dance performances, intramural sports events such as cricket and soccer, and other events and activities. I tapped into these virtual and in-person communities by circulating my study announcement on Indian-community-specific company Listservs, message boards, and through word-of-mouth referrals.

While my focus was initially on the Pacific Northwest, during the course of my study, I found that some transmigrants were preparing to return to India or had decided to move back in the time that I got to know them. From January to April 2009 and in January 2013, I interviewed thirty-five former H-1B and H-4 visa holders who had returned to India (or, as is it often phrased, made the "R2I"). While in India, I interviewed "returnees" who resided in neighborhoods that service the high-tech industries in Bangalore and Hyderabad. Most had not actually lived in the Indian cities to which they had moved "back," so they occupied a hybrid space between transmigrant and local resident. My initial contacts were either relatives or close friends of Seattle-based transmigrants, and many of them had lived in the same Eastside neighborhoods or worked on the same teams before moving to India. Through these meetings, I was drawn into the social life of a midsized housing complex situated on the outskirts of Bangalore's city center, part of the growing suburbs that are especially appealing to returnees and other residents working in the city's technology industries. Located near the better-known neighborhood of Whitefield, I met with "Lake View" residents in their spacious homes and soon familiarized myself with the gated community and surrounding areas.[42]

I traveled next to Hyderabad, where I connected with the extended relatives of Lake View residents. I spent time in a similar housing complex called "Mountain Meadows," which was located in the "IT suburb" of Gachibowli a few kilometers from the Microsoft India Development Center campus and other technology firms, such as Infosys, Wipro, and Computer Associates. This area is also home to the sprawling steel- and glass-enclosed campuses of several research and educational institutions and is part of the city's "Knowledge Corridor." It has experienced skyrocketing land prices and real estate development as the wealth from the technology industry has transformed the region. The majority of my participants in India were women and men between the ages of thirty and forty-five years old. At the time of our meetings, most had returned to India within the previous six months to five years. Spending hours in individual homes, as well as in common spaces such as community clubhouses and playgrounds, I gained insight into how transnational households are reproduced across borders.

In addition to ethnographic narratives, I examined images and representations of Indian temporary migrant workers in media stories, policy reports, and congressional debates over immigration reform. I also drew on blogs, online message forums, and social media sites such as Facebook, which offered decentralized and firsthand user-generated accounts of the migration experience.[43] These sites were of particular importance for women seeking pragmatic advice on legal issues related to the H-4 visa, translating job skills from India to the US, looking for tips on cooking Indian food with American ingredients, raising children abroad, moving back to India, and coping with the experience of being a house-bound wife. Covering issues from the mundane to the political, blogs and social media offered a glimpse into the social and professional worlds of individuals within this transnational class.

Grounded in this evidence, I start in chapter 1 by exploring how transmigrants position their work in American IT industries as valuable and necessary, even as they are the subjects of intense national debate over temporary worker programs. In doing so, workers recode their precariousness as advantage, and, through their professional work and their volunteer activities, position themselves as appropriate bridge builders between the presumptive modern/liberal US and backward/illiberal India. In chapter 2, I demonstrate how transmigration not only informs notions of citizenship and national belonging but also shapes life events for Indian IT workers. For the smaller numbers of women arriving on the H-1B visa, migration provides a space for personal development and, in some cases, contributes to their ability to remain single in the absence of their Indian kinship networks. At the same time, for both women and men, time spent on the H-1B increases their desirability on the Indian marriage market, due to the presumed boost in status that accompanies living and working in the US, though these effects are contradictory and gendered. Transmigration also offers individuals the opportunity to start families with mixed citizenship status, as children of temporary workers can now claim US citizenship and offer a link to future migrations. Consequently, transmigrants strategically use the H-1B to create transnational connections through heterosexual marriage, reproduction, and social networks that can be mobilized regardless of their desire or ability to remain permanently in the US.

I then shift to the household to examine the experiences of women who must contend with immigration and return. In chapter 3, I show how the transnational household emerges as a site constituted through patriarchal assumptions and contradictory discourses about the Indian family and Indian culture. As dependent spouses, women on the H-4 visa negotiate their economic disempowerment by occupying the role of transnational housewives, though not necessarily by choice. Many turn to the domestic sphere to create new channels for personal development and self-expression, while also grappling with deep challenges to their identities as educated, modern women with potential for launching careers of their own. While some women embrace their reproductive roles, others resist their classification as wives and mothers and continue to pursue avenues for professional fulfillment. In chapter 4, I follow transmigrants through the process of return migration. As transnational housewives, women are central to this repatriation. Once back in India, they are almost exclusively in charge of setting up and running households in new housing developments, where they seek to emulate life in the US suburbs while relying on Indian domestic workers and household staff. Their daily engagements are simultaneously linked to the production of the transnational household, as well as to gender, class, and national identity.

In chapter 5, I demonstrate how returning to India is not the end of the circuit for transmigrants, per se. For some prodigal sons and daughters who receive a warm welcome, returning to India represents a positive shift away from US immigration bureaucracies, cultural incompatibilities, and xenophobia. For others, the move back is short-lived, as work differences, family pressures, and concerns about future opportunities for their children leave them disappointed with their decision. Due in part to the challenges returnees encounter and the pull of their previously established networks abroad, some seek to "re-return" to the US, thereby creating another set of displacements. I conclude the book by offering a consideration of how circulation operates as a state of being for transmigrants and has implications for future scholars of transmigration, citizenship, and community formation.

1 Transmigrants

Identity, Nationalism, and Bridge Building

AS A YOUNG UNMARRIED MAN IN HIS LATE TWENTIES, HARSHAD is like so many H-1B visa holders who are eager to work abroad soon after completing their undergraduate degrees in India. Having obtained a degree in computer engineering, Harshad sought admission to a master's degree program and, upon being accepted, moved to the United States immediately after graduation. Once he finished his master's, Harshad located a contracting job at the Microsoft headquarters in Redmond, Washington. When we first met, he had just completed the first three years on his H-1B visa. He was in the process of applying for a renewal in the hopes of staying with the same team. Harshad recounts how his passion motivated him—both for his chosen field of IT and also his desire to move abroad: "I was one of those blind candidates who thought of USA as the land of opportunity." Harshad did not really know what to expect once he entered the country, but he was convinced that living in the US would be personally and professionally beneficial. In practical terms, this meant successfully trading in his student visa for an H-1B visa, even though he understood that locating a permanent position was not guaranteed.

Despite political debates about the overuse of temporary worker visas in IT, securing an H-1B visa is actually a complicated process that shuts out many eager applicants each year. Though a persistently popular avenue for Indian migration, since its reformulation as a skilled worker visa in 1990, the H-1B program has generated a hailstorm of controversy. More recently, the program has faced restrictions under the Trump administration, which has argued that reducing immigration will create more jobs for US-born workers and inhibit possible terrorist threats. In light of travel bans for people from Muslim-majority countries, reduced admittance of refugees, and assaults on undocumented immigrants, restricting temporary visa programs has become part of a partisan and populist attempt to pit "native" workers against foreign competition. The H-1B visa offers US corporations a competitive advantage by allowing them to hire the most talented workers, regardless of nationality or country of origin. These workers pay income and Social Security taxes.[1] They are granted permission to work in the US for short periods of time, but do not have the same rights as permanent residents or citizens. Supporters of the program claim that the lack of qualified labor makes hiring foreign workers necessary. Critics of the program argue that when US firms look to countries such as India and China to fill information technology jobs, US workers are unduly displaced. They argue that the program depresses wages for all technology workers and effectively shuts out women and minorities from the field who might otherwise have been hired.

However, as Payal Banerjee has argued, the importance of the program also "lies in how the visas define and construct the terms through which immigrant workers enter into relationships with employers, capital, and the state."[2] Though these terms generally benefit the companies that hire temporary workers, the visa transforms foreign nationals into transmigrants who view time working abroad as pivotal to achieving career success. They also use the skills and habits they learn while in the US as a way to claim membership in a highly sought-after class of global workers. At the same time, some workers feel resentful of the restrictions placed on them, and their expectations often do not match the realities of life in the US.

Considering the debates over transnational migration as they intersect with temporary work, in this chapter I ask: How do workers position themselves as intractably valuable in the US and India, while also navigating the constraints placed on them through the US visa and immigration system? Through interviews with current and former H-1B workers, I argue that as part of a "middling transnationalism," or the non-elite transnational middle classes, these workers embrace their liminality even when accepting relatively insecure jobs abroad.[3] Once in the US, they position themselves as bridge builders between the West and the Indian nation-state. I analyze their involvement in India-oriented social welfare organizations to show how they internalize and apply neoliberal and techno-capitalist cultures of IT to volunteer development efforts in India. Through this civic work, transmigrants seek incorporation into the imaginary of their home country as ideal nationalists, even when they are dislocated from the nation-state. Transmigrant agency is undoubtedly limited by the tangible constraints of visa restrictions and job markets. However, the transmigrant narration of professional and personal aspiration adds a critical dimension to debates that go beyond exploitation or valorization to describe temporary worker programs. As the cases here demonstrate, temporary worker visas allow

Indian IT workers to create a transmigrant identity that both supersedes and is closely aligned with the nation-state.

A BRIEF HISTORY OF THE H-1B PROGRAM

The juridical and bureaucratic backdrop to Indian IT transmigrant experiences is the H-1B Specialty Occupation Visa Program. The H-1B program has existed in its current form for nearly three decades and is a flashpoint in ongoing debates about immigration reform and the role of the US in the global economy. A central part of the Immigration Reform and Control Act of 1990, H-1B visas dramatically expanded the number of individuals migrating to the US to work in the technology, education, health-care, and finance sectors. The 1990 law increased the cap for total employment-based immigrant visas from 58,000 (the limit since 1976) to 140,000 annually.[4] The H-1B visa allows employers to sponsor workers for permanent residency, rendering it a "dual intent" visa with pathways to citizenship. If employees are unable to find an employer who is willing to sponsor them for permanent residency before the end of their visa period, the workers must return to their country of origin.[5] H-1B visa holders can change jobs only if a new employer files a new petition; they can also switch roles in the same company if their current employer is willing to apply for a new visa. This regulation keeps many from changing jobs, since doing so often delays transmigrants in the process of applying for permanent residency.

The 1990s also marked the beginning of the dot-com boom, as the demand for information technology services grew at an exponential rate. Pockets of industry such as Silicon Valley and the Seattle suburbs grew quickly from sleepy West Coast outposts to centers of global technological commerce and innovation, all fueled by immigrant labor. Almost half of H-1B visas are awarded to staffing companies, or "body shops," which provide contract workers for US-based companies. The majority of these companies, such as Wipro, Tata Consulting Services, Infosys, and Hindu Computers Ltd., are based in India or supply Indian workers to US companies. Between 1999 and 2001, anxiety about making adequate technological preparations for the turn of the millennium, or "Y2K," accelerated US dependence on hiring foreign technology workers, as companies scrambled to update various banking, data processing, and other computing systems. After 2003, the number of new visas available was capped again at 85,000.[6] All H-1B visas are allocated through a lottery system. In 2015, United States Citizenship and Immigration Services (USCIS) received 233,000 H-1B applications within a month. In 2016, they reached the lottery cap within six days of opening, after receiving 236,000 applications. In 2017, the USCIS received over 336,000 applications for new visas and renewals. Of these, 69 percent were for workers in computing-related industries.[7]

The H-1B visa program also created measures for family reunification through the H-4 visa, which has been used primarily for H-1B workers to bring spouses and children to the US. The spouses or children (under twenty-one years of age) of H-1Bs are issued H-4 visas. The visa restricts its holder from working formally and is classified as a dependent visa, which means that it is valid only as long as the primary H-1B visa holder is in good standing. In 2014, President Obama signed a major executive order that allowed H-4 visa holders to apply for the Employment Authorization Document (EAD), which authorized them to work legally.[8] According to the USCIS in 2015, as many as 179,600 people were eligible to apply for the EAD in the first year alone, and up to 55,000 could apply annually after that.[9] Although many welcomed the rule change, new backlogs also emerged, as applications poured in from eager H-4 visa holders who have been waiting for years for the chance to work. While unrestricted in terms of employment type, work authorization for H-4 visa holders is still tied to the H-1B visa holder's legal standing. Thus, if the spouse's work authorization is revoked, the H-4 visa holder's authorization will very likely be rescinded soon after.

Under the Trump administration, new legislative efforts to reform the program continue to create uncertainty about the future. As of April 2017, Trump issued his own set of executive orders limiting the "premium processing" of H-1B visas, which some companies have used to fast-track certain visa applications by paying additional fees. Attorney General Jeff Sessions also has indicated that the White House will not support work authorization for H-4 visa holders, though there have not been definitive policies crafted to rescind President Obama's executive actions. In Congress, advocates continue to argue for an increase in the numbers of available visas. They have argued for a market-based escalator and for eliminating the backlog of green card applications from current H-1B visa holders.[10] In contrast, detractors play on claims that foreign guest workers are cheaper, less qualified, and are conspiring to depress US wages.[11] This negative perception has spilled over into the debates about the H-4 visa program, as spouses of H-1B visa holders are also seen as competitors for US jobs, if they were granted work authorization. This latter perspective has grown even more virulent under Trump, who, through his presidential campaign and subsequent policy agendas, has successfully linked globalization and terrorism with immigration as a major cause for the decline in white working-class stability and US security. Trump's administration has signaled its intention to severely cut back the program, even though the industries that use the visa have voiced strong opposition to these plans. Trumpian logic, while not a new idea, holds that foreigners (particularly nonwhite, non-Western ones) pose a growing and insidious threat to US safety and economic growth, and must be curtailed. What has been alarming has been the backlash that workers themselves are facing daily and the attempts made by the White House to dismantle Obama-era immigration reforms, regardless of the legality of those actions. These anti-immigrant, Islamophobic, and xeno-phobic sentiments have led to a slight waning in foreign workers' desire to apply for the program, as news media outlets have reported anecdotally.[12] Considering the instability and potential backlash that temporary workers face, what appeal does the program hold for young Indian IT workers?

AMERICAN DREAMS AND VISA NIGHTMARES

Despite the ambivalent reception guest workers may face, H-1B applications continue to exceed the annual cap, and over 70 percent of all applications come from India. The reasons that the H-1B visa holds such sway are complex. In practical terms, the visa offers training opportunities that workers view as better than what they enjoy in India. Additionally, H-1B visas typically lead to more permanent affiliation in the US and often ensure future mobility once workers are able to establish residency or become citizens. Salaries are also generally better in the US, and even a short stint abroad allows workers to amass capital. However, workers are also motivated by additional factors, such family encouragement, the desire to experience life outside of India, and the opportunity to expand their professional networks and develop interpersonal skills. These reasons constellate beyond economic understandings of migration and shape young IT workers' desire to become transmigrants more broadly.

PURSUING THE H-1B VISA

Soon after finishing his undergraduate degree in India, Sandeep, a twenty-six-year-old working at Microsoft at the time of our interview, was eager to migrate abroad on an H-1B. As part of a large upper-caste South Indian extended family, he had several cousins living in the US. Also, his school peers tended to viewed migration as a rite of passage and a natural extension of their training. At top universities across Indian metropolises every year, recruiters from the world's major software and technology firms stand in partitioned booths eagerly disseminating company brochures to prospective graduates, who shuffle anxiously from table to table, clutching their résumés. These job fairs have become standard for Indian students as they transition into the working world. Indian contracting companies compete with Microsoft and Google to hire graduates for employment opportunities that range from providing technical customer support to developing new products and services. For many, the potential to travel abroad shapes their decision to join a particular firm.

After Sandeep completed his engineering degree at a regional college in Chennai, he wanted to pursue a master's degree that would give him the training needed to access higher tiers of jobs. He had his heart set on a degree from one of India's highly selective Indian Institutes of Technology (IITs), but found the competition for admission to be too fierce. He began working for a small Indian software development firm, but continued to apply to graduate school. Sandeep felt that he had a better shot at getting into an American university, where Indians are welcomed as foreign students with strong math skills who pay higher tuition rates. Rather than join an Indian IT company directly, Sandeep first obtained a student visa, which allowed him to work immediately after graduation as part of the "optional training program." The OTP allows students to remain in the US for up to twenty-seven months in order to gain practical skills in some fields.[13] After that, he would have to obtain an H-1B work permit. When I asked why it was so important to him that he come to the US, Sandeep was clear that his future job prospects hinged on his ability to work here, even if only briefly:

> I'd say [it's about] the American dream, more than anything else. Also, to just get the firsthand experience of what things are like, what the real computer software game was like. I was working in, I should say, a second-tier software company in India. They aren't, like, the core software companies in India. Whoever has a real passion for software and IT, they don't mind leaving India if they want to, if they are really passionate. They would want to pursue what they won't get in India. I have some friends who got some good jobs after graduation in India, but they wanted to pursue their US dream. So they got in some American university and now they are working in very good software companies here.

Here, the "American dream" is a simulacrum for economic success for transmigrants, but also a way to describe what it means to be at the center of the IT universe. Sandeep connects this dream to his "passion" for the IT field and the chance to prove himself in the more competitive environment of the US software sector. He points to the geopolitical imbalance between sites like India, which is considered an auxiliary or second-tier site for software development, and the Western countries that host the corporate headquarters and research and development branches of major IT firms. International offices tend to employ cheaper on-site labor and provide opportunities to redirect or altogether avoid corporate taxes in the US, even as they fortify foreign markets. Nevertheless, when compared to US IT sites, they are rarely considered the center of innovation, where the major decisions about design, implementation, distribution, and strategy are made.

The so-called American dream also is an expression of mobility and the key for future opportunities. In a survey of nearly 1,000 Indian graduate students in the US, Venkatesh Kumar, David Finegold, Anne-Laure Winkler, and Vikas Argod found that 53 percent wanted to work for some period of time in the US in order to gain exposure to cutting-edge technologies, research, and projects.[14] Many hoped to leverage that knowledge into better opportunities in India upon their return or to find positions permanently in the US. Similarly, among Chinese nationals, Lisong Liu notes the vital role that foreign work exposure and credentialing plays for negotiating better salaries or jobs when workers return to China.[15] As a result, transmigrants such as Sandeep are willing to risk insecure jobs and endure the long and often painful gyrations of the immigration process in the hopes of securing better opportunities in the future.

While conducting interviews, I also spoke via Skype to Situ, another young man from the South Indian state of Tamil Nadu. At the time of our conversation, Situ was in Canada, waiting to obtain a new H-1B visa. He had moved in 2008 to the US as a consultant for an India-based company that contracted with Microsoft. After a few years of contracting, he had his heart set on staying on permanently. Finding that Situ was a valuable addition, the project manager of his team agreed to hire him as a direct employee, which meant initiating a new H-1B visa application. While waiting for the H-1B visa, Situ began working at a Microsoft facility located just over the Washington State border in Vancouver, British Columbia. After obtaining a Canadian work permit, he hoped that he might qualify for an intracompany transfer, or the L-1 visa, which is used by businesses to move employees from overseas branches to the US for short-term projects. They are easier to obtain than the H-1B, as they are not subject to a lottery. Canada's relatively less restrictive skilled worker immigration policy provides real advantages to companies such as Microsoft, which can employ foreign workers who are able to work in the same time zones as their team members and travel relatively quickly across the border between Redmond and Vancouver. For this reason, Microsoft has a growing presence in British Columbia, and, with the opening of a new engineering facility in 2016, the company anticipates doubling the size of its workforce in Vancouver. Situ described his Canadian office like a global holding pen: "There are so many people here from Turkey, Romania, Hungary, and, of course, India. There's a big gang of people from Egypt, and Ethiopia and Russians." While waiting for visa approvals to cross the border, many of these foreign nationals were already working remotely for Microsoft.

Despite waiting almost two years for his visa petition to be approved, Situ was eager to cross the border and join his former colleagues in the Redmond office. Like Sandeep and Harshad, Situ noted:

> There is a lot of glamour associated with America. In the sense that it's just the poster-boy or poster-girl of countries. A lot of fame associated with it. Like, every Indian parent's dream is that their child should go to America. Go to any matrimonial website, you'll see, "Looking for boy in America." It's ridiculous . . . well, very common. I knew it would mean a lot more for my parents than it would for me, but I wanted to also see what this country was like that we had heard so much about. We listened to music that [came from America]. I wanted to try it to see what it was like.

Though he downplayed his initial desire to move abroad, Situ decided to migrate in part because of his exposure to US popular culture, music, and media representations, along with the perceivably improved status he would enjoy as a result of working abroad. Despite the high salary and prestige he might earn as a software developer in India, and the relative class and caste privilege that he had already experienced, Situ was seduced by the notion of America as the land of glamour and opportunity and bet on the additional social capital that foreign work experience would provide.

Beyond his own aspiration, his wish to fulfill his parents' vision for his life also pushed Situ to embark on a multiyear and multinational process to come to the US. Time abroad is desirable for not only potential workers but also for their family members, whose status tends to increase as a result of having their children work in Western epicenters. Xiang Biao's ethnographic study of tech workers circulating between India, Australia, and the

US shows the power of foreign affiliation, particularly through the higher dowries that tech workers can demand on the Indian marriage market.[16] Technology workers who go abroad generally earn better salaries than their domestic counterparts and become desirable as grooms. Migration also helps open the door to future job prospects, thereby improving the entire family's economic and social position through remittances and financial investments at home.

While moving to the US may result in a dream come true for many young IT professionals, the steps they take to achieve this dream—pursuing particular educational trajectories in their home country, applying first for student visas and then transferring to work permits—are arduous, and the results are often out of their control. Even though class and educational advantage aid them, transferring from one visa to another can create delays and setbacks, leaving transmigrants in a state of limbo. Situ's migration story is an example of the kind of purgatory that transmigrants potentially face as they move between statuses, while Sandeep's and Harshad's cases point to the complex layers of international bureaucracy that transmigrants must navigate if they hope to have a shot at their "American dreams."

THE RIGHT KIND OF TRANSMIGRANT WORKER

Beyond the glamour of the US, transmigrants view the H-1B as an opportunity to build their technical skills and fashion themselves as global ambassadors who can easily interface with Western companies and clients, as well as foreign development teams. By developing habits, proficiencies, and tastes that align with corporate IT culture, transmigrants signal their status as ideal immigrants in the West and as valuable global workers. The ability to adapt quickly to Western work environments, standardized work practices, and cross-cultural communication strategies are all part of a process that Smitha Radhakrishnan calls cultural streamlining. As part of a transnational class that strives to "create a simplified, influential notion of a new Indian culture that is compatible with the economic and geographic mobility of the global economy," IT workers strive to position themselves as "appropriately different, but recognizable as part of global corporate culture regardless of location."[17] Adopting these practices shapes Indian IT workers' professional engagement, but also crafts their personal subjectivities as ideal workers who can bridge the West and the rest of the world. Companies also benefit from hiring transmigrants who are willing to relocate and work to improve coordination between geographically dispersed teams, offices, vendors, and customers. This desire to become seen as an effective global liaison is closely tied to specific practices, such as learning to speak unaccented English, using an American-sounding nickname, and eschewing traditional clothes, food, and customs in the workplace.

At the same time, H-1B workers are only valuable for as long as their labor suits the needs of capital and the state allows pathways to migration. If they are no longer economically productive, or their employment capacity becomes obstructed, there is an almost immediate change in their status and the state retreats from its formal obligation to them. Moreover, in the turbulent political climate created by the Trump administration, there is a deep-rooted suspicion of all immigrants, particularly those who come from developing nations or countries with substantial Muslim populations. H-1B workers are increasingly the target of racial profiling by border control agencies and the Department of Homeland Security. As South Asian migrants, they are positioned as inherently alien and threatening to American workers (read: white workers) and US national interests. If they are welcomed into the fabric of the nation, it is usually through model minority discourses that prioritize economic and educational achievement and inherent cultural traits, such as "family values" that paint them as ideal liberal subjects in relation to negatively racialized citizens and immigrant populations.[18]

Such a narrow rendering of immigrant identity contributes to the precarious employment and immigration scenarios that temporary workers face. On the one hand, as Harshad shrewdly articulates: "When they give [the] visa, they give it on the basis that we are not going to stay here forever. That's their assumption. But they would like to keep good talent. This is the land of opportunity and immigrants. Even though they know some people might stay, they give the visa. But if the job is done or gone, so are you." Harshad lays bare the contradiction embedded in issuing a temporary visa that allows employers to initiate the permanent residency process, but only after transmigrants have proven that they are valuable to a specific company that is willing to take the time and expense to sponsor a green card. This contingency has historical roots. The conditional inclusion (and exclusion) of Asian Americans has been couched in terms of the needs of US imperialism and capitalism, as evidenced by the passage of the Chinese Exclusion Act of 1882 and the creation of "Asiatic Barred Zones" throughout the twentieth century. By the end of WWII, even before the passage of the game-changing 1965 Immigration and Nationality Act, US immigration policy had already pivoted toward welcoming *select* Asian immigrants who fulfilled specific labor needs or had family ties, a pattern that was repeated

across the Western world.[19] Using the example of the rapid growth of educated and middle-class Korean American immigrant populations between
1959 and 1965, historians Madeline Y. Hsu and Ellen D. Wu argue that the
trend "illustrate[d] broader transformations in Asian immigration patterns,
including growing emphasis on economic considerations privileging individual employability and educational attainment that produced Asian
immigrants as a predominantly well-educated and professionally or technically employed minority group."[20] The immigration laws that followed the
1965 Hart-Celler Act continued to solidify those group characteristics and
began to explicitly prioritize immigrants that fit the model minority mold.

Beyond the qualities ascribed to model minorities, such as strong math
skills or subjective notions of work ethic or family values, Sareeta Amrute
has argued that Indian IT workers are envisioned as ideal employees because
they are stratified into groups of workers who possess the kind of "flexibility"
that benefits the IT industry.[21] This means that transmigrants must be willing
to take on less desirable assignments, work late when required, and be willing
to move around as needed. The flexible nature of the H-1B visa also ensures
that they are pliant and easily categorized as a group whose parts are interchangeable. While they must have a specific set of skills, knowledges, and
proficiencies, they are also lumped into a general category that presumes one
worker could easily replace another. Such flattening increases the urgency
for transmigrants to both blend into the work culture they seek to enter and
to set themselves apart as exceptionally useful by being willing to sacrifice
and adapt to the needs of the companies that hire them.

As a result, IT transmigrants internalize discourses of value and utility
encoded in the visa and seek to distinguish themselves from other types of
immigrants, many of whom arrive via family reunification or through less
secure labor streams. Situ was critical of the ways in which visas create
hierarchies and divisions between different classes of immigrants. Yet, he
reiterated that transmigrants' class and educational advantage, as well as
their ability to "do something directly to help the USA," is grounds for
preferential admittance. While waiting for his H-1B in Canada, Situ reflected
on the large Punjabi-speaking community in Vancouver, which, in some
ways, projects greater class diversity than the South Asian community he
encountered in Seattle. He noted,

> You can see second- and third-generation Indians. In the cafeteria in
> Seattle, the people who worked in the café were from Latin America. Here
> you find people from India. The perception people have in Vancouver of

Indians is that they are less educated. The difference between the US and here is that if I meet someone [who has] grown up in America, and they saw Indians around, the general reaction is that "oh, you have very good schools there and you must be in IT." Like if I'm going through the airport they always ask if I have a laptop computer in my bag. In fact one time they said, "You have to put your laptop here." And I wasn't carrying one! That is the stereotype. In US, Indians are assumed to be rich and prosperous, doctors and stuff. But that's not the perception they have of Indians here in Vancouver.

While Situ perceived a distinction in Indian communities in both locations, he did not attribute it to class or caste advantage or to the different immigration histories that resulted in the wake of British colonization in Canada and India. Nor did he attribute these distinctions to education and labor policies that have created different immigration streams in both locations.[22] Instead, he assumes that the respect he commands is a function of his individual merit and credentialing, which theoretically works to supersede the negative racialization that comes from being a foreigner. Because he is an Indian IT worker, which is a high-status occupation globally, he presumes that he will be treated equitably.

However, this desire to distinguish oneself as the ideal transmigrant worker is moderated by hierarchies that create uneven distinctions among different types of IT workers, such as those who remain in India (lowest tier), those who come through "body shops," or third-party contractors for short-term positions (mid tier), and the H-1B workers who were first students or whom major firms hired directly (highest tier). There are material differences between the three categories, as the workers in India and the body-shoppers are likely to be paid less, are more readily terminated once the project no longer requires their skill, and are often positioned on the lower rung of IT teams. Often thought to be unable to work independently, solve problems without supervision, or interface effectively with Western co-workers or managers, these lower-tier workers are sometimes referred to as "code monkeys." *Code monkey* is a term used in the software industry to describe easily interchangeable software developers whose skills are best used for the routine and mundane work of line coding, rather than more creative or collaborative architectural or design work. Beyond their technical skills, there is a presumed cultural distinction between these categories of IT workers globally. As Situ and Harshad noted, many body-shopped workers might possess the same level or quality of skills as they do, but because they remain segregated and culturally removed from the American workplace and social life, they will not be as successful as those who can traverse the global IT world with greater ease. Harshad critically argued that they are less effective than "real" transnational workers because they have not "learned the culture." Relating a story about a friend of his that came on a short-term contract for two years and then returned to India, he noted:

> His main motivation was to save some money up and then go back. Obviously the project, company, everything requires them to go back to India unless they ditch the company and change to a different company, which nowadays has become another pattern. This is not what my friend did. He went back. He was different than me because I saw perspectives from both ends. You should not come only to just save money and see your workmates. You should learn the culture. But they are still in that Indian mode—save and go take care of the family. We are a little more advanced beyond those people because we have been here for a little longer and have been here in different modes: student mode, then work mode. Those people aren't.

Having moved through various "modes," Harshad is able to position himself as a "new economy subject," in contrast to his compatriots, who are more concerned with remittances and returning to India to, as he states, "go back home and collect a nice dowry."[23] Harshad argues that the temporary workers who come to the US only to earn and save money lose out because they do not participate in American leisure activities, develop new food preferences, or learn about other cultural practices that would signal their cosmopolitanism and integration. Writing about young technology workers in India, Carol Upadhya has found similar patterns emerging. As their incomes rise and they become more exposed to Western companies and lifestyles, they begin to place higher priority on consumption and leisure activities as a marker of their global sensibility.[24] Among the workers I met, such capital is demonstrated by attending music concerts and movies, taking hikes in the nearby mountains, or dining at the suburban strip mall cafés and restaurants that punctuate the landscape between Bellevue, Redmond, and Kirkland. Harshad blames the individuals who do not work hard enough to develop these hegemonic qualities and tastes, rather than pointing to the ways in which the IT system itself relies on a revolving door of easily contracted and expanded labor that creates stratifications between workers. Moreover, his perspective reinforces the notion that transmigrants are able to legitimate their value by "deliberately cultivat[ing] a global sensibility by embracing cultural diversity in their friendship and professional networks, developing tastes for foreign music and food, and participating in lifestyle choices."[25] By neutralizing their cultural difference, or encoding it in nonthreatening and socially appropriate ways, transmigrants can successfully distance themselves from the stigma of being a foreign and raced body in an industry that divides the value of workers by national origin.

At the same time, the issue of cultural integration is complicated. Unlike the earlier groups, H-1B workers are entering a demographically diverse landscape that already has several temples, gurudwaras, mosques, restaurants, Indian dance and music classes, and even movie theaters that broadcast primarily Indian-language films, while serving chai and samosas. A statue of Mohandas Gandhi adorns the front lawn of the Bellevue Public Library, which is situated within walking distance of the bustling downtown and is flanked by high-rise towers that house Microsoft offices. In contrast to earlier generations, who were part of linguistically, ethnically, and religiously varigated South Asian communities, the wide array of South Asian spaces now available allows many transmigrants to connect to socially homogenous friendship circles that are centered on their work ties rather than more diverse community ties. As Harshad mentions, most of his friends are from the same region in India and share his language and religious background; all are IT workers or associated with the industry. When I asked him about his typical weekend, Harshad replied: "Well, I mostly hang out with other Telugu speakers. What do we do? We go to see movies, go out to eat, go to the mall. Now and then we might go to the temple, but if it's some festival or holiday, then we go and cook with each other." This segregation has roots in India, where regional politics, history, and language traditions create distinctions among national subjects. Despite maintaining a language- and culture-specific friend network, Harshad nonetheless sees a key distinction between himself and the lower-status Indian workers: he spends his disposable income rather than just saving it or sending it back, and he is able to "pass" successfully in social and work contexts. The difference between the ideal transmigrant and the lower-tier worker is thus marked through the social capital that the former demonstrates; it's not just a matter of cultural isolation. One can still spend the majority of his time with people from India who seem similar, but how and what they do together is what sets them apart.

Likewise, in a conversation I had at a dinner party with Mitsy and her husband, Kamal, in Kirkland, Washington, the discussion about whether or not foreign workers should work to fit into the US echoed Harshad's sentiments. Mitsy was living in London when Kamal first came to work as a contractor, or a body-shopper, in Seattle. Even though she was anxious to join her husband, he cautioned her against working for a contractor, since she faced the distinct possibility of being placed in a low-status job or stuck waiting for a position between clients (a process that is referred to as "benching" in the IT industry). Instead, he encouraged her to wait until she could directly obtain a position with a software company. When she did begin working, Mitsy was eager to distinguish herself, not as just another Indian IT worker, but as someone with valuable Western work experience. When I asked about whether Mitsy had experienced any discrimination as a temporary worker, she was clear that negative feelings toward H-1B workers were normal and unsurprising. She noted, "It would happen in India too . . . if we were taking a bunch of foreign nationals and putting them in certain positions, like when Coca-Cola came to India in the 1970s, they were pushed out!" Instead, she argues, it is up to the individual to adapt to US social codes and professional environments. Mitsy's friend Malini, who was also at the dinner, quickly chimed in: "In the corporate world, I never had the experience that anyone has made me feel that I'm an outsider." As part of the well-educated and global world of IT, Malini argued that discrimination is rarely a problem as long as Indian workers are familiar with the culture of work in the US and do not offend the wider public socially.

However, Malini further noted that, outside of the IT sector, monitoring and adapting one's behavior is not enough; rather, "there are some areas in the US where there are some issues. Sometimes you see that attitude, that its an Indian who has walked in and they do not respect us. We won't get the same customer service that they would give to other white-skinned people." However, Mitsy and Malini read this as an issue of class discrimination, not race or national origin. Mitsy interjected: "I agree, I agree. But this is the exact conversation I've had with some American colleagues at work. But I what arrived at was that it wasn't that they particularly looked at Indians in a bad way, but it's the way you dress up, the way you carry yourself, how you act. That will determine the treatment you'll get in a shop or on the street." By disciplining one's decorum, dress, and public engagement to align with preconceived expectations of Indians as ideal subjects, Mitsy presumed, transmigrants should be able to avoid outright discrimination. Unwilling to categorize discrimination as tied to their status as nonwhite foreigners, Malini and Mitsy's focus on demonstrating appropriate class and social capital perhaps allows them to bypass the discrimination they still face as educated, middle-class workers who possess valuable skills. Moreover, class mobility through behavior modification and comportment becomes a more achievable metric for transmigrants, whereas shaking off the impact of racism and negative stereotyping that is based on national origin is a much harder task.

Thus, for Mitsy, Malini, and Harshad, the difference between acceptance and discrimination emerges partly as a result of their association with the IT industry, but also because they are able to display the correct social codes that allow them to pass as the "right" kind of foreigner. By emphasizing outward appearance, behavior, and consumption, as well as demonstrating facility with Western work environments, social spaces, and the ability to glide easily between domestic and foreign assignments, transmigrants seek to blend in as appropriate neoliberal subjects who can make their cultivated social capital legible to a broad global audience. The H-1B thus offers individual workers the chance to build their professional skills, but also the opportunity to learn the cultural norms that help them transform from generic Indian IT workers into valuable global liaisons.

BACKLOGS AND BACKLASH

Despite the efforts that transmigrants make to fit into US companies as foreigners, they still face intense scrutiny politically and professionally. Kamal was candid about the juridical limitations of being a temporary worker, limitations that existed regardless of how appropriately he behaved. Kamal initially moved to California through a body-shopping agency in 2001. After enduring months "on the bench" without work, Kamal finally found his way to contract work and eventually a permanent position in Redmond. He applied for several jobs, and even though he was qualified and subsequently vetted, he found that smaller companies were unwilling to hire him because of his temporary worker status. Kamal's wife Mitsy chimed in to explain that by the time they were eligible to apply for a green card, they were facing a severe backlog in the processing of applications: "Actually, at the time, we didn't know about the retrogression. You figured you had a fixed amount of time, you file it and you'll get it. So we didn't know what we'd run into." She noted that she was initially ambivalent about staying in the US and thought, "Oh, theek hai . . . mila, to theek hai, na mila, to kyaa hua [If we get it, great, if not, who knows, it will be fine]." But after several years of working for the same companies in the same positions, while their compatriots with green cards were able to move into higher-ranking positions, Kamal and Mitsy wanted to pursue permanent residency.

They experienced firsthand how the structure of the visa effectively moors workers to the companies that sponsor them, but does not necessarily allow for advancement within those firms. In order to navigate around this issue, companies might give workers additional responsibilities or move them into different teams, but often without a corresponding change in rank or salary grade. This period of stasis has long-term effects on IT workers' careers. A 2017 report of the San Francisco Bay area technology workforce from Ascend, a nonprofit Pan-Asian organization for business professionals in North America, found real barriers for Asian upward mobility. The report, which examined data collected from 2007 to 2015, found that "despite being outnumbered by Asian men and women in the entry-level professional workforce, white men and women were twice as likely as Asians to become executives and held almost 3x the number of executive jobs." Even though Asians made up the largest proportion of the IT workforce in the Bay Area, they were the least likely among all races to be managers or executives. Asian women, in particular, were the least likely of all to become executives.[26] While there are other factors at play, such as race, networking, and gender norms, the immigration status of many Asian workers also keeps them in lower positions. For Kamal and Mitsy, this means they were stuck in the same jobs as they proceeded with the green card process, which lasted several years.

Malini also found herself in a difficult situation because she actually switched jobs while on the H-1B. Though she had been working in the US for almost eight years, she was still waiting for her green card application to be processed: "Probably because of the retrogression, it will be about another two years. I made one mistake and should have filed my green card when I was a systems engineer, because for systems engineers, you can file under an EB2 category and there are more visas available." After switching to a new position within the same company, Malini's application was pushed back in the processing line, which she regretted. Because of the danger of having their permanent residency petitions pushed back, foreign workers often avoid pursuing valuable management or business development experiences that would further their careers. It is only after the green card process is complete that they are fully free to move to other jobs. Malini went on to note:

> It is unimaginable that a country that can be efficient on so many fronts, they just do not have the right ethics to make the immigration policy work. I think it is just because it doesn't really benefit them. They feel that it's fine to have people dangling. Unless there is an exodus of H-1Bs

all over the US, which I don't think would happen, they won't look at
reform. What benefit does the government get out of these reforms?
They probably don't. People have to wait for years and years without
any knowledge—they don't have a timeline of when they will move
forward. . . . But nobody really cares, so it doesn't change.

Although Kamal and Mitsy had moved through the immigration system
successfully and become citizens, they remained frustrated by the long
backlogs in processing permanent residency applications that mark many
H-1B workers' experiences. Kamal's, Mitsy's, and Malini's stories underscore how the H-1B operates to extract surplus labor from flexible workers,
as the US immigration system not only facilitates but creates conditions that
keep workers in limbo for several years. Without H-1B workers, the US
technology sector might suffer; however, there is little incentive to change
the process, which ensures a steady stream of new, disposable workers ready
to replace others as needed.

Beyond the backlog, as an Indian Muslim, Kamal underwent additional
delays and layers of scrutiny when his green card application was finally
processed. Following new restrictions that were established after the World
Trade Center and Pentagon attacks of September 11, 2001, he had to endure
a lengthy background check. While the majority of my interviewees were
from Hindu families, as IT workers tend to be overwhelmingly drawn from
the Hindu upper castes, the inflammation of anti-Islamic sentiments across
the US has created new barriers for South Asian Muslims coming to the
US. Their applications are often subjected to higher levels of vetting by the
Department of Homeland Security. Another Muslim H-1B worker, Shirin,
had her green card for several years before she decided to apply for citizenship. At the time, she and her husband were considering moving back to
India and desired US citizenship in case they decided to return in the
future. With the green card, residents are required to return to the US
regularly to keep their status active; however, with citizenship, individuals
can live abroad indefinitely. However, as Gujarati Muslims, it took over two
years for them to finally obtain citizenship, despite having successfully
completed each stage of the process. Shirin related: "So there was the problem with September 11 and my husband's last name is Mohammed. We
always had extra background checks. All our friends walked in, did the
interview and had their oath ceremony. Not us." She concluded by noting,
"I can't believe it [was random]. . . . because we are of a certain sect, this
is how we get treated?" For Muslim transmigrants like Kamal and Shirin,

the H-1B visa, green card, and citizenship processes are an opportunity to formalize their belonging in the US. At the same time, they are also imbricated in geopolitics that stratify immigrants on religious, cultural, and regional grounds.

Since Trump's election, the discriminatory immigration and border control practices that Kamal and Shirin experienced have gotten worse and will likely continue to do so in the near future. In September 2017, the Department of Homeland Security instituted new rules that would require *all* immigrants (including permanent residents and naturalized citizens) to disclose their social media aliases and other highly personal information. Such politically motivated actions promote the idea that immigrants are categorically untrustworthy and a security risk to the nation. The rise in nationalist and xenophobic sentiment has had deadly consequences for Indian IT workers. In February 2017, two Indian H-1B workers were shot in Olathe, Kansas. Srinivas Kuchibhotla and Alok Madasani, software engineers on H-1B visas working for the GPS company Garmin, were at a bar watching a basketball game when a white Navy veteran got into an altercation with the men. The shooter demanded to know if the men were "legally" in the US. He then screamed at them to "get out of my country" before opening fire on the two men, murdering Kuchibhotla and severely injuring Madasani. In an emotional press conference after the incident, Kuchibhotla's father pleaded with Indian parents not to send their sons and daughters to the US, especially as incidents of racially and nationally motivated hate crimes increase. A few days later, Kuchibhotla's wife made a heart-wrenching statement detailing how much her husband had loved the US and how he had dreamt of building a life in Kansas. Kuchtibhotla's and Madasani's stories are a chilling reminder about the very real dangers that immigrants continue to face, even those who have mastered the appropriate skills as ideal transmigrants.

Though the path to becoming an H-1B worker is complicated by political and bureaucratic factors and an increasing risk to personal safety, workers still seek the H-1B visa because of perceived benefits of working in the US that go beyond economic rationales. Working in the US becomes an aspiration that is tied to developing professional skills and networks, but also to learning specific cultural codes and practices that mark visa holders as valuable workers and global liaisons. As discriminatory, anti-temporary-worker, and anti-foreigner sentiments grow in the US, this transnational connection becomes even more significant. Though transmigrants still have to contend with immigration systems that do not align with the purported "flatness" of IT or globalization and, therefore, must overcome concrete barriers posed by visas, green cards, and citizenship applications, transmigration nonetheless becomes both a coveted process and an identity for Indian workers.

"BEING LIKE BENJAMIN FRANKLIN": H-1B WORKER AS BRIDGE BUILDER

Even as they seek desperately to come abroad and establish a foothold in the US, many transmigrants actively maintain material and emotive links to their homelands. As transmigration and diaspora studies scholars have shown, transnational community formation takes place by re-creating customs and traditions abroad,[27] traveling frequently between locations,[28] maintaining virtual networks,[29] volunteering to create new local networks,[30] and improving the home nation from afar.[31] Among the transmigrants in this study, volunteering for India-oriented development organizations has become an important avenue for creating communities while living abroad; such activities also serve to push against the idea of the "brain drain," reframing the skills they have gained abroad as vital to their homeland's development. These volunteering activities help transmigrants position themselves as bridge builders who view their liminal status as a way to both create local communities and maintain links in their homelands.[32] Volunteering for ethnic or nationality-specific organizations in the US has long been a facet of immigrant community life; as with older generations, the H-1B transmigrants I profile here view their philanthropic and organizing activities as a way to connect with local diasporas socially. However, rather than devote their efforts to building community institutions in the host nation, they seek to apply to Indian development efforts the neoliberal and managerial practices they have internalized while working for Western companies.

This sort of long-distance volunteering allows them to give back to the homelands they have left behind and is also interpolated by the Indian nation-state as a way to better harness the economic and political clout of this transnational class. As the Indian government creates new opportunities for the greater integration of its diaspora through the development of partial dual-citizenship categories, it also symbolically deploys the entrepreneurialism of the transnational IT worker as a replacement for a state-sponsored vision of national progress. This neoliberal nationalism, which prioritizes skills, technical education, and global connection, becomes a substitute for state-led development and it has been amplified under prime ministers Atal Bihari Vajpayee, Manmohan Singh, and Narendra Modi, whose administrations have presided over the global technology boom that coincided with the rise of the H-1B program in the United States.

VOLUNTEERING AND LONG-DISTANCE DEVELOPMENT

With the explosion of Indian populations in the Pacific Northwest, new nonprofits, annual charity events, and family foundations aimed at development in India have grown rapidly in the region. Two institutions were particularly important among transmigrant communities: Children's Rights and You (CRY) and the Association for India's Development (AID). Nearly all of the participants in this study had volunteered with or attended an event sponsored by one of these two groups. The Seattle chapter of CRY is one of the most active chapters of the organization, which has twenty-five "action centers" in the US. The Seattle chapter was founded in 2003, and its main goal is to raise funds for partner nongovernmental organizations in India that are working to improve children's access to education and other social rights. It also seeks to mobilize individuals "to take responsibility for the situation of underprivileged children, especially Indian, and so motivate them to seek resolution through individual and collective action thereby enabling children to realize their full potential, and people to discover their potential for action and change."[33] The CRY Seattle chapter hosts four to six major events annually, including a Holi festival, which drew over 4,000 people in Bellevue in 2015. They also sponsor an annual fund-raising gala, several music concerts with local and traveling Indian musicians, and a garba celebration during the Navratri season.

Events such as the gala dinner and the Holi festival take place in downtown Bellevue and Kirkland, while concerts, movie nights, and dance events often take place at the Microsoft campus in Redmond. The technology company's offices have become a space for community gathering and also blur the line between work and life, thereby encouraging IT workers to spend substantial portions of their private time at the office. There has been much written about the design of IT offices as self-enclosed campuses that strive to provide everything a worker needs on-site to increase productivity. Companies such as Google, Salesforce.com, Microsoft, and Amazon offer "perks" such as gyms, massage chairs, nap stations, free food, and happy hours, which are intended to create enticing workplace environments and extract more labor from workers, who need not leave the office to meet their basic (or leisure) needs.[34] In addition to the ubiquitous video game stations and ping-pong tables that dot the corridors, the Microsoft campus in Redmond hosts a massive food hall and indoor shopping mall. As Jay Yarow notes, "It's more like a town than a headquarters."[35] Neon signs above reception desks read "Live, Work, Play," and several groups and clubs meet in common areas during lunch breaks. During the late afternoon, cricket leagues and soccer teams play alongside one another on the expansive lawns that surround the sprawling campus. In the evening, café tables and chairs are pushed to the edges of the cavernous dining halls of the campus "commons" to make space for Indian dance rehearsals. Conference rooms that normally hold meetings for product developers and marketing teams are transformed into speaker halls where NGOs host presenters or show films. The audiences for these events are drawn from the nearby apartment complexes that surround the area, which are filled primarily with recently arrived IT workers and their spouses. Such spaces are particularly important for transmigrants who might not feel as integrated into other social sites in the region, or who lack transportation.

Organizations such as CRY and AID also use these environments to recruit Indian IT workers to become volunteers who can connect with their homelands through philanthropic efforts. AID Seattle meets weekly on the Microsoft campus, and the CRY Seattle homepage even displays specific instructions for Microsoft employees to make donations and receive a matching corporate gift (no other companies are specified). While the stated mission of CRY is to fund-raise for development projects abroad, the majority of its day-to-day focus is on orchestrating social events in the Puget Sound area. Transmigrants are often motivated to volunteer by the opportunity to network, create social bonds in a foreign land, and to validate their identity in places where they are normally considered minorities. As Sandro Cattacin and Dagmar Domenig note, by participating in formal organizations, "the experiences of foreignness and alienation are not only made understandable, but are also normalised through exchange within the group and, in the process, are de-individualised."[36] These NGOs organize bike rides, running events, dance parties, concerts, films, and speaker series that function as fund-raising events and also vital social spaces for personal connection. Even beyond the large public events, which draw thousands of people, the regular chapter meetings, happy hours, planning committees, volunteer nights, and rehearsals for performances create opportunities for transmigrants to participate in communities comprised of others occupying similar positions. Having the opportunity to meet other H-1B workers also increases resource and information sharing, and leads to friendships that endure outside of the office.

These spaces, both physical and organizational, help transmigrants craft subjectivities as bridge builders who can aid the Indian nation-state. No longer living in India but not fully integrated in the US, transmigrants turn to such organizations to help bridge the displacement they experience while living abroad. Appealing to the "domestic abroad," such organizations blur the line between citizen and transmigrant, as they rely on diasporic networks for funding initiatives that might otherwise be led by the state.[37] In fact, Situ credits his time abroad with heightening his sense of obligation to development in India and with opening his eyes to different poverty-alleviation solutions. He remarked:

> When I was in India, it's ironic, I had a very capitalistic view of the nation in the sense that all you should do is make factory-like schools all over the country. That's it. When I came to volunteer, I saw that's not really what's plaguing the educational system. I got to know real social workers because they come to America to give talks. My understanding of India deepened *because* I was in America. I don't think there is such a well-organized social group in India that does this kind of work simply because the means of communication—email and meeting spaces that we have [at work] or in community centers—they are just not as available in India. Traveling in India too, it's just harder than in the US. My conclusion was that I could actually do more for India by being here.

Like Situ, Malini noted that she volunteers as a way to give back to India, but also because she feels as though those who reside in India are unwilling or unable to do so as effectively as she and her fellow transmigrants can:

> We've used every amenity to do the work. In whatever and every way you can give, you give. And it's just the true feeling of helping that is guiding these people. But when I go to India and I sometimes see the corruption, it totally pushes me down. Am I doing all the work for this? We are like the top [country] for corruption. I feel the attitude that Indians develop here of helping, giving back, and doing honest efforts to do that, it's really, really good. And I feel like somehow, the Indians staying back in India, they should see how much effort we put in here. How many hours, how many numbers of people, how much honest effort we put in. Of course, we are having a good time doing it.

Situ and Malini both assert that they are neither tainted by the corruption nor frustrated by the red tape that often characterizes Indian bureaucracies, precisely because they do not reside in the country. By living as transmigrants, both Situ and Malini see themselves as leaders for the nation they left behind, and as strong advocates for expanding children's access to education. This transformation from passive (and skeptical) Indian citizen to active transmigrant occurs on several levels. First, while historically US ethnic organizations have been directed toward helping new immigrants integrate, all the while preserving cultural traditions and customs abroad, transmigrants are not simply working with these NGOS as an assimilatory gesture. Rather, they are using their links to the IT industry as a way to mobilize and organize around Indian development issues, presuming that they will likely return or spend substantial amounts of time in India, due in great part to their lifestyles as circulating and migratory workers. They are not motivated by the desire to find ethnic organizations where they might celebrate native customs or even to preserve these traditions in a new country (though they do participate in such spaces); rather, the specific mission of these groups is to create new constituencies of transmigrants who are willing to offer time and money to the benefit the home nation. Moreover, as they travel regularly between India and the US, transmigrants are able to check in on the projects that the NGO sponsors in India, which allows them to maintain a visceral and regular connection with the work they believe they are supporting financially. This affective engagement and neoliberal confirmation of a "return" on their investment of time and money motivates them to continue volunteering.

Second, Situ and Malini attribute the transformation in their attitudes about civic engagement to their exposure to Western workplaces and society. They believe that after they came to the West, they were able to offer more to development efforts than they could have while still living in India. Situ's motivation for volunteering is grounded in what he presumes is a more authentic understanding of Indian development challenges because he is removed from the day-to-day politics of the nation. From his vantage point in the US, he has had a chance to expand and clarify his vision of the "real" problems plaguing Indian education or child welfare efforts, the most important of which, in his mind, is the lack of an accountable state. He argues that because of this change in perspective (geographically and mentally), he sees the individualized or private-sector responses, such as self-help groups or privately funded schools and clinics that CRY and AID support, as better solutions to poverty or providing empowerment. These solutions become closely aligned with the entrepreneurial rhetoric of IT itself. State-led economic reforms are not enough to create change. Instead, the individual middle-class subject becomes the catalyst. Technical, agile, and project-based solutions are valued over systemic investment or structural reform. Even as he critiques his earlier "capitalistic" perspective, Situ's activism still reinforces neoliberal models of development, whereby private solutions to poverty are developed by those located outside of the communities most impacted. Situ praises the systems of communication, processes for fund-raising, ease of travel, and even the comfort and cleanliness of physical spaces that foster the NGO activism in the US and seeks to help cultivate those attributes in the Indian context. As part of this cadre of transmigrants who view themselves as situated outside the webs of corruption that control Indian politics, he and his comrades believe they can leverage the cultures and wealth of the global classes to mitigate the failures of the state. The market, the entrepreneur, and the NGO emerge as the sites through which fissures created by sedentary inequality are to be resolved—not the state. Thus the liberal promise of forging an enlightened nation-state capable of uplifting all of its citizens is eschewed in favor of anti-state solutions that draw on the transmigrant as a vital change agent.

Expressing his admiration for a colleague who quit the software industry altogether and opened a school in India, Situ confessed that he once felt that leaving India meant that he was turning his back on his homeland. But, like other transmigrants who work with NGOs in the Seattle region, Situ can engage in an alternative vision of "giving back" that accommodates his own life goals and desires to work in the US without feeling that he is betraying his country. He noted,

> It was one of the most important factors that kind of made me decide that I can be here and still work for the country. I had read Benjamin Franklin's biography and learned that he was in France for ten or twelve years during the War of Independence, and still he was a good example. And even Mahatma Gandhi had stayed in South Africa for twenty years, so I thought, yeah, it's OK!

Situ references figures of anticolonial nationalism in both the US and India as models for his own philanthropic practices and sees his location as a class- and caste-privileged member of the Indian diaspora as carrying the same revolutionary potential. More than an economic link between a developing nation and the global economy, the H-1B transmigrant comes to inhabit and rework his or her subjectivity as part of the vanguard that will bring the lessons of responsibility, self-empowerment, and neoliberal change home, while also using the experience of volunteering to create social and professional networks with other transmigrants.

GLOBAL INDIANS AS NATIONAL NEOLIBERALS

Scholars of Indian political economy such as Leela Fernandes, Paula Chakravartty, and Rohit Chopra argue that such diasporic engagements can also result in the consolidation of a narrow vision of Indian identity that is steeped in retrogressive nationalism while valorizing the global over the domestic.[38] Indian state efforts to bring transmigrants back into the imaginary of the nation also work to conjoin the global with the nation.[39] For example, with the extension of new citizenship categories such as the "Overseas Citizenship of India (OCI)" or the "Person of Indian Origin (PIO)" initiatives, Indians living abroad or even those enjoying foreign citizenship are able to invest more easily, retain funds, and buy property in India, thereby exerting greater economic influence within the nation.[40] Seeking to entice higher numbers of technology workers and other wealthy diasporics to invest in Indian real estate, financial products, or banks, such efforts elevate the nonresident Indian middle class as a major economic driver within the bounds of the nation.

Speaking to a crowd at an annual celebration of the Indian diaspora (the Pravasi Bharatiya Divas), former prime minister Manmohan Singh capitalized on this connection by recalling his predecessor's "India Shining" campaign, intended to use technology to catapult the nation into modernity.[41] In his speech, Singh praised government-run programs that were slated to train 200,000 emigrant workers who would be well positioned to "fill the large labour supply gaps emerging in the western world."[42] Through such efforts, the Indian state has taken up responsibility for expanding opportunities for migration through greater investment in educating future workers of the nation, but also future workers of *foreign* nations. These workers hope that their training will translate into jobs abroad, while the Indian state sees transmigration as a way to increase remittances and investment at home. As Singh notes: "In this increasingly inter-dependent and inter-connected world, overseas Indians are becoming 'global citizens'. The overarching idea of a shared culture and shared values bonds us together. . . . The idea of India transcends the narrow barriers of religion, language, caste or class, both within and outside the Indian nation."[43] Such a declaration of "Indianness" discursively redefines the nation as a transnational construction. As

Anita N. Jain argues, "By imagining the nation and diaspora as occupying the same affective space, through neoliberal terms, the state promotes a form of nationalist discourse predicated on economic exchange."[44] Since Indian independence, the nation has struggled to integrate people from various linguistic, regional, and religious backgrounds into a single populace under the banner of "unity in diversity."[45] Singh resolves the tension between sectarianism and the homogenizing impulses of nationalism here by drawing on an ahistorical notion of "shared culture and values," which are de-linked from territorial formation or political context. Thus, the transmigrant becomes the ideal Indian subject whose individual actions can bring about change within the nation, even when residing outside of its boundaries.

This embrace of neoliberal nationalism among IT workers has also led many of them to support conservative and right-wing political causes, such as the rise of militant Hindu groups and nationalist parties, including the Bhartiya Janata Party (BJP), which recently brought Narendra Modi to power as prime minister.[46] Modi has been implicated in the spread of bloody riots in the state of Gujarat in 2002, when he was chief minister of the state, and for inciting subsequent waves of sectarian strife during his reign. Under his leadership as prime minister, there have been new forms of communitarian violence aimed at religious, caste, and sexual minorities.[47] At the same time, Modi has fashioned himself as a pro-business, technically savvy, and globally oriented champion of neoliberalism in India and beyond. With an active Twitter presence competing on an international level with Trump, he has a broad reach across the diaspora and has found purchase among IT workers, who have been particularly impressed by the economic redevelopment in Gujarat under his administration.[48] Because he is a vocal proponent of the Indian technology industries and consistently hails transmigrants through speeches and media events, workers who see him as their advocate in India and abroad have embraced Modi. Here, IT transmigrants, as the source of indirect remittances, foreign direct investment, and new entrepreneurship opportunities, are interpolated by the state and held up as the example by which India ought to model its development.

Poonam, a CRY volunteer, Microsoft employee, and former H-1B worker, finds resonances in Modi's Indian neoliberal strongman approach. When we met at his Redmond office in 2015, Poonam was clear in his admiration:

> Narendra Modi? I think he has been fantastic for the country. Yeah, there
> is all the Hindutva stuff and all, but overall he has brought more good than

bad. He has the majority in Parliament, so he can actually bring about change. He has already been starting with improving IT infrastructure and enabling youth to bring change. Like his "Discuss and Do" website— it allows you to get involved and offer your opinions on change in India. It's hard to do this as an NRI—discuss topics and people can bring it to the government. But now, youth get more involved and empowered. He also uses technology as much as he can. I think India is moving in the right direction under Modi.

In this discussion, Poonam side-steps critiques of Modi as an ideologue and conspirator in genocide. Instead, he embraces Modi's neoliberal vision of an open democracy (even though there have been arrests, censoring, and even attacks on his detractors since his ascent). Poonam is not unique. Even though Modi had been previously denied a visitor visa to enter the US because of his link to the Gujarat atrocities, when he launched a formal state visit as the new Indian prime minister in 2015, he was greeted with wildly excited crowds of Indian supporters. During his election in India, it was reported that over 10,000 US-based Indians returned home to campaign for him, while the US chapter of the BJP (which claims almost 2 million members) sent out "supporter" teams across major US cities and university campuses to generate enthusiasm for Modi's candidacy.[49] Many of the same supporters of Modi who embraced his virulent anti-foreigner and anti-Islamic sentiment in India have admired the Trump White House's stance on banning refugee and visitor visas from Muslim-majority countries, even as Trump also threatens to cut back the H-1B program. While Poonam is careful to distance himself from the radical elements of the BJP, his whole-hearted support for Modi's message of neoliberalism and modernization is grounded in a version of an Indian nationalism that favors the technologically savvy and transnational classes, without corresponding structural transformation.

CONCLUSION

The H-1B program emerges as a site of contradiction, especially with xenophobic and isolationist ideologues in the White House paving the way toward a new world order that is enflaming resentment and distrust of immigrants. Labeled as perpetual foreigners, Indian workers nonetheless still see the program as a way to engage in personal growth and self-discovery while living abroad. At the same time, workers face long delays in transferring from temporary to permanent residency and remain trapped in the liminal space of midlevel workers who cannot advance their careers because of immigration restrictions. In response to these constraints, H-1B workers discursively represent themselves as vital to US technology industries while also acknowledging the ways in which the industry benefits from their labor and insecure status. As Saskia Sassen has argued, subjects with liminal status work to situate themselves as civically engaged and model citizens, even when they do not formally possess the necessary status to claim social and political belonging.[50] By participating in long-distance development and nation-building efforts, H-1B transmigrants reject narratives about the low value of temporary workers. Even amid real danger and constraint, transmigrants are able to recast their time spent away from India as a positive development that helps them professionally and personally. In that way, temporary migration can transform the Third World subject into a legitimate neoliberal subject in the US while also allowing him or her to retain a cosmopolitan and nationally oriented identity that is valorized at home.

2 Engineer Brides and H-1B Grooms

Visas, Marriage, and Family Formation

WHEN I MET AMINA IN 2010 IN REDMOND, WASHINGTON, SHE HAD been working on an H-1B visa for a major software company for a few years. At the time of our interview, Amina had just initiated a trial separation from her husband. They met while living in Bangalore and had been dating for a short period of time when she learned she had been admitted to a graduate program in computer engineering in Seattle. She was determined to come to the United States, but her family insisted that she get married before she moved abroad. Since her boyfriend was also planning to attend graduate school (in Boston), their families encouraged them to marry and travel together, even though they would have to reside in separate households. Upon graduation, they converted their student visas to H-1B visas after finding jobs, but they were unable to find work in the same part of the country. After four years of a long-distance marriage, they decided to end the relationship. Although Amina's mother had even made a special visit with the intention of helping the couple reconcile, Amina was determined to move forward—alone.

Unmoored from her marriage and on her own for the first time as an adult, Amina enjoyed financial independence but struggled to figure out her next step. She noted that during her marriage, she had been committed to the idea of moving back to India: "My husband wanted to buy a house and it made financial sense. But we never did because I felt like I'm going back to India. I'm going back to India. All the time. I don't want to be tied down with a house." However, after living on her own and establishing a new community of friends through work and her volunteer activities, Amina changed her mind. When I asked about whether she would want to go back now, she admitted it would be very difficult for her to adjust to the scrutiny she would face about her personal life in India, particularly after the dissolution of her marriage. She noted:

> The main thing I love about being here in US is that it gives women, especially Indian women, so much freedom. Whereas, back in India, that's not so. You have to live there to feel the different ways in which society—everything—is so restricted. I mean, for example, here, if I just felt like, I could take my car and go off somewhere for a drive. Or come back late at night. And that is something that is not possible there. Even in the daylight, even if you have your own vehicle and means in India, you couldn't just go off on your own anywhere.

Here Amina associates living in the US with a certain level of privacy and as a way of shielding herself from the scrutiny of neighbors and family members. Amina recalled, "It was harder for young, unmarried girls to get an apartment [in Bangalore]. People would say, oh, there'll be guys coming or . . . so it's always harder for us to get apartments than similar, unmarried young men. Whereas here, I never faced that kind of problem." After growing used to the relative independence she experienced in the US and because she was on her own H-1B visa and not tied to her husband's employment status, she was free to stay in the US, pursue her own interests, and live outside of the constraints of marriage and family. "See, this hiking and all? That is what I like to do and now I can spend my time with people who share my interests. I get to be someone that I want to be. Not have to be," Amina said during our interview. An avid outdoorswoman, Amina had been training to scale Mt. Rainier with friends in order to raise funds for AID. Proud of her ability to support herself and to engage in the lifestyle of her choice, Amina pushes against gender norms suggesting that Indian women should prioritize marriage and family concerns over their own desires or ambitions.

While the cases profiled in the previous chapter demonstrate how transmigrant identity is partially consolidated through the internalization of corporate IT cultures and long-distance nationalism, Amina's story shows how ideas about gender, marriage, and friendship also are shaped by the experience of transmigration. Beyond their professional and social service, some transmigrants use their liminal status to push against cultural norms, as Amina's example suggests. Although Amina's case may not characterize the full breadth of transmigrant women's experiences and could be considered an outlier, her story importantly demonstrates how intimate decision-making is calibrated through the process of migration and can lead to changes in gender norms and expectations. At the same time, transmigrants use migration as a way of facilitating traditional marriage and family formation, even as they face restrictions and backlash in the US. In some of those cases, transmigration also can sediment retrogressive cultural aspects of those same institutions, as many women end up becoming dependent housewives after marriage. This contradiction leads to the question: How does transmigration both challenge and consolidate gendered expectations around work, marriage, and family formation?

THE INTIMACIES OF IT MIGRATION

The differential experiences of women engineers and software workers—an underrepresented but important segment of H-1B visa holders—offer insight into how transmigration is not simply economically or employment driven, but also structured by gendered decision-making that has repercussions for social institutions across borders. Statistically, women make up a much smaller percentage of IT workers in general, but their numbers are increasing in India. Drawing on IT industry data, Parvati Raghuram notes that "in India software engineering has proved to be more open to women than any other field of science and engineering with many companies actually preferring to recruit women as the attrition rate is lower than that among men."[1] In the US, the lower number of women pursuing STEM is often ascribed to gender socialization and the characterization of those fields as "unfeminine," whereas in India, there are fewer stigmas attached to women entering science- and math-based fields.[2] Computer science and engineering are highly valued fields for women in India, presumably because working in these fields tends to enhance a woman's ability to balance work and family demands after marriage. Working in these fields may also add considerable income to the household and is associated with work in offices and laboratories, which are seen as high-status places of employment. Moreover, the IT industry is seen as more "woman friendly" because of the stability, cleanliness, and respectability associated with working in a globalized office environment.

At the same time, family pressures play a major role in women's pursuit of STEM degrees and whether or not they can actually put them to use. Namrata Gupta attributes the "feminization of science" to the higher prestige associated with scientific fields and the growing preference of families to look for a bride that can work.[3] As other studies of women STEM students have shown, the decision to study engineering or science is often determined by parents, rather than individual students, and is tied to cultural and gendered notions of appropriate work-life balance.[4] Even though women's enrollment in science and engineering has been rising in India, after joining the workforce, more women are still concentrated in quality assurance or testing, areas that are considered less technical than the more rigorous and more lucrative development or research sectors. Historically, women's education in India has been regarded as a "consumption luxury" rather than a "productive investment." While having an education is important to finding a suitable marriage partner, a woman's skills and education ultimately benefit her husband's family, who have greater say over her ability to work.[5] Thus, while a woman's education is an added bonus in matrimonial arrangements, there is no guarantee that, upon marriage, she will put those skills to work, or have the opportunity to pursue her own career ambitions.

As a result, the number of women in India actually working in IT after finishing their degrees is much lower than that of men who possess similar qualifications, and the number drops significantly after marriage. Such patterns are present across sectors in India: between 2005 and 2015, there was a notable decrease in women's labor force participation, even though women's employment rates rose globally.[6] Even when women enter engineering programs, educators and future employers assume that they are not as serious as male students, and will likely prioritize marriage and childrearing over the pursuit of competitive jobs. In turn, women are less likely to be chosen for short-term foreign work assignments, and they often must obtain the consent of their families before applying to graduate programs overseas. This gender imbalance is reflected in the pool of H-1B visa holders. Xiang Biao notes that "women made up only 24 per cent of all the temporary workers and trainees who entered the USA in 2002."[7] Although it is nearly impossible to obtain gender-disaggregated data about the H-1B visa, and the USCIS has turned down repeated requests to provide such information, in 2013 Professor Karen Panetta testified in front of Congress that only about 15 to 20 percent of visas were issued to women.[8] These figures confirm that there are far fewer women H-1B workers from India, and even fewer who come on their own before marriage.

TRANSMIGRATION AND CHALLENGES TO MARRIAGE

Many of the women who do travel on H-1B visas find it difficult to subscribe to traditional gender roles or give up their careers in favor of their husbands' jobs after building their own careers. Many face a paradox: on the one hand, they are encouraged to pursue STEM degrees as a way of increasing their marriageability; on the other hand, they are expected (or required by immigration policy) to relinquish their own ambitions and adhere to patriarchal norms once they are married. Madhu's story exemplifies the gendered expectations that women face on the H-1B visa and the dissonances that migration created for her personal life. She migrated to the US in 2006 for graduate school and, at the time of our interview, she had been working in Redmond as a contractor for six months. Unlike most women in her peer group, she was still single and, as a result, faced intense pressure from her conservative South Indian Tamil community to return to India to get married or consent to a marriage abroad arranged by her family. Defiantly, Madhu asserted that her time in the US was a precious opportunity to escape the obligations of family and the pressures to "settle down." She relished the economic and physical independence that came with earning a generous paycheck and sharing an apartment with other young Indian women who worked in IT. As an H-1B visa holder, she also remained suspicious of the intentions of young men in India who were eager to come to the US and who, consequently, would jump at the chance to marry a woman with a foothold in the US immigration system. Acknowledging that she would eventually acquiesce to her family's expectations, she wanted to enjoy the freedom of a young, single woman while she could.

Madhu is not alone in her desire to remain unattached while living abroad. Among unmarried Indian students, there is a lower preference to return to India after studying in the US.[9] In part, this is because of the pressure they face to marry and start families once they return. A similar desire resonates among H-1B workers, who grow accustomed to what they perceive as greater openness in US culture toward dating and premarital relationships. Single women and men on the H-1B see the visa as a pathway to independence outside of family expectations for early marriage, as well as a chance to develop their own career and educational opportunities. While few outright reject marriage as a pathway, especially in light of the prescriptive role that heterosexual marriage plays in India, H-1B workers do tend to delay marriage.[10] Many choose to tackle time-consuming assignments that interfere with family life, hoping to establish their careers, to be seen as "team-players" willing to work long and hard hours, and to increase their earning capacity.[11] These assignments also help them demonstrate their company loyalty and work ethic, thereby improving the chances that their employers will support their permanent residency petitions. For this reason, work is seen as an acceptable substitute for marriage; however, men are more likely than women to avoid scrutiny for staying single.

Take Malini, for instance. When she considered coming to the US after gaining H-1B approval, she experienced strong family pressure to get married before migrating: "My dad was hesitant. Because he was like, 'Why don't you get married and then go. You'll be away, you've never stayed away and that will be tough. It will change you.'" Concerned that the experience of living on her own in a foreign country would make it difficult to find a suitable partner for her later, Malini's father was reluctant to grant her permission to leave at all. However, the chance to work with a prestigious company such as Microsoft ultimately convinced him that living and working abroad would improve Malini's economic and social prospects. Subsequently, he allowed her to go. In her study of Indian engineering students in the US, Debalina Dutta finds that there is the sense that women experience an "in-betweenness" that pulls them "between working towards occupational efficacy by gaining 'successful' engineering careers that take time and commitment, and fulfilling their obligation to their parents by adhering to patrifocal Indian customs."[12] Malini was caught in this same trap. She was determined to establish herself professionally but had to mitigate her family's fear that her migration as a single woman would open her to potential dishonor, render her vulnerable to danger, or make her too old to find a suitable match. Her family, who would not be able to maintain a close level of oversight over her behavior from India, was also caught between supporting her pursuit of a career and wanting her to resolve her marital obligations.

In some ways, Malini's father's fears came true. The longer she lived abroad independently, the harder it became for her to give up her own career to accommodate a partner. Malini was clear that she would rather wait to find a good relationship rather than jump into a hastily arranged, and potentially unhappy, marriage. However, she felt that she was at a disadvantage because she was older when she came to the US for work (rather than school) and was less connected to communities of single Indian men who were already residing in the US and would share her perspective on modern womanhood. She was unwilling to step outside of the Indian community to date for fear of her parents' rebuke, and was resigning herself to the possibility of staying single for the long term. She noted, "The girls like me who have come here on H-1B, we find it really hard. It's better if you are here as a student, you get to know other boys like you, too. I do know girls who got lucky eventually and found someone. But I've also seen girls who are still single and still more elder to me and they are still looking out." She was not completely closed off to the possibility of redirecting her professional ambitions for the right person, but only under certain conditions: "If I meet the right person and feel like giving up everything and moving, I'll do it. But only after I take my green card, then I'll see other opportunities." Malini's insistence on getting a green card before leaving the workplace is linked to the problems that women face when they are on spousal visas such as the H-4 visa or when they do not have independent immigration status, which I explore in greater depth in the next chapter. As an H-1B holder, Malini can work, but if she were to marry another temporary worker and quit her job, there is little guarantee that she would be able to obtain another visa or easily reenter the job market. As a result, Malini was reluctant to give up her independence or her visa for marriage, despite her desire to start a meaningful partnership.

While Amina, Madhu, and Malini saw working on the H-1B as an opportunity that allows them to temporarily create lives outside of heteronormative and gendered expectations around family life in India, they still faced substantial pressure to marry (or in Amina's case, stay married). All three women were encouraged to enter IT because it increased the likelihood that they would find suitable marriage partners, but in practice, it also diminished their desire for the type of traditional marriages that would require them to give up or curtail their careers. While Madhu and Malini specifically did not reject marriage and were looking actively for partnership, they were discerning about finding a partner who would support their ability to work and advance in their jobs. While their cases do not represent all women on H-1B visas, and many decide to marry without completely sacrificing their careers, these women's stories show how some remain trapped between maintaining their independence and potentially compromising their ambitions in order to marry, especially if their husbands' opportunities and desires override their own.

MAKING SUITABLE MATCHES

While transmigration may challenge traditional ideas about gender and family for some, the process can actually work to consolidate marriage and gender norms for others. Prakash, whom I met in 2009, invited me to his home to meet his wife Reena, who had traveled to the US on the H-4 visa three years prior. Prakash had moved to the US in 2000 to pursue a graduate degree in computer science engineering. After finishing his master's degree, he moved to Seattle and found a job with an Indian contracting firm that supplies workers to large corporations such as Microsoft. Embedded in a team working on a core product at the Redmond headquarters, Prakash still was not a full-time employee, or "FTE," a point that came up several times during our conversation. Without FTE status, Prakash did not have the benefit of long-term job security. Instead, he was subject to the vagrancies of annual contracts and shorter term assignments. Even without a permanent position, he had wanted to get married while on the H-1B visa rather than after entering the green card process. Immigration lawyers working with H-1B visa holders at Microsoft regularly advise workers to get married while on the temporary visa since they will face greater restrictions as they move further along the process of applying for permanent residency. Whereas H-1B workers can bring spouses to the US almost immediately after marriage, in contrast, green card holders must wait at least six months before sponsoring their spouses to join them. The differences in the immigration process for temporary migrants and permanent residents points to the racial logics of exclusion that underpin US immigration policy. Historically, while the marriage and family life of non-nationals has been subject to state regulation through, for example, legislation that banned Asian women from migrating in the nineteenth century or through contemporary policies that curb family reunification for immigrants of certain visa categories, the H-1B visa offers temporary and nonresident transmigrants a quick pathway for family reunification or to start families. As "non-immigrants" who are presumed to return to their home countries after a period of time, H-1Bs presumably are less likely to become part of growing immigrant populations, even though they have the option of becoming permanent residents and citizens. This assumed temporariness allows H-1B holders to sponsor family members to join them immediately, in comparison to green card holders, whose spouses and children would also qualify for green cards and be subject to greater scrutiny.

Prakash felt the time crunch created by his H-1B visa, and so his family began the process of finding an appropriate match for him, even though he did not have FTE status. Prakash did not drink, smoke, or eat meat, and he wanted to marry someone who was well educated, of the same caste and linguistic background, and someone who shared his social values. As a result, he wanted his parents to arrange his marriage, which is a common practice across India and the diaspora. According to the Center for Studies of Developing Societies–Konrad Adeneur Stiftung (CSDS-KAS) survey of Indian youth attitudes in 2016, 84 percent of those who married when they were fifteen to thirty-four years old had an arranged marriage and of those, 97 percent were from within the same caste.[13] When seeking a spouse, the majority of Indian IT workers prefer to find partners with religious, cultural, and linguistic commonality, and also emphasize education and a global orientation as key criteria. Smitha Radhakrishnan argues that this emphasis on finding a match with the correct "background" has led families to prioritize technical education, as well as traditional cultural demographic factors.[14] However, there are fewer women of appropriate backgrounds eligible for marriage, thanks in part to the long history of son preference in India, which also has led to what demographers refer to as a "marriage squeeze," making educated women harder to find. While Christopher Fuller and Haripriya Narasimhan report that among Tamil Brahmin IT workers there is a preference to maintain caste stratification, they also argue that education levels and professional compatibility have become more important than family position or horoscopes, as has been the case in the past.[15] This "occupational or professional endogamy" has come to override more traditional matchmaking criteria.[16] Women who are educated (often to the same level as men) and who are also flexible enough to move between the workforce and the home when necessary are in high demand. Even among Indian IT workers who have pursued "love marriages," as Michiel Baas documents in his study of IT workers in Bangalore and elsewhere, the emphasis on appropriate background "has led to the formation of what could be seen as a new caste— an 'IT caste'—which is highly upper-caste in nature and which consists of highly-educated people who work in the local IT industry."[17] As a result, the caste and class hierarchies that structure IT work in India are reproduced through the dating and marriage selection processes.

Reena's family answered the advertisement placed by Prakash's parents in a local temple in Chennai. After a few rounds of negotiations and several late-night conversations between Reena, who was living in Chennai, and Prakash, who was in Seattle, Prakash decided that Reena met his criteria and he proposed to her. Prakash was pleased because Reena had an engineering background and worked in a call center before her marriage, though she had a graduate degree in the social sciences as well. When I asked why having an engineering degree was so important for a marriage partner, Prakash answered: "I think it's because the culture here—if you have an engineering degree, it's easier to get a job." In India, engineering degrees require four years of undergraduate education and are more likely to be equivalent to US bachelor's degrees, whereas humanities or social science degrees are often not recognized as full degrees. Having an engineering degree thus aids in transnational matchmaking, as families presume that it will increase the likelihood that both partners will be able to find work abroad.

Likewise, Bala, who had been married for three years at the time of our interview, recalled that his family was very insistent on finding a girl with an engineering background. He related, "A lot of girls, they come here and they don't have the proper education or anything. It's hard for them to be in a different country, not being able to go outside, not being able to work. Just be stuck in the house." At the same time, he linked the pressure to find a girl in engineering to his location in the US:

> If I were in India, they would not go for an engineering girl. They want someone to take care of the house stuff, so they'd go for a good degree in the arts or something. Just a degree so she would be able to teach our kids, but they wouldn't bother as much about engineering degree.

As Bala noted, he would not care as much about his wife's educational credentials were they to remain in India, but the prospect of migration changed his perspective on what would make an ideal partner.

Potentially, going into computer science or engineering creates agency for women to marry men of their choosing and to migrate abroad. For example, Radhika, who grew up in the northern Indian city of Ahmedabad and who had been living in the US for five years when we met, noted that while she found engineering easy enough, she really didn't have much interest in the subject. Instead, her boyfriend at the time intended to come to the US after he finished college, and she was eager to join him. Realizing that her family would not approve of her moving in with her boyfriend before marriage, Radhika decided to enter IT so that she could apply to graduate school in the US. She recalled: "I did my engineering and then my basic decision to come here was based on: (a) everyone else is doing it, and (b) I had a boyfriend here. Usually that happens, I'd say in 90 percent of the cases: the guy comes here, so the girl wants to or the other way around." For Radhika, going into IT was more about being able to travel abroad to pursue the relationship of her choice, rather than simple interest in the field or even future economic gain. Being part of the IT sector increases the likelihood of marrying another IT professional (or at least someone who has the ability to work in the field), and in Radhika's case, made her love marriage to her boyfriend possible.

A survey of matrimonial websites like Shaadi.com or Bharatmatrimony. com further demonstrates the desirability of women with STEM education as potential brides. A search of the first twenty profiles on Shaadi.com of prospective grooms working in the IT industry in the US reveals advertisements like "We are seeking suitable alliance for our son . . . We are looking for a suitable educated, beautiful, preferably IT professional." Others read: "Mohit . . . expects his partner to be good-looking, fair with average body type, height between 165 cm and 170cm, and well-educated in engineering and/or computer software development"; or "Would like to meet a girl who is well-educated or pursuing professional career or enrolled in higher education; is family-oriented and can support and complement him both professionally and personally." Marisa D'Mello finds that while many Indian families fear that women working in IT might not fit "the preferred stereotype of a 'home-loving' patriarchal ideology for women," there also is a strong preference to find a girl who can, at least theoretically, traverse the same employment and social landscape as her future husband.[18] As a form of symbolic capital, women's education can be understood as an important metric of appropriate womanhood that allows Indian families to reproduce cultural norms while aspiring to modern notions of class and status. As many feminist scholars have articulated, this tension is at the core of the "new Indian woman," who is educated and career driven, but is still a diligently attentive wife and mother who is willing to sacrifice her desires for her husband and family.[19] As a result, women must walk a fine line between demonstrating their education and ability to work while also foregrounding their desire to conform to traditional gender roles.

ENGINEERING BRIDES, HOMEMAKING WIVES

For some H-1B visa holders, such as Sarkar, who was living in Redmond when we first met and waiting to getting married, the desire to have a partner who could put her engineering or IT skills to work was a top priority. He explained that he pushed to delay his wedding so that his fiancée could apply for her own H-1B visa rather than come to the US on a spousal reunification visa and give up her career: "I would have been married earlier, but I waited. I didn't want her moving to a different part of the US because I was on contract first. I didn't want her to come here and then not be able to work on her own." Encouraging his fiancée to build her software development credentials while waiting, Sarkar underscored the practical and symbolic importance of having an engineering or IT background in transmigrant nuptial decision-making. However, while many IT transmigrants claim that education and work exposure represent an important aspect of spousal selection, such prerequisites are not necessarily an indicator that women will actually be encouraged to pursue work after marriage. For the majority of the men with whom I spoke, even though they wanted a bride with a STEM background, having their wives at home was an expression of their ability to provide financially and was tied to notions of masculinity that view men as natural breadwinners. As Prakash declares, "It doesn't matter if she's working or not. I can take care of her. It's my responsibility to take care of her. If she can't work, that's perfectly fine." Likewise, Carol Upadhya and Aninhalli R. Vasavi found that among IT workers in India, "many men said that they would not like to marry women working in IT, and even those who preferred working women wanted wives who would give priority to the home and family."[20] The 2016 CSDS-KAS survey of Indian youth confirmed this sentiment, finding that even as the Indian economy becomes more globalized and liberalized, younger generations retain highly patriarchal attitudes about marriage and family life. The study found that 51 percent of respondents agreed that women should be obedient to their husbands and 41 percent thought that women should not work after marriage.[21] Transmigrant desires to find educated but traditional brides are grounded in the expectation that a woman's career should be secondary to that of her husband's, and that women are primarily responsible for taking care of the home and any future children the couple might have.

Even as working women experience increased gender equality within the household, professional mobility, and input into household finances, the burdens of household labor have not shifted significantly. Women's work-loads are often multiplied, rather than reduced, when they work outside of the home, which can lead them to drop out of the formal workforce. Examining women who work in IT, Parvati Raghuram argues that women's exit from the labor market "do[es] not arise out of the particularities of women per se, but out of social norms that limit women's mobility and social expectations around their contribution to and responsibility for undertaking unpaid reproductive labor within the household."[22] For professional women, marriage and family responsibilities can be a hindrance to the flexibility and high mobility expected from IT professionals and point to the pervasive nature of gender norms that tie women to the domestic sphere.

This exit from the labor market amplifies men's expectations of women's reproductive labor after marriage. As single transmigrants, many H-1B men save money on rent by living with several roommates and learn to do the work of the household, even though almost none of them performed such tasks prior to migration.[23] However, after marriage, especially if women are unable to work, men quickly revert to more traditional divisions of labor. For those couples who move back to India after being on the H-1B, this division is even more pronounced, as the presence of household domestic workers further diminishes men's reproductive labors. Thus, even when transmigration potentially offers women a chance to resist gendered expectations about work and family, most still face patriarchal norms about their labor and domestic duties. In the next chapter, I explore in greater detail the implications for this enforced gendered division of labor as it intersects with limitations placed by family reunification visas.

BIRTHING MOBILE CITIZENS

Transmigration also shapes decisions around family formation. In response to a report about the challenges associated with the H-1B and H-4 visa program, a San Francisco Chronicle reader commented: "H-1B provisions are generous and in many cases allow employers to seek permanent immigration status for the workers. No need for us to shed tears yet. Another benefit I've seen these couples almost always take advantage of: they quickly bear children in the States."[24] As a condition of birthright citizenship, children born to transmigrants are US citizens.[25] In recent years, anti-immigration advocates have fixated on the racial implications of nonwhite or non-Western immigrants having children on US soil. Much of that discussion has centered on the figure of the criminalized and hypersexualized Latina, whom many accuse of taking advantage of state benefits such as public school, food stamps, or health care. But temporary migrants also are linked in discourses about "anchor babies," a phrase that has gained prominence in recent political debates and campaigns.[26] Though immigrant women often have longer and more complex community ties in the host country before having a child and rarely cross the border for "just-in-time" reproduction, they are regularly demonized in the media and Congress by anti-immigration advocates.[27]

More recently, concerns over the citizenship rights provided by the Fourteenth Amendment have shifted to Asian women who come to the US on temporary visas, both for work and for tourism. Writing for the conservative journal *The Social Contract*, Edwin Rubenstein asserts, "In case you're wondering, the anchor baby loophole applies to guest workers also. H-1Bs and H-2Bs are allowed to bring in spouses (and children). These are *not* counted towards the 'cap.' And, as with illegal aliens, a baby born here means they are hard to deport and can ultimately be sponsored by their citizen child."[28] In contrast, Tierney Sneed warns that curtailing the Fourteenth Amendment would harm US technology industries: "High-skilled immigrants already face a number of obstacles when coming to the U.S. to work, immigration experts say, without having to worry about the legal status of their children born after they arrive."[29] Quoting a technology industry lobbyist, Sneed relates, "Why would we tell an engineer at a startup or a doctor or a small business owner, 'You're contributing, you're paying taxes, you're building a better life for your family but your child should forever be denied citizenship?' It just flies in the face of everything we cherish about opportunity and American values."[30] On the one hand, the family formation of immigrants is rejected by nativists, who fear the further "browning" of the US; on the other hand, advocates argue that family reunification is an integral part of the immigration process—necessary to keep "quality" migrants in the US.

Such concerns over the national status of children preoccupy transmigrants, whose time in the US often coincides with proscriptive time frames around childbearing and childrearing. For many, reproduction is deployed strategically, and the decision to have children while living abroad often is deliberately calculated. For example, Mita was a twenty-eight-year-old woman who was six months pregnant when we met in September 2008. She and her husband had been in Redmond for five years and were planning to return to India for a trial period in the following year. Concerned about maintaining residency status in the US because she and her husband had not yet converted their H-1B visas into green cards, Mita was nervous about moving back to India without having some way to maintain a connection to the US in the event they decided to return in the future. When I asked Mita about the timing of her pregnancy and her return to India, she noted:

> It makes sense to have a baby that's a US citizen. It's good for the future. I know that I lost out because my mother was pregnant with me when she was living in London and she went back to Bombay to deliver me. I could have had more opportunity if I had been born in London. I wouldn't have to deal with the visas. I'd be able to move through the European Union now! It wasn't a big thing, but we wanted to try to have a child here before going back to India.

Mita and her husband were convinced that having a child with US citizenship would ease their ability to return and would open opportunities for their family in the future. In her studies of wealthy Chinese entrepreneurs, Aiwha Ong has argued that the family is a primary facilitator of migration and transnational circulation.[31] Describing how some family members reside in the US while others move between other metropolises around the globe, she notes that this sort of dispersed national strategy works to increase mobility and wealth accumulation. Many members of the Chinese transnational class in Ong's study send children to the US for high school and college as a way to establish residency rights, "a process which enables them to escape to some extent the disciplining of the state because of their flexible deployment of capital."[32] For transmigrants such as Mita, who may not have a permanent claim in the US, having a child that would not have to engage with the red tape of visas and work permits allows for a future connection to the US and opens the possibility for new migrations. Since children are embedded in family units, the differing immigration and even national status of family members can create both opportunities and barriers for transmigrants. Caroline Bledsoe argues that "through connection to a child, an adult gains more attributes than his/her own: attributes that might be used to make additional claims on society. In an increasingly 'connected' world, children may offer new pathways for their families' mobility and the security it can bring."[33] Thus, some "immigrants at the margins of political legitimacy" make decisions about childbearing as a way to establish links to a specific nation or state and as a way to increase their own social standing.[34] Thus, the decision to start families while living abroad acts as a form of place-making, even in transient conditions. As parents of US citizens, they can ensure mobility for their children but also lay claim to a form of national belonging that is otherwise closed to them as transmigrants and foreigners.

At the same time, there is deep ambivalence about the realities of forming a family with transnational affiliation. Not unique to Indian transmigrants, anxieties over how to raise children in a culture different from the parents' social milieu are present across immigrant communities.[35] In my study, transmigrants echoed concerns about raising children in the US such as potential alienation from family members and grandparents who still live in India, lack of exposure to Indian culture, overexposure to "American values," compromised safety, intercultural and intergenerational communication challenges, and difficulties in maintaining households without nearby familial support systems. Mita reflected on these fears:

> It's difficult if both the parents are working. It's not so difficult if at least one parent is at home. But if both parents are working, you have to do the things like school and day care. And if you want your child to have all the cultural stuff from India, I don't think the parents can in any way give that kind of time and attention to inculcate that into the child. And this is something that takes place early on in your childhood, up to a certain age. After that, it's too late. So in that sense, I find it much more

challenging here. It's kind of the same in India if both the parents are working. But again, you have more support in the sense maybe you have some relative or your mom at home. Grandparents may be at home. That kind of social support is more in India.

Mita makes the point that having both parents in the workforce diminishes the exposure of children to "the cultural stuff from India" even in India, but the lack of cultural context and intergenerational transmission creates particular challenges for transmigrants. Women often are charged with bridging the gap for a child's cultural and religious upbringing; as Denise Spitzer et al. argue, women's caregiving roles in the immigrant family work to "demarcate ethnic boundaries and operate as ballast against the potential onslaught of competing values that threaten transnational communities with dissolution."[36] In their roles as mothers and wives, women shoulder the burden of teaching children about religious practices and holidays, Indian languages, and traditional foods. Moreover, they are tasked with ensuring that children develop the "correct" values of education, hard work, modesty, and discipline. This expectation is heightened as transmigrants live away from the social milieu that would (presumably) naturalize such cultural learning.

Without the benefit of grandparents nearby or other family networks, the work of cultural reproduction falls almost entirely on the nuclear family. In order to provide some exposure to extended family members, transmigrants try to invite grandparents to visit after a child is born and for regular visits over the course of their time in the US. The parents of transmigrant women often try to come on a visitor visa immediately after a grandchild's birth, which is generally valid for up to six months. After the visa expires, couples often will sponsor the male partner's parents to come for another six months. By using short-term visitor visas, the H-1B couple is able to reconstruct a semblance of the caregiving networks they would have experienced if they still were living in India. After the visitor periods end, alternative childcare arrangements typically are made, unless women resume primary care for the children.

Even though transmigrants worry about the consequences of having children abroad, such family formation offers workers a way to maintain connections to life in the US in the future. Rather than settle in the US permanently to ensure that children have access to the educational resources and opportunities they associate with living in the West, as previous generations of Indians have done, transmigrants see their children's citizenship as an insurance policy that eases the pathway to return if they decide to leave the US. By using short-term visitor visas, transmigrants are also able to bring family members over to the US to help with childcare and provide some connection to India, especially in the early part of their children's lives. In this way, creating a family with partial affiliation in both India and the US allows workers and their spouses to establish a household unit that is presumed to circulate, rather than commit entirely to one location or another.

CONCLUSION

Marriage and reproductive practices allow transmigrants to use their liminal standing as a way to disrupt and undergird family obligations and expectations while also carving out a foothold in multiple locations. For some women, the H-1B visa offers a chance to explore professional and private lives away from the prying eyes of local family and kin networks. In other cases, an education in IT or engineering, coupled with the ability to move to the US on a temporary visa, becomes a way for women to increase their own desirability on the marriage market. At the same time, there is a gendered discrepancy. For women, IT is often seen as a way to improve the chances of making a good marriage match, but only if they also remain appropriately devoted to family and home life. As such, women must perform the role of the "new Indian woman," who is modern, educated, and global in her outlook, but also primarily concerned with the reproductive labor of the household. For men, obtaining an H-1B visa and being associated with the global IT industry also improves their chances for marrying well, though they are able to rely on traditional divisions of labor that support, rather than hinder, their career aspirations.

However, the glamour of life on the H-1B has begun to diminish, as India has become the site for new entrepreneurial opportunities, and fewer people are willing to move abroad for short stints, preferring to take advantage of the prospects at home. The economic instability in the US, coupled with more stringent immigration restrictions and increasing job insecurity for foreign workers, has led to a decline in the number of families seeking grooms who work abroad. Representatives from popular matrimonial sites such as Jeevansathi.com, Shaadi.com, Bharatmatrimony.com, reported a drop of between 15 and 20 percent in the demand for grooms living abroad, particularly those working in less stable sectors the American economy like finance or technology during the height of the US recession between 2008 and 2009.[37] The economic downturn had been linked to a change in attitudes about the value of H-1B visa matches; according to a representative of Shaadi.com: "With promising careers, independence and the need to spend more time with one's family, some of the eligible Indian women are not looking to move abroad after marriage . . . also, despite the slowdown, jobs in India are still secure, which is one of the reasons why Indian grooms are in higher demand than NRI grooms."[38] By 2012, the US job market started to improve, but the demand for suitable brides remained high among H-1B workers. Writing for the *Hindustan Times*, Shalini Singh speculated, "With the rising level of affluence and job opportunities, successful women today have more choices within India and their own cities, when it comes to choosing a life partner."[39] More recently, attacks on H-1B workers in the US in 2017 and the increasingly open xenophobia faced by immigrants have impacted migration and marriage.[40] For women who might be potential marriage partners for men holding H-1B visas the idea of moving abroad into uncertain circumstances is becoming less attractive.

Despite the constraints imposed, the H-1B visa has improved young men's ability to compete in a tight marriage market and to engage in place-making activities at the same time that they are also positioning themselves as flexible and adaptable workers. In his study of changing marriage and dowry practices in South India, Xiang Biao finds that family practices and gender relationships are critical to sustaining the mobility of IT transmigrants to Australia and eventually the US. Arguing that among the highly educated and high-caste communities of Brahmins in Andhra Pradesh who practice the custom of dowry, it "can be seen as the price paid by wealthy families with daughters to purchase those highly profitable men in whom there has been heavy investment."[41] From the perspective of women's families, men in IT have a high likelihood of earning good salaries and finding steady work; therefore, the prestige associated with having a son-in-law with a job in the US is worth the investment and risk.

Finally, marriage, intimate relationships, and expanding one's family all emerge as strategies for workers who are not committed to living in one location or another and also allow H-1B workers to claim a sense of belonging, despite their legal classification. The marriage and family formation strategies that H-1B holders employ also point to the ways in which workers are navigating their paradoxically precarious position in an effort to further their life and personal goals. Using the temporary visa to create new family units that are mobile and often linked to the US through birthright citizenship are examples of how transmigrants negotiate the opportunities and constraints of global capital. However, while transmigration can benefit men's careers and open opportunities for good matches, the story is often more complicated for women. For women who migrate on H-4 visas, there is a darker side to transmigration because they must contend with an enforced dependency and loss of their careers, as I show in the next chapter.

3 Transnational Housewives

Work Restrictions and the Gendered Division of Labor

SITTING IN AN APARTMENT LOCATED ABOUT TWO MILES FROM the Microsoft campus in Redmond, Washington, Mani spends most of her day waiting for her husband to return from work. Tucked into a dead-end development, the apartment complex is close enough to the main thoroughfare that you can hear cars passing. Along the little pedestrian space that edges the road, young women and elderly Indian and Chinese couples crowd the narrow sidewalks. Some wait in shelters for the infrequent suburban buses to arrive, while others walk a mile or more to the nearby shopping centers. Inside the apartment complex, each of the housing units has a door that faces the parking lot, while interior windows look onto the "garden view," which is really a small patch of green lawn edged by concrete curbs. Though the apartment management company claims luxury amenities and spacious quarters, in reality, the apartments are squat, grim little spaces.

I enter the dank, narrow hallway leading the way into a small living room that was hardly big enough for the couch, coffee table, and an oversized TV. Mani spent the majority of her day puttering in this space. A desk with an expensive computer monitor sat against the back wall, while a galley kitchen and small dining area completed the main room. Though the apartment was basic, Mani made efforts to cheer it up. A bouquet of plastic flowers sat in a vase in the window. A corner of the dining area had been converted into a small Hindu shrine, with small idols, colorful pictures of deities, and incense. It was clear that Mani, who came to the US in early 2015 as a young bride, was eager for the company of a guest in the middle of an otherwise listless July afternoon. She was twenty-one years old when we met and had been married for eight months. Mani recently had completed an engineering degree from an Indian regional university, but never had the chance to work after graduation. She came from a strict Tamil Brahmin family who felt that arranging her marriage was more important than her work experience, so they quickly found a match within their community networks for her. She was a quintessential example of an "engineer bride," whose education credentials made her desirable on the marriage market.

Mani did not anticipate moving to the US so soon after finishing her degree. She had hoped to work in India, but the groom whom her parents selected was based in Seattle. After completing his master's degree in computer science, he worked on an H-1B visa at Microsoft for a couple of years, and he wanted her to join him in Redmond soon after they married. Though she was hesitant to get married so young, she was hopeful that because her new husband was living abroad, she would have the opportunity to start working after she joined him. She worried that if she stayed in India, she would be expected to stay at home instead of working on her own terms. However, after migrating on the H-4 family reunification visa, she was unable to work legally. She lamented: "I wanted to come to the US so I could start my own career. But now, I am sitting at home, nothing to do." Since migrating, Mani has been "suspended between the two countries, two realities, and two identities: independent and dependent."[1] She is an educated and ambitious young woman who is now a housewife primarily because of her immigration status. "Every day," Mani said, "is like a jail."

H-4 visa holders face a strong stigma as dependents and in terms of media accounts and policy debate.[2] They are assumed to be economically privileged women whose migration is the result of family decision-making; at the same time, they are viewed as either Third World subjects caught in culturally backward relationships or as potential economic threats to US workers who are taking advantage of a "backdoor" to immigration.[3] I nuance and move these discussions forward by asking: How do less visible, "non-economic" subjects negotiate the constraints and opportunities produced by transmigration and temporary worker programs? What roles do these dependents play in sustaining transmigration? The marriage preferences of Indian IT transmigrants, along with family reunification policies, have created a new class of highly educated and technically skilled women who are proscribed from formal employment. Instead, these women are expected to become what I describe as "transnational housewives" who conform to gendered norms about reproductive labor and family management while also supporting migration for the family unit. This transformation often has a negative impact on women's self-esteem, mental and physical health, and long-term career prospects. Along with facing an intensification of domestic chores and parenting responsibilities, many women also find themselves combating a sense of loss, shame, and frustration over an immigration system that keeps them out of the formal labor market. However, even as their visas legally limit them, many women both resist and embrace their position in the household and use the time spent out of the workforce to develop new skills, invest in education or additional training, undertake creative pursuits, and maintain connections between life in India and abroad. It is their unpaid and hidden labor that sustains the system of temporary labor underpinning the global IT industry.

THE EVOLUTION OF TEMPORARY FAMILY REUNIFICATION

As the number of Indian H-1B visas holders has grown, the migration of family members who accompany them has also expanded. Discussed in greater detail in earlier chapters, the H-4 comes with work restrictions and is only available to H-1B visa holders' spouses and children under twenty-one years of age. In order for companies to recruit and retain high-quality labor globally, family reunification has become a key issue, even for short-term migrants.[4] Compared to employment-based categories, refugees and asylum seekers, or the general visa lottery, family reunification is the largest stream of new immigration.[5] Under the H-1B program, more H-4 petitions are approved each year than H-1Bs, and the family reunification elements of the program have resulted in many women moving abroad as spouses.

Kerry Abrams argues that family reunification played a key role in the earliest iterations of US immigration policy, with both positive and negative effects.[6] Historically, the US government sought to limit the migration of family members, particularly among temporary laborers. Starting with the Chinese Exclusion Acts of 1882 and the Asiatic Barred Zone Act of the early twentieth century, Asian migrants who came to work in the railroad, timber, fishing, and other labor-intensive industries were barred from bringing spouses with them, and single women were prohibited from migration under the enactment of vice laws. While there was a substantial demand for Asian labor, anti-immigrant sentiment pushed the US government to deploy bureaucratic and legal means to restrict settlement by targeting the migration of women and family members. These restrictions were intended to limit the establishment of permanent Asian communities in the US, as anti-miscegenation laws also made it difficult for immigrants to find brides from their own racial and ethnic backgrounds.[7]

However, even though formal race- and nation-based restrictions were in place during the late nineteenth and early twentieth centuries, the family still was mobilized as a way for some, predominantly European, women to migrate: "Under coverture, a man had the right to determine the domicile of his wife and children; the right to bring his wife and child with him when he immigrated was analogous."[8] By the time the 1924 National Origins Act was passed, wives of citizens were incorporated into a non-quota category that included children under eighteen years of age. This act made it easier for male citizens to sponsor their immigrant wives, but still prohibited women citizens from sponsoring immigrant husbands. It also gave citizens and legal permanent residents the power to sponsor their family members, a point that was recodified in later immigration acts, such as the Immigration and Nationality Act of 1965, also known as the Hart-Celler Act.

Hart-Celler is best known for abolishing country-based quotas and opening the door to non–Western European migration through the prioritization of skills and US labor needs. It also enshrined the right to family reunification as a cornerstone of US immigration policy, mirroring the United Nations' Declaration on Human Rights, which establishes the right to form a family (defined predominantly in heterosexual kinship terms), and the UN's International Covenant on Economic, Social and Cultural Rights, which holds the family as the "the natural and fundamental group unit of society."[9] Despite this outward embrace of family reunification in 1965, members of Congress had hoped that the change in policy giving preference to family members would privilege Northern European immigrants. However, what Congress did not anticipate was how quickly non-European immigrant populations would grow as a result of using those same family preference categories.

By 1990, there was deepening concern that the existing immigration policy was not accomplishing what congressional leaders had hoped. Family reunification was leading to the overrepresentation of family-based immigrants from non-Western countries and creating a backlog in permanent residency application processing. The Immigration Act of 1990 was passed in part to rebalance immigration away from family reunification and toward labor categories. The act established a three-pronged preference system that still included the family, but also addressed employment and country-of-origin diversity and introduced new categories for temporary non-immigrant admission.[10] The law expanded certain forms of migration (temporary, non-immigrant, and employment-based) while seeking to curtail others (undocumented or family-preference based). At the same time, there was a growing global recognition of the foundational role that migrant labor plays in modern economies and of the need to address family reunification as part of those flows.[11] Conventionally, family reunification is a

contra-indicator to future migrations and seen as the precursor to settlement in a host country.[12] However, the 1990 act effectively dislodged this
correlation by increasing the reserve of expendable workers and by allowing
their immediate family members to migrate, although it simultaneously
established limits keeping those dependents out of the labor market.[13]

Such family reunification policies benefit capital by creating a surplus of
migrants whose unpaid or underpaid labor is subsumed by the household
or other economic spheres. It does so while allowing the state to appear as
benevolent and protective of some migrants' right to form a family, even as
it undermines the integrity of the family unit for others.[14] However, it cannot be overstated that family reunification for temporary migrants is always
dependent on the good standing of the primary visa holder. This point was
driven home dramatically in 2017 in the case of Sunayana Dumala, the
widow of slain H-1B worker Srinivas Kuchibhotla. Dumala, whose immigration status was tied to her husband's employment visa, found herself "out
of status" after her husband was murdered by a white supremacist. She was
eligible for deportation and were she to leave the country, as she planned
to do in order to attend her husband's funeral rites in India, her reentry to
the US would be in jeopardy. Dumala's congressman in Kansas intervened
personally to help her obtain work authorization for twelve months and to
begin the process of applying for a "U" visa, which is reserved for immigrant
victims of crime. Even with this temporary immigration relief, her case
brings home the precariousness that the dependents of temporary immigrant workers face. Even for women in less extreme circumstances, family
reunification is both an opportunity and a disadvantage.

FROM CAREER WOMAN TO H-4 HOUSEWIFE

Dipti is an example of a software engineer who came to the US to complete
her master's in computer science, and who regretted her decision to transition onto a family reunification visa. She met her husband while completing
her graduate work, and they both successfully secured H-1B visas, although
he resided in Seattle and she worked in Silicon Valley. Even after getting
married, the couple tried to maintain a long-distance relationship for nearly
three years, and then they reached a breaking point. Dipti recalled:

> So I finally said, OK, this isn't the way to be married. I will come to you.
> What was terrible, what I didn't realize then, was that my company was
> going to sponsor me. If I had waited another year, I would have been in

the process of getting my green card. But then I couldn't move and would have to stay through the processing. I couldn't wait that long, so I left to be with him.

Even if Dipti had known she was on the path to being able to secure a green card, she might have hesitated because once she entered the application process, she would have been unable to leave her position and join her husband. Instead, she quit her job and was issued an H-4 visa, which allowed her to move to Seattle. She was sure that after moving, she would quickly find another job. However, she no longer had a work visa and found that few companies were willing to sponsor a new H-1B for her. Fed up with staying at home, she started a master's of business administration program in the hopes that she could redirect her career path. After finishing her degree and receiving a job offer in a different city, Dipti found out that she was pregnant. Again, she chose her family over her career: "So here I am again. Back in Seattle, no job, another degree in hand, and with a baby on the way." Dipti felt completely trapped by her situation and, even though she was happy about the pregnancy, it became another hurdle for her to navigate on her way back to the job market. Although women like Dipti willingly enter into marriages that require them to be flexible about their careers, many are unprepared for the frustration they feel once they actually migrate or make the choice to leave the labor force. They become financially dependent on their husbands and risk deportation should their husbands lose their jobs, become incapacitated and forced out of the labor market, or perhaps even more alienating, decide to leave them.[15] These conditions create considerable strain on their emotional well-being and on their marriages, as I show in this next section.

SHAME, FRUSTRATION, AND ANGER

On discussing her transition to the US, Mani related: "I felt really lonely. Here I don't have any friends—it is my husband's friends only. I'm thinking I want to do something because everyone is working here. No one is housewife! I started thinking, what is happening with H-4?" Likewise, Dipti noted that her visa status made her feel ashamed of her inability to work. She described a recent encounter at a social gathering with some friends, which sharpened her feelings of frustration:

> So when we meet, they all talk about Microsoft, everything, their world . . . and I'm kind of lost. There are other people in the neighborhood who are

on H-4 or are at home for some reason. Maybe they have gotten a green
card but decided not to work. It's like, these are people who have decided,
"Oh, I have to do this because it's the best for my family," or maybe this is
what they've always wanted. I don't know. Oftentimes we just have awk-
ward conversations because they ask me what I do, where I work. I try to
find out if they're in the same boat. If not . . . then they really don't get it.

Because she had a vibrant career before going on the H-4 visa, Dipti often
felt like an outsider among friends who were immersed in the culture of
work. When she was employed, she participated easily in cocktail party
conversations regarding new innovations on technology platforms, workflows, or even just industry or office gossip. But now that she wasn't working,
she felt left out of the loop and, even worse, as though she was not as capable
or effective as her compatriots who were able to secure H-1B visas. Among
transmigrants, working is symbolically meaningful for women, particularly
because many have had to work hard to obtain their credentials abroad or
in India, where they are often compelled to push against patriarchal norms
that devalue women's education. When they are forced out of the labor
market, their education is rendered meaningless in the face of an economic
system that equates skills with wages.

Such exclusion from working can result in women losing status socially
in the private sphere as well. Relating the experience of three of his friends
who recently returned to India to get married after studying and working
in the US, Hareesh noted:

So coming back to my friends—all three of the wives are not working.
Are they happy? Definitely. Are they unhappy? Definitely? Unhappy,
because they don't have their own identity. Don't get me wrong. My three
friends are very, very good in nature. But they happen to make all the
decisions. It may be a bad thing, but not always the best option. The
women applied for H-1B for the second year consecutively because the
number of applications went down. Unfortunately, their applications were
not picked up. Again, my friends are not bad. They are trying for their
spouses to have some identity, to work. I mean, not just by working you
have some identity . . . but that importance is there.

In this articulation, Hareesh reads his friends' wives' desire to work as a way
of maintaining their identity as independent from their husbands, even
when their marriages would appear to be satisfying otherwise. In these

cases, or even worse, when they are not in supportive marriages, women on the H-4 have the potential to remain trapped in a state of economic and emotional dependency, which can hurt their mental health. In the film *Hearts Suspended*, immigration lawyer and activist Shivali Shah argues, "These are people who are being brought in only as the most base function as women: housewives, baby-makers, and sex partners."[16] Since the majority of H-4 visa holders move to the US after getting married, they must deal with marital expectations and getting to know a new partner while living away from family networks. Since many find themselves without other anchoring identities outside of the heterosexual family unit, they can feel reduced to a singular role. This feeling of becoming one-dimensional is worsened by the fact that, as detailed in the previous chapter, women on H-4 visas are often equally as educated or as qualified to work as their husbands. But, because they must put their career aspirations on hold, some women begin to view themselves negatively while adjusting to a life narrowly defined by being a wife and mother. While these experiences are not unique to H-4 visa holders, the structure of immigration policy functionally prohibits them from changing their circumstances without significant changes in other parts of their lives.

FIGHTING SOCIAL ISOLATION

In addition to feeling shame or frustration upon the halt of their careers, H-4 visa holders also must negotiate social and geographic isolation. For example, the geography of the Seattle suburbs is dramatically different from the dense urban settings in India. Since the majority of technology companies are housed on sprawling campuses, rather than urban downtowns, transmigrants opt to live close to work, where they can take advantage of company shuttles and save money on cheap apartments. Newly arriving South Asian immigrants are more likely to move directly to the suburbs than concentrate in urban centers. In her account of Indian families living in the "Little India" section of Edison, New Jersey, Kalita S. Mitra shows how immigrants bypass traditional urban ethnic enclaves and move directly into suburban communities where they can find others who share their ancestry, religion, and cultural beliefs.[17] Like other US suburbs that have transformed from enclaves of privilege for whites fleeing increasingly diversified urban centers after World War II, Seattle's Eastside has experienced a rapid growth in foreign-born populations, who have contributed to a visible "Asianization" of the region.[18] Such suburban spaces are not necessarily separate from urban ethnic communities, nor do they imply greater assimilation; rather, they offer immigrants the chance to form new ethnic communities in a high-status setting. The Eastside has experienced a spectacular rise in real estate prices, particularly as foreign nationals buy homes and land for commercial development and IT salaries compound the concentration of wealth.

In contrast to Indian high-rise apartment complexes, where neighbors frequently visit one another, the quiet, wooded stretches of the US suburbs tend to be socially isolating. Almost all of the transmigrants with whom I spoke found that the lack of common gathering spaces and the seclusion of apartment living (which is a direct result of urban planning that separates commercial and residential areas) lent few natural opportunities to make friends outside of work. For those who are employed, some choose to tap into the volunteer or social networks that are tied to their companies or area institutions, but their dependent spouses are often excluded from easy opportunities to meet others. Moreover, without reliable modes of public transportation, many find the lack of density disquieting and the distance between locations difficult to traverse. When I asked Reena about her initial experience migrating from Chennai in 2005, her response was less than enthusiastic. Reena had a vibrant career working with an NGO conducting relief and reconstruction work following the 2004 Indian Ocean tsunami in South India, but after her marriage, her career came to an abrupt end. When she transitioned from a life filled with meaningful work and robust social and family obligations in a metropolitan city to the sleepy suburban apartment, where her husband Prakash's long hours at work left her alone for most of the day, she found it depressing: "Even though I didn't have any major concerns, but because you are at just home all the time, gray skies, nowhere to go." She would volunteer at the local library and seek out other pastimes to fill her long days, but the loneliness was hard to resolve.

TENSIONS AT HOME

These feelings of stigma, isolation, and loneliness can breed marital tensions. Whereas men may have the option to absorb themselves in work or their own social lives when strife arises at home, women on the H-4 rarely find such outlets because of their lack of autonomy and own social networks. They have few avenues for dealing with their frustration, and as Anika found, being a dependent spouse negatively impacted both her and her marriage. She related:

> I want my freedom. That's not something just related to H-4, but it's
> one ingredient of my frustration. So, initially if we argued, the most

frustrating part was that he'd take his bag and go to the office. [I would think] "You have an office. What do I have?" If you are angry or frustrated at home, then once you go out, you meet people and your mind kind of changes. He can feel, "I'm angry—I'm angry at my wife," or something and then it gets better. For me, I also want to go out, meet people, get dressed up, but I'm stuck at home. Now, I have another tension . . . more tension.

For Amisha, domestic discord bloomed into disaster. Amisha had completed a master's degree in the United Kingdom and was working in India when she met her husband through family connections. Her future husband suggested they marry quickly and that she migrate on an H-4 visa, since his green card processing date was quickly approaching. Once he moved into that stage, it would be harder for Amisha to join him, so they accelerated their marriage plans. As soon as the henna was dried on her hands, she was ensconced on a jetliner headed to the US Midwest. Unbeknownst to both Amisha and her new husband, the priority dates for their green card applications had been pushed back, and they were unable to file for permanent residency. Instead of job hunting, as she had planned to do after arriving, Amisha found herself in a new town with little to do. Even worse, initially, the newlyweds did not find an easy rhythm with each another. Though they had chatted over the phone and via Skype dates, Amisha found their chemistry misaligned when they met in person: "It wasn't just that we didn't get along—we did. It's just there was something off, you know, when it was just the two of us. And yeah, sex and all, that was tough at first." They both struggled with adjusting their lifestyles and expectations to accommodate the other person, particularly since Amisha was used to a great deal of independence. Now she was reliant on her husband for everything, from buying groceries to driving the car, or even leaving the house.

The conjugal problems grew as she spent more days at home and he continued to spend longer hours at work. Though they met other Indians living nearby, they struggled to make friends, particularly because they were from a different part of the country and did not speak the same language. The recurring source of their tension was Amisha's frustration with being forced to remain home and her husband's inability to meet her emotional needs. One evening, things escalated between them and a loud argument drew the attention of neighbors, who subsequently called the police. Because of mandatory arrest laws in domestic violence complaints in the state where they were living, Amisha was taken into custody and held in jail, even though no violence had occurred and her husband did not press charges. After a harrowing two days, during which she was unable to contact anyone, she was released. Amisha became withdrawn and depressed in this period and was ordered to surrender her passport. Though her husband never had any intention of calling the police, let alone pressing charges, Amisha's case was caught in a snarl of bureaucracy that had long-term consequences. Only after spending several thousand dollars were they able to have the charge reduced to a felony misdemeanor. Because of her visa status, her arrest was reported to the Federal Bureau of Investigation. Now, each time she wants to leave or enter the country, customs agents who see her name in a database of felony arrests almost always detain and interrogate her.

When her husband got a job that brought the couple to the Pacific Northwest, his new employer handled the transfer of his H-1B visa. But, compounding their difficulties, the wrong start dates were entered when the new visa was issued. They discovered this only as they were attempting to travel outside of the US. They soon learned that because of a clerical error, their visas were "out of status," or functionally expired. This meant that the company's lawyers had to file a new visa. Otherwise, they could only hope that the Department of Homeland Security would eventually correct the date. Because of these issues, travel within and outside of the US has been challenging for the couple, and adds to their feeling of being trapped in their current situation.

The restrictions of the H-4 can lead to even more serious legal problems for some women, particularly when they experience domestic violence.[19] Survivors of abuse, unless they are able to convert their H-4 to a U visa, are at high risk of deportation if they report their husbands or try to divorce them. The state is more likely to blame their vulnerability on Indian cultural norms rather than the immigration policies that strip dependents of economic and political autonomy. As Sharmila Rudrappa has shown in her study of South Asian domestic violence cases in Texas, South Asian culture has been mobilized as a defense to excuse the battering and killing of women, and "marks Third World immigrants as carriers of dysfunctional gender, familial and social traits all attributable to culture."[20] This perspective pervades the agencies that are charged with enforcing US immigration policy. For example, as part of my research in 2009, I interviewed US Department of State employees in the US Consulate General who evaluate and issue H-1B and H-4 visas within India. Some employees were empathetic toward the numerous young women who apply for H-4 visas immediately after marriage. Many feared that upon migration, these women would become victims of abuse, presuming that Indian men were inherently patriarchal and potentially dangerous. In an attempt to forewarn these women of the dangers that possibly awaited them after migration, State Department employees in Chennai created and distributed pamphlets in languages such as English, Tamil, and Kannada with resources about domestic violence in the United States.[21] At the same time, some State Department employees who were unfamiliar with arranged marriage practices tended to be suspicious of couples that had only met a few times (or perhaps not at all) before marrying, and sought to actively root out fraudulent uses of family reunification and fiancée visas. It is standard practice to ask new brides to show pictures of themselves with their spouses or of the wedding itself, or to ask intimate questions about the couple's relationship. As Dipti recalled, "When I was coming in for my worker visa, I used to see these people carrying photo albums and trying to prove that I am the wife . . . I used to look at that and think, 'Why are these women doing that?' And little did I know that I would be one of these people someday." Foreign passport holders already are policed to ensure transmigrant marriages are legitimate, but H-4 visa holders are further identified as susceptible to abuse or fraud as a result of cultural and racialized assumptions about marriages and gender norms.[22]

These cultural assumptions are not tied to H-4 visa holders exclusively. In her study of women of color and immigrant women negotiating the Canadian legal system, Sherene Razack argues that such women are often seen as subjects worthy of state protection when their oppression is grounded in the experience of cultural patriarchy.[23] Likewise in the US, family and culture are strategically deployed by the state, which allows for certain recognitions—for example, a gay male subject in need of protection from a homophobic Islamic society—while enacting other exclusions that reinforce the hetero-patriarchal family by limiting family reunification for same-sex couples.[24] These subaltern subjects only become legible as potentially in need of state protection because of their cultural deficiencies, even though state policies that limit their economic autonomy paradoxically heighten their vulnerability.

INCREASED HOUSEHOLD AND FAMILY RESPONSIBILITIES

As women contend with their role as housewives, unsurprisingly, their labor is redirected to the household. Bhanu had been living in a suburb of Redmond for almost a decade when we met in 2015. She had a master's degree in computer science and had been working as a software engineer for multinational companies in India before her husband had an opportunity to take a short-term position at Microsoft. Bhanu recalled:

> We thought it would take a month or two, so I came with a paid vacation. Then it dragged, so I had to quit the job from here itself. It was unexpected. But at that time it was a big relief because working in India as a software engineer is a stressful job. But after coming here, we really had a very good time together.

As the contract turned into a more permanent position, Bhanu began to second-guess her decision to take a break from working. Bhanu notes, "Without a work permit here, life in America is hell. It's really frustrating . . . volunteering is fine, but when you do the full-time volunteering, school or anywhere, you get the feeling that, are we servants just to work and not get paid?" This shift from the paid employment sector to the home has been described as a "de-skilling," "re-domestication," or as "cumulative disadvantage" that places women in economically marginalized positions.[25] The compromises that women like Bhanu make to meet the needs of their families often come at high personal costs: "Instead of me working, I'm just sitting here at home." Bhanu reflects that even though her life seems content from the outside, when she sees her friends moving ahead in their careers or, because they are earning, reaching their savings goals, she begins to worry about her future. Thus, women such as Bhanu must "achieve a fine balance between the competing responsibilities of career and home postmigration, a transition whose costs include disrupted careers and an intensification of domestic responsibilities."[26] Transmigrant women are caught often between the opposing forces of their personal ambitions, their family's needs, and their legal circumscriptions.

This struggle over gender roles, work, and household labor becomes even more acute for women who have as much education as their spouses and who are more likely to expect greater equality and freedom inside and outside of the home. Asmita Bhattacharayya and Bhola Nath Ghosh argue that among relationships where men and women are both earning, there is a greater division of housework, childcare, and support for both spouses' professional mobility, as well as joint decision-making in intimate arenas such as the use and type of contraception, family planning, and sexual engagement.[27] Additionally, women are more likely to participate in financial decision-making once they have had exposure to education and formal employment. As a result of the enforced dependency that H-4 visa holders face, however, the balance of power within heterosexual transmigrant relationships has the potential to reinforce men's patriarchal control over women's reproductive labor. Because women's labor is uncompensated, it is not regarded as real or valuable. At the same time, because of this "free" labor, men are untethered from domestic tasks and able to take more risks in their careers, develop new skills or hobbies, and carve out great authority over family decision-making as the primary (or only) income earners. As a result, even as the family unit may experience upward mobility, skilled migrant women may personally experience individual downward economic mobility. Even though the household is the primary site of social reproduction, the often unpaid and gendered labor that women perform in the household is devalued, rather than seen as foundational to the functioning of modern capitalist economies.[28] Women's reproductive labor thus masks the true cost of waged labor in an economic system predicated on freely exchanged work for market-determined wages, and becomes naturalized through the conditions of transmigration.

Since the majority of women who come on H-4 visas were either students or full-time employees prior to migration, it would have been rare to find them assuming the primary role of directing a household in India. Moreover, the reliance on domestic workers in India limits their exposure to the exigencies of managing daily life. However, living abroad, the household becomes the primary domain, where they spend their time learning how to keep up with the cooking and cleaning that is required of them. For example, when I met Samreen, she and her family had recently moved to Hyderabad, where they relocated after spending more than a decade in the Pacific Northwest. When she first married and moved in with her husband in Redmond, Samreen had trouble dealing with the burdens of household labor. A designer with a degree from a prestigious fashion institute in New York City, Samreen gave up a paid position when her husband got an offer at Microsoft, moving across the country on an H-4 visa. On the first evening she and her husband spent together after she joined him in Redmond, Samreen experienced a rude awakening to the realities of her married life: "The next day, when I realized I had to do my own dishes . . . I still remember that day. He picked me up when I first came, cooked a great meal and then left the dishes. The next day I saw the sink and thought, 'Oh god! I have to wash this?'" Eventually, after several years of being at home, Samreen found work, but had trouble finding an employer willing to sponsor her permanently. She and her husband had a child during this period of employment uncertainty, and her childcare obligations severely curtailed her ability to commute to downtown Seattle from the Redmond suburbs where they lived. After her son turned three, she learned that she was pregnant again. Her desperation to continue working and not to go back on the H-4 led her to seriously consider aborting the pregnancy. Ultimately deciding to carry the pregnancy to term, Samreen found herself back at home, with her aspirations once again stunted. Her frustration was a major reason that she and her husband decided to move back to India, where she could avail herself of networks of domestic workers to care for her house and children while pursuing her career.

Likewise, Bhanu decided that she should start a family while in the US on the H-4 visa, but found that having children greatly complicated her ability to pursue work. She gave birth to her daughter, and within a year, she unexpectedly became pregnant with her second child. Even after her second child was born, she hoped to get back into the labor market:

> I applied for my H-1B and I got it, but I couldn't work because we decided to not put our kids in day care. Our parents were really hesitant to take care of two little kids—they were like twins. So I had to get back to H-4 again. Even after that, my kids needed me so much, so things were good. But after they started going to school, I really wanted to get out of my home and do something. Last two years, it's been really frustrating.

Even though Bhanu was actually able to obtain an H-1B visa, she felt compelled to prioritize her role as caregiver for her young children and framed the matter as a pragmatic decision. Childrearing takes up a great deal of the time of transmigrant women with kids and requires a substantial reordering of their daily lives. As men are often expected to work according to their company's product development timelines and cannot necessarily control their schedules, women end up becoming primary caregivers. In order to transport kids to and from school and other activities, women must learn how to drive, navigate the school systems, and become self-sufficient in handling the tasks related to children and the household. These reproductive responsibilities cut into the time that they ordinarily would spend looking for work or furthering their skills.

Many of the women I interviewed who had not yet started families were adamant that they wanted to delay or space out having children until they had an opportunity to establish their careers. Anika was direct about her reluctance to pursue a family: "I think there is a mutual understanding, but I never talk to my husband about that stuff, indirectly or during friends hangout or something like that, it's like, '*Chalo . . . time ho gaya.*' But like, I'm still a kid. Please. Let me live. Let me work first!" Mani, too, noted that the pressure to have a child was strong from her friends and family, but her own lack of career options made her reluctant to do so:

> One friend, one month before, she got her baby. She lives near my house. She is twenty-four only. Before one year ago, she got married and then suddenly she got pregnant after four months. Here so many Indians are like that. Even my relative in Texas, even she got a baby suddenly because parents and relatives are forcing them to get a baby early. Even my parents and relatives, when I am calling them, they are asking if I have some special news. But I'm very young. In US, there are so many things to do! I don't want to waste my life. Since I came to US, my mind has changed so much. I don't know what's happening inside my head! But here, everyone is working and everyone is settled and they are happy and they are enjoying also. My mind is totally changed.

Mani was clear that she was not ready to get pregnant and, even though she faced significant family pressure, she wanted to have the opportunity to try working first. Some of those who did have children entered into motherhood reluctantly. While they did not regret having children, they also were aggressively pursuing other tracks, including graduate school, additional certifications, and internship/professional volunteer opportunities, in an effort to keep their skills competitive. Dipti's daughter was born soon after she finished her MBA. She noted, "I mean, I love babies, but I also want to focus on my career. And I've been that person from the beginning, so this part was hard for me. I used to wait until my husband returned from work so I can actually go get a shower. That's not what I expected." With an advanced degree and experience in software, nevertheless, Dipti decided to enroll in another certification program at the University of Washington: "I had assignments that I had to finish, it keeps me thinking, and I would still be in the zone and not out of touch. It wouldn't just be about babies and diapers." Even though adding in an intensive online course created demands on her time, Dipti saw this attempt as vital to her well-being and ability to reenter the job market, which she desperately wanted: "I wouldn't even consider another baby until I actually have a good career." While higher levels of education often result in delayed childbearing globally, women still face a conflict as their prime working years intersect with the time frames for "optimal" childbearing. Pamela Stone's research on women "opting out" or being pushed out of the labor market suggests that many professional women must choose between having kids and potentially taking a break from the workforce or delay starting a family until after they achieve certain career milestones.[29] The transmigrant women in this study were forced out of the labor market during the period of their lives when they would have been career building, and some used that opportunity to have children earlier than perhaps they might have. Others delayed childbearing even further, until they were able to figure out their next career step. Even though having children in the US with citizenship gave them a stronger foothold in the country regardless of their own visa status, childbearing and childrearing affected their work and personal lives for years after.

MAKING IT WORK: JOB MARKET REENTRY, INFORMAL EMPLOYMENT, AND COMMUNITY CREATION

Many women who leave the job market (either voluntarily or involuntarily) find it difficult to reestablish themselves in their fields when they try to reenter. Pamela Stone suggests that a host of complex factors push women out of the workforce, such as generous maternity leave policies that encourage them to stay home (and thereby miss out on professional opportunities) or the lack of leave policies (or low pay), which leads women to quit in an attempt to save on childcare costs.[30] In both scenarios, when women spend time away from the working world, they have a harder time maintaining professional relationships, are less likely to be assigned to projects or roles that lead to promotion, and miss out on more prestigious growth opportunities. After leaving, they have fewer employment networks to mobilize and are competing with younger and more recently trained workers. This issue is particularly acute in the IT industry, where technology changes rapidly and workers must actively maintain their skills and keep up with industry changes. Furthermore, the longer women stay out of the workforce, the more difficult it becomes to find jobs, as employers are less likely to invest in retraining them. H-4 visa holders face a double disadvantage because they lose out on valuable work experience and because, as foreign-trained women, they must prove that they are as capable of doing the work in the first place. In the next section, I show how some women turn to building new skills and furthering their education in order to maintain their competitive edge, while others use the time to volunteer or work without authorization, hoping to add concrete line items to their résumés.

COLLECTING CERTIFICATIONS

While waiting for employment authorization, many women spend their time building skills they hope will translate on the job market. One common strategy is to enroll in local universities or online graduate degree or certification programs, as detailed in Dipti's case. In my study, women had amassed degrees and certifications in areas ranging from business administration, social media, program management and coding languages such as C++ and JavaScript, to nonprofit management, preschool education, and many others. Even though they approached their courses seriously, many saw these pursuits as a way to pass the time until they could really start working. Others hoped that these certifications would signal that their skills were still sharp, and they were proud of their ability to keep abreast of changes in the field, even if they were not working in knowledge economies formally. When we met in 2015, Abhina had already completed a graduate business degree at the City University of Seattle and was working on a certificate program, this time in social media management at the University of Washington. Prior to migrating, she also had completed a master's degree in engineering. Abhina noted, "I worked for almost two years and then I came here and got my MBA. Now I'm doing more certs. I have also been doing some volunteer and part-time work here and there—not getting paid, obviously, because I cannot get paid legally. But I just keep trying, hoping this will all pay off!" While Abhina hoped to demonstrate her skills to future employers and to broaden the types of jobs for which she might be considered, the fact that student visas are easier to obtain and can be more easily transferred into work permits through the optional training program (OTP) is another reason that graduate and postbaccalaureate programs are so popular with H-4 visa holders. The OTP allows students to stay in the US for a period of time after graduation to gain more specialized experience, giving them a grace period that allows them look for jobs with employers who can sponsor work permits. Many H-4 visa holders see this as a pathway to work and a way to ease their transition to the H-1B.

VOLUNTEERING AND UNPAID WORK

H-4 visa holders are also able to build their marketable skills by applying for internships or volunteering with smaller companies.[31] While volunteering represents a way to keep a foot in the job market, often these positions do not live up to their promise, and companies take advantage of women's time and labor. Dipti, whose long history of work in the US is rare for an H-4 visa holder, still had difficulty finding a position. She decided to start volunteering as a way to create a professional network, but soon grew frustrated after she tried working for a friend's company. Though she was helping on a variety of projects, she was unable to truly "own" a particular sector and offer it to potential employers as an example of her substantive work experience. Though she dedicated substantial time to the venture, even paying to send her daughter to day care to free up more time, she began to feel as though the company owners did not treat her as seriously as a full-time employee or paid contractor, precisely because she was volunteering her time. While the entire point of working without pay was to continue building her résumé, ultimately she felt as though she was spinning her wheels.

Other women on the H-4 sought out internships as a way to get more formalized job training, but were rebuffed because they had too much experience or were not as competitive as recent US graduates. Bhanu also tried applying for an internship that was intended to bring more women into the tech sector, but she was unsuccessful. Revati, too, pursued other unpaid work avenues. She eventually won an internship after spending years applying: "I worked at the organization for two projects. The last project which I did was designed curriculum for new people and also did all their visa processing and everything." I remarked on what an important role she played for the organization and how that position sounded more like a full-time job rather than an unpaid opportunity. She noted, "Yeah, that is the way it is though. They can just ask you to do anything and you will do it because you want the experience." As Ann Vogel and Iain Lang argue, a rising "crisis of work" has driven many vulnerable individuals to accept unpaid and underpaid work in the name of gaining experience.[32] According to the Society of Human Resources Management, 44 percent more firms were offering unpaid internships in the wake of the 2009 US recession.[33] As the economy recovers, a growing premium is still placed on experience and companies have moved away from internal apprentice-style training programs that would have offered compensation. As a result, volunteer positions and internships offer potential employees the chance to stand out in a crowded job market. As Vogel and Lang note, because it is considered "work for a 'higher' cause, it appears intelligible as individual sacrifice that is offset against an anticipated future pay-off."[34] Even though volunteering and internships are couched in the framework of reciprocity, or even altruism, whereby a benevolent employer willingly helps support H-4 women's ambitions, such programs overwhelmingly advantage companies, which benefit from their unpaid labor to subsidize the true cost of their operations.

Because H-4 women technically cannot be paid, their labor is even more likely to be used to the profit of companies that want their experience without having to sponsor them. As for the women, they are cognizant of their exploitation. Bhanu noted, "Volunteering is one thing, but let's be honest. You want that paycheck. You want your work to matter." While transmigrant women are willing to take on unpaid work, they are also aware that their labor is being consumed for someone else's gain.[35]

The women who are eventually able to obtain an H-1B or wait long enough to survive the permanent residency process remain hopeful that they will finally be able to jump back into the game. More often than not, though, women have difficulty finding jobs that fit their skills and lifestyle demands. Bhanu had never worked in the US and had been out of the labor market for ten years before she finally obtained her employment authorization. She noted, "I'm a little nervous because I really have to brush up my knowledge. So after ten years, becoming a software engineer again, it's going to take a lot of time for me to appear for an interview. But only the fact that I did my master's when I was on the H-4, it makes me think I should get back to IT. I've been dreaming of it so much." After a decade away from IT, Bhanu was apprehensive about finding work in the field again. There are several reasons for this. First, while job market reentry challenges are not unique to H-4 visa holders, as detailed above, these women have a harder time finding jobs when they are finally able to work because of the combination of their long exit from the job market and their lack of US work experience. Women who are employed before taking a break from the labor market, for reproductive reasons or otherwise, are more likely to reenter and find work more quickly than women who have not worked previously.[36] The women without previous work experience fare much worse on the job market, as has been the case with H-4 visa holders, who generally did not work in the US before migrating. Second, women with children are less willing to take jobs that require long hours, extensive travel, or much time away from their families. This limits their opportunities and makes them more selective about the positions they will seriously consider. Third, most H-4 visa holders have completed the bulk of their education in India. Women with degrees from foreign universities are less likely to be employed than women who have studied in the host country.[37] Since most women on the H-4 visa have not worked in the US and possess foreign degrees, they are doubly disadvantaged. Even if they earn certifications or volunteer while on the H-4, their experiences are not recognized as valuable in the US context.

CREATING COMMUNITIES AND DEFYING DEPENDENCY

Considering the issues that H-4 visa holders face as a result of being shut out of the labor market, it is easy to reduce them to victims of an immigration system that benefits patriarchal forms of capitalism that rely on women's unpaid labor to subsidize productive labor. However, transmigrant women do not necessarily view themselves in those terms. Beyond the formal employment sector, H-4 visa holders turn to new spaces of community formation and cultural production to make their time in the US meaningful. While H-4 and H-1B workers are less integrated into traditional community institutions, they create informal spaces for communal gathering and cultural transmission. H-4 visa holders play an important role in these spaces, redirecting their energy to making family- and community-level contributions. Examining the case of recently arrived Asian immigrants in Canada, Shibao Guo and Young-joo Lee and Seong-Gin Moon argue that volunteering can offer immigrants opportunities for informal learning and help them acclimate to their new country.[38] Stacey Wilson-Forsberg and Bharati Sethi further argue that immigrants tend to volunteer to gain work experience in their host country, to hold onto shreds of their professional identity, and to negate the loneliness and boredom they face at home.[39] Volunteering can also foster a sense of social cohesion within ethnic community groups. From the perspective of civil society, such community groups are vital to filling the gap between the services that the state might provide and the demand for those services. In the final section, I explore how in-person and virtual spaces offer H-4 visa holders an opportunity to create communities and resist their devaluation as non-economic subjects.

CULTURAL PRODUCTION AND FAMILY SERVICE

Just as transmigration reinforces men's roles in the household as patriarchal breadwinners, it also reinforces women's obligation to carry the burden of cultural continuity and maintain transnational and local kinship ties. Some women engage in this cultural work by organizing functions for Indian transmigrants to celebrate holidays and festivals, while others turn their energies toward their children's schools, libraries, or local groups. In order to combat the social and economic isolation they face, historically, many immigrant women have flocked to community institutions such as temples and religious groups.[40] As "custodians of culture," unemployed women play a pivotal role in these institutions and are often the primary conduits for maintaining and transmitting religious and cultural customs to the next generation.[41] In the Pacific Northwest, established groups such as the India Association of Western Washington or the Hindu Temple and Cultural Center in Bothell have provided those vital community-gathering spaces. However, some temporary visa holders are less likely to integrate into community institutions because they may have to leave at any time or because they find that their concerns and interests are different from those of older generations of South Asian immigrants. As a result, many transmigrants seek out other H-1B visa holders whom they meet through work, which amplifies the link between transmigrant work and cultural reproduction over more traditional forms of community-based sociality. Bhanu describes her work with a nontraditionally organized religious group as a way for her to feel productive and connect with other transmigrants:

> We have a religious gathering every Saturday. I'm big time into that. We regularly go there and we even have a nonprofit organization. For birthday parties, we take the Indian stories like Akbar and Birbel and make them into puppet shows. We also go to concerts and have a food stall. We make food and sell it. All the profits from the shows and food go to the group.

Bhanu became involved in this religious community, which is made up mostly of other H-1B families, during the weekend and volunteered around her children's schedules. By adapting Indian fables to children's audiences, she was involved in the sort of cultural transmission work that Namita Manohar describes as vital to immigrant community building.[42] Bhanu described her devotion to the organization in both religious and community terms: "It's a lot of fun, but also this way we can do something here for the others too. I can cook, meet people, and do the fund-raising and all that." For Bhanu, her work with the religious group was as much about her spirituality as it was about finding a place where she could meet other H-1B and H-4 visa holders who were in the same position as she and her family.

There are other outlets for social engagement that replace formal community and religious groups, such as the India-oriented volunteer groups detailed earlier. Anika, a friend of Mani's who lived in the same apartment complex, was part of an Indian dance troupe that helped break her isolation. Having been married for six years, she migrated on a H-4 visa but was unable to work formally the entire time. Though she migrated with a master's degree in chemistry and then earned an MBA and certification in social network management from universities in Seattle, being excluded from the workforce left her feeling incapacitated. Like Mani, she spent long days at home waiting for her husband to return and feeling as though she was losing a sense of herself with each passing day. The dance troupe allowed her a regular outlet wherein she connected with others: "I would say, because of this dance group at least now I have something to do in the evening. So, daytime is pretty boring. I don't like the days." She also depended on her husband to drive her places when she first arrived, which exacerbated Anika's feelings of isolation and confinement. After she obtained her driver's license, she started attending events without relying on him, which improved her sense of independence.

H-4 visa holders also participate in informal-sector work activities that often are tied to their social and cultural reproductive roles. A quick scan of bulletin boards posted in Indian shops and restaurants in the Eastside reveals a large number of women seeking under-the-table employment as nannies, cooks, or seamstresses for other Indian families. Others market their small businesses applying henna for weddings or parties, hairstyling, cooking, or teaching music, language, and dance lessons. Many of these services provided by transmigrant women subsidize the cost of running other immigrant households, as they are often cheaper than if purchased through formalized companies or businesses. At the same time, they allow women the opportunity to earn money informally while also providing new outlets for self-assertion. Anika revealed that she uses her artistic talents to make some money on the side: "I did a couple of dance classes for my friend's studio, also some henna. So, she used to pay me cash and that helped for a few months." Unlike other immigrants who work under the table for family businesses[43] or in South Asian specific settings that are considered culturally safe spaces for women to work,[44] H-4 visa holders are likely to pursue entrepreneurial activities on their own. Anika and Bhanu offered private music and dance lessons, mostly to children of H-1B visa holders who wanted to learn more about classical Indian arts. Anika even worked at a few weddings and began to promote her henna designs on social media. However, for both women, visa constraints stopped them from pursuing these business ventures formally. Instead, informal work allowed them to gain a small bit of financial freedom, even if did not compare to what they could have earned in the formal sector.

In addition, H-4 visa holders with children spend considerable time volunteering in schools and for their children's extracurricular activities. Chase Billingham and Shelley Kimelberg report that there is a substantive rise in middle-class parental involvement in public schools, particularly in urban and peri-urban settings, where schools rely on private funds and parent involvement to counter shrinking state support for education.[45] Women who are either out of or marginally attached to the formal workforce, provide much of this labor. Sharon Hays has described the philosophy that motivates such women to devote considerable time, money, and personal resources toward parenting children as "intensive mothering."[46] This form of intensive mothering is overlaid with the desire/expectation for transmigrant women to act as key conduits for their children's social and educational success, particularly when they are unable to redirect their efforts toward their own careers or self-development. Writing for the *Seattle Times,* Lynn Thompson reported that in the Eastside schools, where IT transmigrants tend to live, there has been an explosion in the foreign-born and second-generation population of students who attend public school. The number of Asian Indian students enrolled in the Bellevue School District increased by 356 percent between 2004 and 2014, while the numbers of students whose primary language was either an Asian or Indian language quadrupled. Meanwhile, the number of Mandarin, Cantonese, or Taiwanese speakers grew by 90 percent. This demographic shift has also meant that more immigrant and transmigrant parents are becoming involved in their children's schooling.[47]

Bhanu experienced this phenomenon firsthand. She not only assumed an active role in her two young children's studies at home but also regularly attended parent-teacher association meetings, volunteered to staff the annual science fair, and visited her kindergartner's classroom to bring snacks, read stories, or otherwise act as a teacher's aide. Reporting on H-4 visa holders in the San Francisco Bay area, Anastasia Ustinova writes that volunteering around children's activities is a common strategy for H-4 visa holders to demonstrate their civic engagement in lieu of formal pathways.[48] She describes how H-4 visa holders combine playdates with volunteering for community centers to develop curriculum for preschools and elementary classrooms. By pouring their energy into the education and social development of their children, H-4 visa holders see themselves as contributing to the well-being of their families and to US social institutions. Moreover, in the absence of formal work opportunities, these gendered reproductive acts allow transmigrant women to claim belonging in the US and push against their status as non-economic or dependent. Another respondent, Reena, who lived in Seattle and the Bay Area and moved back to India in 2009, recounted that she was integral in helping establish an

Asian Parents' Link at her child's school in an effort to help teachers communicate more effectively with immigrant parents. She worked on a committee that met to translate important documents into a variety of Asian languages to better incorporate parents with limited English-language skills into school governance. Her case supports Namita Manohar and Erika Busse-Cárdenas's contention that there is a strong desire to perform self-sacrificing and upwardly mobile motherhood among racially minoritized immigrants who are excluded from other modalities of social belonging.[49]

Transmigrant women's gendered roles as mothers and wives are also reinforced by the expectation that they are responsible for teaching children about religious customs, Indian languages, traditional foods, and the "Indian" values of education, hard work, modesty, and discipline.[50] Though she initially wanted to work, Amina reframes her time at home as a way to ensure a certain level of cultural continuity for her children. She noted:

> It's not so difficult if at least one parent is at home. But if both parents are working . . . you have to do the things like school and day care. And if you want your child to have all the cultural stuff from India, I don't think the parents can in any way give that kind of time and attention to inculcate that into the child. And this is something that takes place early on in your childhood, up to a certain age. After that, it's too late. So in that sense, I find it much more challenging here. It's kind of the same in India if both the parents are working. But again, you have more support in the sense that maybe you have some relative or your mom at home. Grandparents may be at home. That kind of support is more in India.

Amina insisted that having both parents in the workforce diminishes children's exposure to "the cultural stuff from India"; her sacrifice made intergenerational cultural transmission possible. By "mothering for class and ethnicity," South Asian women mobilize appropriate gendered and cultural codes to position themselves as vital to both the family and the wider host nation.[51]

VIRTUAL COMMUNITIES

In addition to the place-based communities in which H-4 visa holders participate, virtual communities offer spaces for women to alleviate their isolation and recode their domestic preoccupations as empowering. Many women spend their time on social media or websites that are aimed at dependent spouses and offer a platform where they can share information and connect with others. The proliferation of online portals catering to non-resident Indians dispersed globally and the ubiquitous use of information and communication technologies within the diaspora creates a "bridge-space" between "home" and "abroad."[52] These sites offer opportunities for sharing resources, tips, and ideas that help women adjust to life in the US and also allow them to stay connected to friends, family, and cultural traditions in India. With relatives just a click away, thanks to video conferencing technologies like Skype and internet-based text messaging services like WhatsApp or Viber, transmigrants engage in various techno-scapes that keep them linked to networks located outside of their immediate geographies.[53]

Sarika noted that such virtual forums were crucial to alleviating her depression and feeling of entrapment after she first arrived on the H-4 visa. Though these groups were online, they also facilitated local, in-person connections:

> One of the things I have appreciated, especially about Microsoft is that they have created this spouse network . . . and they have been really interested in trying to keep on top of the changes and regulations happening around visas. I think they realize that it is hard for their employees if they have an unhappy wife at home, so they have been interested in pushing to get the dates back [for the visa applications] and helping people process their applications.

Here, Sarika references the Microsoft Immigration Family Network, which was developed specifically to address the needs of the spouses of transmigrant workers and has the mission of "enabling spouses/partners to learn, thrive, and grow, while developing a strong sense of community among our members."[54] The network runs webinars on career counseling and navigating local school systems, and offers a place for women to share resources such as how to find nannies, where to find the best Indian groceries and goods, and how to procure services. For H-4 visa holders who seek advice on issues such as obtaining a driver's license or tax identification number, volunteering, and filing immigration papers, as well as navigating the educational system or applying for graduate studies, these digital forums create a space of information sharing and community. Such networks offered Sarika the chance to connect with other women with whom she could relate. Though she had met some people through the local Maharashtra community group, which hosts events and regular meetings for people who speak the Marathi language, it was not her primary community. She noted, "It's an older group, which is nice enough, but no one would go out of their way for us. They don't really need any help because they are settled here and understand how things work. We can't really ask for help and they won't offer it either." Instead, Sarika found online networks to be most useful in her initial adjustment. For the corporations that hire H-1B workers, such online communities offer a low-stakes way to demonstrate concern for the entire transmigrant family. At the same time, such sites also consolidate gendered norms, as they hail H-4 visa holders primarily through their domestic roles and dependent status.

Even more visible are Facebook groups such as *H-4 Visa: A Curse*, which is an online community that is dedicated to mostly Indian dependent spouses and seeks to offer real-time support and answers to issues that H-4 visa holders face.[55] This community uses social media not only to connect with members but also to launch campaigns to lobby for changes in H-4 visa restrictions. Summer Harlow and Dustin Harp argue that the online forms of activism that occur on social networking sites have a real potential to translate into "offline" actions that seek social change.[56] One example is a letter-writing campaign initiated by the *H-4 Visa: A Curse* site moderator to advocate for granting work authorization to H-4 visa holders. More recently, the site has been a forum for collecting personal testimonies to be used by immigration advocacy groups. H-4 visa holders are often reluctant to engage openly in political activity because of the fear of retaliation or endangering their visa status. However, these online groups offer more anonymity and transform dependent transmigrants, who are geographically dispersed and isolated, into a politicized constituency that can organize and support immigration reform in a relatively protected way.

In addition to online community sites, individual blogs are a way for women to document their experiences for broader audiences. Paul Adams and Emily Skop argue that techno-social tools such as blogs or websites help to heal the fractures created through the migration process and also operate as "the means of establishing mobility and communication [that] permit women to control their situations and gratify desires for inward and outward discovery."[57] Many of the transmigrant women I met used Facebook or other user-generated sites such as Wordpress or Tumblr as a way to write about their migration experiences. Sarika decided to start a blog on her own experiences of migration, partly as a way to engage in creative forms of self-representation, mixing her thoughts on daily life with fiction, film reviews, recipes, and advice for others intending to move to the US. Another blog, *The Involuntary Housewife*, has generated a community of followers. Having moved from India to the US on an H-4 visa to follow her husband, the *Involuntary Housewife* blogger wrote, "I guess, I belong to an entirely different generation of women who never thought of ever being financially dependent on anyone—even their husbands."[58] Desiring to reconcile her new status with her sense of personal independence, the *Involuntary Housewife* blogger reaffirms her sense of self-worth by sharing her experiences with other women who live in similar situations. Blogging offers women on the H-4 visa a chance to reframe their skill building, housekeeping, and childrearing activities as productive and entrepreneurial. A fellow commenter on *The Involuntary Housewife* blog shared:

> I stumbled on your blog by chance . . . and it is indeed a big surprise to see an echo of my feelings by so many others trapped in the same situation. I kind of felt guilty for having those feelings as I felt that this is a life most people back home dream about. I am an architect, worked for two years and got a Master's from IIT Kanpur. After a few months of job I got married, moved to US with my hubby and ever since I find myself in the same state of gloom and despair which was exponentially grown by demise of my parents. I have joined a bowling league which is a good stress buster, trying to get another masters if I get scholarship, regularly visit public library, volunteered once for an International Conference, [I] keep digging food blogs and try new dishes regularly.[59]

For women who feel trapped at home, blogging becomes a way to demonstrate liberal self-development, entrepreneurialism, and empowerment. Akin to the proliferation of "mommy bloggers," who focus on the struggles of raising children, balancing family and career demands, and sharing recipes, fashion, and housekeeping tips, transmigrant women's blogs blur the line between being a platform for one's interests and creating an active community of like-minded users.[60] While some bloggers reinforce stereotypes about women's roles as mothers and caregivers, others challenge dominant representations and use their virtual platforms to create new narratives. In an analysis of the rise of immigrant food blogs written by self-identified IT professionals, Radha Hegde highlights how bloggers actively construct identities that are in opposition to the dual forces of patriarchy and a racist immigration system that undervalues their labor and interests.[61] Blogs, therefore, offer a space for documenting cultural adaptations, as women write about creating home country recipes with new ingredients or re-create religious rituals or festivals through carefully staged photographs. Blogs also allow them to maintain an internet presence that demonstrates their technological savvy and keeps them linked to IT. Moreover, as Hegde argues, "Using interactive modalities and synchronous communication across borders, the blogs fill the spatial gaps and temporal disconnects that have historically clinched the isolation of the diasporic experience."[62] In this way, transmigrant women's online activities create transnational exchange circuits that maintain an active and affective connection between home and host nations and push against linear notions of migration, settlement, and assimilation.

CONCLUSION

While the H-4 visa offers temporary workers a chance to create family networks in the US, visa restrictions reinforce a patriarchal household model in which men are supposed to be breadwinners and women, homemakers. When women at home provide the reproductive labor needed to sustain the immigrant family, men are freed to dedicate themselves to their jobs. Deploying a neoliberal logic that is intended to both maximize the quality and supply of labor and diminish its cost, family reunification benefits corporations that presume that dependents at home will make workers less likely to pursue more risky immigration strategies or move to other positions. In this way, the heterosexual family operates as a grounding force in an industry characterized by high and frequent worker turnover.

In practice, the paternalistic logics of H-4 visa actually work to disquiet the transmigrant household, rather than act as an anchor. Though Indian women migrate in substantial numbers through the H-1B program, their threat to US workers is neutralized by their location in the household as wives and mothers. At the same time, racialized representations of Indian women on the H-4 visa paint them as either caste- and class-privileged housewives or as downtrodden victims of Indian male patriarchy. This depiction obscures how actual immigration laws and policies are experienced and the ways in which they benefit the companies that hire H-1B workers. While allowing family members to migrate does increase the appeal of temporary work, it is at the expense of women's careers and aspirations, as they are caught between opportunities for their spouses and their own ambitions. As Sharmila Lodhia has argued, "The creation of a partial and derivative citizen-subject, through the H-4 visa program, allows the U.S. to resolve its current 'capitalist contradiction,'" whereby the labor of foreign workers is welcome, but only when it is tightly linked to nationally defined need.[63] The same calls for unfettered labor are deployed to deny rights for dependent spouses, ensuring that US companies ultimately benefit the most from temporary worker programs.

As dependents, H-4 visa holders feel a great sense of loss and constraint. Their education and work experiences are not valued in the US job market, while their visa status creates hurdles for potential employers to hire them. As the patriarchal family unit is codified through transmigration, H-4 visa holders experience an intensification of domestic responsibilities and reproductive work. In order to negotiate these constraints, many H-4 visa holders either reluctantly or actively embrace the role of the transnational housewife. They do so by striking a patriarchal bargain that exchanges their economic and social independence for creating homes suitable to their husbands and children, participating in entrepreneurial self-development, and creating the conditions to bolster their male partner's career choices. Thus, the unpaid labor of transnational housewives subsidizes the wages and social responsibilities of the H-1B worker while reinforcing women's roles as caretakers and non-wage-earning members of the family unit. As wives and mothers, some transmigrant women experience a deep sense of ambivalence and contradiction about these roles. In some cases, the condition of dependency leads transmigrants to question their decision to stay on in the US, and some seek to return to India in order to ameliorate the alienation they experience while living abroad.

Even while embroiled in the hetero-patriarchal logics of their visa status, H-4 visa holders still refute the notion that dependency alone defines them. The relatively unmediated space of the internet offers an opportunity for diasporic subjects to assert an identity that contradicts the exigencies of daily life and to transcend geographic boundaries. As Radha Hegde writes, "Unlike earlier migrant experiences, for the bloggers, home is always accessible via the screen."[64] For the transmigrant women writing about new Indian recipes using ingredients found in US grocery stores, sharing stories about Indian dance and culture classes, or taking up new hobbies, engaging on the Internet helps them negotiate the multiple displacements they endure through migration and allows them to embrace and challenge the boundaries placed on them through gender roles, state policies, or other social norms.

4 Returnees

"R2I," Citizenship, and the Domestic Sphere

AFTER SPENDING THE MAJORITY OF HIS TWENTIES AND EARLY thirties in the United States, first as a graduate student and then on the H-1B, Hemant was preparing to move back to India the following year. "It's all set," he related. "We'll be going to Hyderabad." When we met in 2015, Hemant was ready to explore work experiences in India and applied for an intercompany transfer to the Microsoft India Development Center in Gachibowli. After years on the H-4 visa, his wife also was eager to move to India, where she wished to return to work as a software engineer. Even though many of their friends suffered through the green card process with the hope that it would give them the option of staying in the US or returning in the future, the couple decided to move back regardless of whether their application was processed in time. As part of a transnational middle class, many technology workers already move back across borders for work and for personal reasons.[1] However, scholars and policy-makers agree that, around the globe, an increasing number of factors pull transmigrants back home for economic opportunities in the home country[2] and as a result of national government policies.[3] At the same time, a number of factors push transmigrants out of their host countries, such as uncertain immigration status, discrimination or xenophobia, the militarization of borders, and job insecurity.[4] Since the US does not track when transmigrants exit the country and because many returnees leave after gaining permanent residency or citizenship, this phenomenon is difficult to quantify; however, the acceleration of new housing complexes marketed toward returnees in India, the growing number of US-based Indians seeking jobs in India, and ethnographic evidence suggests that return is on the rise.

Those who choose to go back must learn anew how to live in India, since most have spent the majority of their adult lives abroad. While some "returnees" are from urban centers such as Bangalore and Hyderabad, where IT is now booming, the majority in my study opted to move to those cities for the first time after living in the US. As Hemant pointed out, "Even though it's not true migration, it is migration to your own home country"; in actuality, the return is not always as natural or smooth as returnees anticipate. Returnees often have varying levels of comfort with the local language, culture, and customs of their new cities and can feel displaced after moving back. As a result, many choose to live in communities with other returned Indians and ex-patriots to find solidarity with those who have lived abroad. Using the same virtual friendship and information exchange circuits that Indian transmigrants utilize, I connected with twenty-five friends and relatives of my study participants between 2009 and 2013, all of whom decided to relocate to such communities in Bangalore and Hyderabad. Through interviews and informal conversations with mostly women returnees, I explored the following questions: How do returnees adapt to life in India after living abroad? How does gender influence both migration and return? And finally, how does "return" fit into their identities as transnational and circulating subjects? Of the interviews that I conducted, all of the participants had lived in the US for six years or longer, were married, and had children. Their stories demonstrate how gender, family life, and community impact this stage of transmigration, as transmigrants have to contend with a different set of work cultures and family expectations upon their return to India. Moreover, they provide insight into how Indian transmigrants conceptualize themselves not just as national citizens, but also as circulating subjects with ties in multiple nation-states.

"MIGRATION TO YOUR OWN COUNTRY": FACTORS IMPACTING RETURN MIGRATION

While reverse migration is not a new phenomenon, as the Indian IT market expands and immigration becomes stricter in Western countries, India has increasingly attracted skilled workers and entrepreneurs who would otherwise remain abroad. The Indian government has redoubled its efforts to attract its "non-resident Indians" (NRIs) home by making regulatory changes in property ownership and voting rights, and by creating partial citizenship categories through the Person of Indian Origin and Overseas Citizen of India programs.[5] India, much like Poland, Bosnia-Herzegovina, and other periphery and semi-periphery countries, has experienced a sustained "brain drain," which led to the adoption of policies that deliberately attempt to increase "brain gain" or "brain circulation" in ways that will strengthen local economies.[6] As repatriates, former H-1B workers carry valuable skills back to India, and are seen as vital to bolstering domestic education, technology, business, and social service sectors, primarily because of their global networks and the social capital they gained by working in the West. However, affective and gendered reasons, such as kinship networks, quality-of-life issues, and women's ability to pursue personal opportunities also play a major role.

ECONOMIC REFORMS AND INDIAN OPPORTUNITIES

Changes in banking and financial systems known as "economic reforms" have also simplified foreign direct investment in India and have encouraged NRIs to maintain reserves of foreign currency in Indian banks.[7] These reforms represent a significant shift away from technocratic solutions and welfarist approaches to economic development that were initiated in the post-Independence period toward a neoliberal embrace of free-market policies, individualism, and entrepreneurialism.[8] One effect has been the opening of the Indian economy through the rapid growth of "new economy" jobs in information technology, call centers, or business processing outsourcing (BPO), rather than in government service or the public sector. India's largest informational technology trade organization, the National Association of Software and Service Companies, estimated that this sector was worth $154 billion in 2017. The IT sector alone makes up approximately 9.3 percent of India's gross domestic product, and is the largest private-sector source of employment.[9] This explosion has driven return migration. As Theodore Davis found in his study of professional migrants, Indian IT workers are twice as likely to return to India than professionals such as doctors or academics.[10] Davis notes, "Being an Indian immigrant working in information technology increased the odds by 140% that they intend to return to India."[11] These IT industry expansions have been supported by Indians living in the West, who are now more likely to invest greater sums and take advantage of job opportunities in Indian outposts of transnational companies.[12]

Economic reforms in India seem to have paid off for the IT sector and have contributed to the rapid ascent of the new Indian middle classes, who have benefited tremendously post-liberalization.[13] A 2009 study estimated that more than 50,000 workers have already left the US and returned to India and China, and that at least 100,000 more would return in years to come.[14] Drops in H-1B visa renewals in 2017 and spikes in applicants searching for jobs in India suggest that the combination of long wait times for green card processing that H-1B workers endure and new opportunities in India are making return a growing reality.[15] Losing talented immigrants to their home countries hurts US industries that are left without a competitive labor pool; yet, on the Indian side, return migration offers an infusion of talent and financial resources. For IT transmigrants, the allure of returning to India is heightened by the sense of opportunity available outside of the US and the chance to escape the process of navigating an alphabet soup of visas. And for those who are able to convert their temporary status into permanent residency or US citizenship before returning, loosened investment and banking regulations mean that returnees can enjoy key benefits open to Indian citizens—without relinquishing their foreign citizenship.

As opportunities increase in India, even second-generation Indians born in the US are moving to homelands where they have never lived and would-be migrants are choosing to remain in the country rather than pursue opportunities abroad.[16] Roli Varma and Deepak Kapur find that among graduates of the Indian Institutes of Technologies (IIT), there is a growing desire to stay in the country after graduation: "Their decision to stay in India does not seem to be based on any altruistic desire to contribute towards India's national development, but rather due to the new economic reality in India as well as abroad."[17] For example, Talal was a high-level Microsoft director when we met in Hyderabad in 2009, and he confirmed this trend in his own hiring. When he initially came to Hyderabad to set up a new team for Microsoft, he encountered a very different set of desires from workers who were desperate to go abroad:

> Literally, in 2005 when I came here, there was this craziness from people who just wanted off-site assignments. Their goal was just to go off-site. If your company did not offer some sort of off-site arrangement, they weren't a very attractive place to go. Given the way things are now, I suspect things would be drastically different now. There aren't enough jobs in the US. We are seeing people come back actively. They are very worried about what they are hearing in the news every day. Obviously, this is compounded by the recession. These are bad times—they go there and see that things haven't changed that much yet, but its impacting everyone. You come over here, and it's all this gloom and doom news and 689,000 job losses and so on—so I think it's having a significant impact. At least for the short term, I don't think the US is as sexy of a place to go work as it had been.

For the young legions of workers that Talal managed, there was a decided change in attitude about how much value working abroad could really add to their careers. In contrast to their peers from even a few years earlier, younger workers preferred to stay in India, where they at least could rely on other networks for jobs if something were to go wrong. More recently, news from the US has showcased the negative reception that some H-1B workers has received and the open hostility to foreigners from the White House have compounded the feeling of ambivalence that some feel about going or staying abroad. Increasingly, the growth in the Indian economy makes the return to India more attractive for midcareer workers, as well as those who feel stuck in their positions in the US. After waiting for years for a green card or being denied promotions because of their visa status, many of these experienced professionals also are looking to India to pursue new business ventures or to work in new subsidiaries or branches of US-based companies, where they can better develop professionally.[18] Talal recounted his own decision to return to India: "It was a good step in the right direction from a career standpoint. And luckily, we saw it as an extended vacation for us. Go to India, try it out there for a while, and if we don't like it, you still have your place and everything else in the US that we could come back to." For Talal, the return to India was part of a larger calculus about where to maximize opportunity for his future career growth, while keeping the door open to opportunities to the US. At the time they decided to return, he and his wife already had become citizens, which minimized the potential risks they faced when returning. For Talal, citizenship did not signal a deeper commitment to the US, but rather a way to enable to his circulation and movement.

Upon returning, many transmigrants anticipate that their foreign experience will translate into higher salaries or result in what Deepanjana Varshney refers to as a "wage premium."[19] The men and women with whom I spoke expressed assurance that if they were to return, they would locate positions comparable to or better than what they currently held. However, as more Indian job seekers return to India, they often are competing with younger workers, not to mention that companies also have a wider selection of foreign applicants from which to draw. As a result, many companies have stopped offering "ex-patriot" salary packages (which often offer US salaries and add in housing or other bonuses), and many returnees are paid equivalent salaries to their Indian counterparts, which is still considerably higher than almost all other economic sectors. What they give up in salary, however, they make up in prestige. Vivek Wadhwa found that while only 10 percent of Indian returnees held senior management positions in the US, after returning to India, 44 percent obtained such jobs.[20]

Even though they might not experience a wage premium, living in India offers other economic benefits. Hemant noted, "A lot of [multinational corporations] have offices in India. In fact, one of my friends just yesterday left for India for good. She was working for Cisco in California and she's now going to Bangalore, in mostly the same position, almost the same salary, but in India. But life is much, much cheaper there." Hemant pointed out that even in cases where people may be getting only half of their US-based salaries in India, "It's enough to keep India as an open option." Though the cost of living is rising considerably in Indian cities where tech workers tend to settle, the ability to live a life replete with domestic workers, drivers, cooks, nannies, and other kinds of services and amenities makes returnees feel as though their money stretches farther than it would in the US.

BREAKING THE ISOLATION OF TRANSMIGRATION

Beyond the economic reasons for returning, the isolation and loneliness of living abroad also takes a toll on transmigrants. Samip, a twenty-eight year software engineer, proclaimed that in India he was perceived as a "rock star" and a desirable young man, whereas in the US he was seen as "just another nerdy software developer from India." Samip's colleague, Karan, also noted that life in the US can feel extremely lonely for H-1B workers, who were not well integrated into older Indian communities and tended to congregate among themselves, thereby reinforcing the feeling of isolation.[21] Describing his average evening in Bangalore before coming to the US, Karan noted that he would get off work, often sharing an auto rickshaw back to his neighborhood, and then go out to dinner with a bunch of friends. They usually went to the mall afterward or caught a film together. After that, they might end up at someone's apartment, chatting until it was time to go back home. He never felt as though he lacked a social life. In contrast, he noted, "Here, most evenings on the weeknights, it's just me. I leave work around 6:30 or 7:00 p.m. and I'll go to the gym or maybe for a run. But then its back to home and you don't really see people. Even if you meet some friends over the weekend, it's still not the same." Being part of a racial minority population within a white-majority region is a new experience for Indian transmigrants, and many find it hard to become close to their US-born and -raised colleagues, who have different cultural reference points and experiences. That dissonance coupled with the insecurity of their visa status keeps some workers from fully integrating either into larger South Asian community institutions or the broader society for fear that, just as they set down roots, they may be asked to leave. This displacement suggests that, as for Talal, even as transmigrants integrate economically and through citizenship in some cases, they still view themselves as displaced from mainstream US communities. As a result, Karan and many of the workers with whom I spoke longed for a deeper connection with their friends and colleagues that go beyond meeting occasionally after work or on the weekend and did not believe they could find that in the US.

In contrast, returnees noted that they were much more at ease socially in India. Suli noted that one big reason she and her husband decided to move back to India was to take advantage of a lifestyle that lightened their domestic burdens; the availability of cheap household labor freed their time for leisure activities and to meet friends and relatives. When she was in the US on an H-4 visa, she felt stuck at home without much of a community. After moving to Bangalore, she related, "At least three times a month, my group of ladies goes out to some bar or party at a club or restaurant. But it's easier here—I don't have to do as much at home. I mean, I still have to manage the servants and all that. But I can just go, socialize and have fun!" Other returnees reported similar increases in the amount of social contact they had with friends, relatives, and neighbors. Sita related, "We have a great time. I love being in India. Everybody comes together, we drink, really good food, it's fantastic! I missed all that in the US. We didn't get a chance to do those things. Even if you do with someone, it's low-key, you see the same people, do the same thing each time." The sense of camaraderie and comfortable belonging to a community ranked high for returnees and played a vital role in their decision to move back to India. Moreover, many followed friends or family members who decided to move first, afterward settling in the same neighborhoods or housing communities where earlier returnees lived. These physical and emotive forms of sociality allowed transmigrants access to the kinds of networks they missed while living abroad.

FAMILY AND SOCIAL PRESSURES

Other major factors that drove the decision to return to India were the desire to spend more time with aging parents, to expose children to life in India, and to draw on family and labor networks to care for the household. As their parents in India began to age and develop health complications, the pull back to India increased for many transmigrants I interviewed. India has experienced a demographic transition in the past thirty years and, as socioeconomic status has improved for the middle classes, birth rates have fallen.[22] As a result, many middle- and upper-class H-1B workers often come from smaller families with fewer children and must shoulder the responsibility of caring for elderly parents. Swati, a former H-1B worker who decided to move back to Bangalore with her husband in 2007, was eager to return in order to spend more time with her family:

> My family is all in India. For me, it was good to come back to the family. Living in the US, your trips back to India are short and a month is not enough time to spend time with everyone. So since we've come back, we've had quite a few get-togethers with my brother and sister and it feels really good to be back. To be able to meet them that often, it's really nice. My parents are still in Delhi, but they've come down twice. They can come longer, too, so its quality time with your parents. They did visit us in the [United] States, but this is nice. I have three [uncles] in the US, in the Washington area. So my parents would travel around a bit and divide their time. But they got totally bored when they came because they were dependent on us to take them anywhere. They didn't know anyone, it's lonely for them. Here it's OK, it's a big community. You go down and meet a lot of people of your own kind.

Rather than wait for citizenship and then continue to live in the US so she could sponsor her parents to come abroad, as was the trend for earlier generations of South Asian immigrants, Swati preferred to move closer to her parents and brother in India, even if it was in a different city. After she and her husband obtained citizenship, they decided to move back to India with their young daughter (who had been born in the US). Finding it easier to associate with "people of your own kind," Swati was able to both socialize more comfortably, but also ensure that her parents were at ease when they came to visit. Nearly everyone with whom I spoke stated that their parents had no intention of permanently migrating to the US, and most preferred to visit for shorter periods of time. As parents aged, however, the only way that they could spend more time with them was to consider returning to India. Among elderly immigrants who do migrate to join their adult children, there are mixed outcomes in terms of life satisfaction. If elders do not have their own social networks, feelings of isolation amplify.[23] The loneliness and boredom that elders face when coming to the US, combined with the long wait for permanent residency clearance, makes family reunification between older parents and middle-aged children less likely.

In India, retirement communities have been growing, particularly with so many children moving abroad permanently.[24] Sima explained: "The concept of the old-age home has now come in to India. They create an old-age home that has all the facilities. You just have to show up at the cafeteria and eat. If you can't do that they'll bring you to a room at a charge. But it's a luxurious resort where you live there, and a lot of parents are choosing that." Sima noted that although this trend has been rising, there is a still a strong taboo against elders living away from their children. Living in Hyderabad, Talal pointed out, "One of the hardest things to manage is thinking about how to best care for our parents as they get older. It's relatively painful." In their survey of Indian IT workers, Carol Upadhya and Aninhalli R. Vasavi found that the high wages IT workers received abroad allowed them to send money back to India regularly, while allowing them to fulfill obligations toward family members. But, even with those monetary links, those living abroad for several years "expressed regret at not being able to devote the kind of time and attention to their families (especially to parents) that is expected of them."[25] Likewise, Talal noted, "Right now the main thing is that both sets of parents are aging and this is a good opportunity to spend more time with them. That was a big part of the decision to stay on." For many transmigrants, while their parents are still in good health, they may continue to live independently abroad. But once parents begin to decline, the expectation for children to return to India to manage their care intensifies and they are confronted with relocating their nuclear household.

In addition to caring for parents, almost all returnees cited the desire to expose their children to the sort of social and cultural life they themselves experienced in India: one filled with relatives, neighbors, and friends.[26] Talal noted, "The quality of life in India is a lot better from a social interaction perspective. My kids are constantly interacting with other kids. In the US, it's fairly typical that unless you have planned activities, you are cooped up in the house watching TV or studying or playing video games." Swati also noted that the return has been good for raising her toddler daughter: "The nice thing for her is that she has made friends here because in the evening, it's like how vampires come out at night, all these kids come out and there's like fifty kids over there. They use the pool, they use the gym, there's a tennis court, and there's a little play area and a basketball hoop." Particularly in large housing communities filled with other returnees, there are often impromptu gatherings in the evenings as children run between houses or apartments and women congregate in the common areas near playgrounds or pools in the late afternoon waiting for husbands to return from work.

Almost all returnees I met found this sort of informal social engagement vastly superior to how they socialized in the US through scheduled play-dates or activities.

At the same time, returnees' intention to expose children to what they perceived as "Indian culture" was strongly mediated by their desire to alleviate the reproductive and economic burdens they faced while living in the West. Sheila, who moved with her family to Bangalore after living in Redmond for several years, noted,

> You know most people say it's for the kids, and definitely there is an aspect to that. You want the kids to grow, to know where you come from and what family is like. But more than that, I think it was also getting difficult for me as parent because I was not working. I had two really young toddlers and it was very difficult because my husband was commuting a long distance. And there was really no help and it created a lot of frustration, you know, I mean taking care of two toddlers. I am managing all the stuff and he was working hard. It was harder than I thought it would be. The school district was not so good where we lived also and then I'm thinking, you know, with one income how are we going to afford to send two kids to private school?

For Sheila, moving back to India meant having the means to afford better schooling for her children. She was also able to rely on relatives and domestic workers to help with the kind of reproductive labor that is expected of nuclear families in the US. Childcare in these cases is not a neutral resource, but a means of cultural transmission as caregivers perform important reproductive roles and provide exposure to Indian food, customs, religious traditions, and other cultural markers. In many cases, familial and social factors act as a strong draw for transmigrants even beyond economic calculations; however, most make the return only when they have the flexibility of US citizenship or permanent residency and the security of being able to circulate if they must in the future.

LIFE AFTER THE "R2I"

So after making the decision to return, what is life in India like for returnees? How do their expectations stack up against the realities of return migration? One effect of this influx of returnees has been the growth of new housing communities situated on the periphery of Indian cities such as

Bangalore and Hyderabad. Both cities are centers for IT companies and are home to large subsidiaries of US technology firms such as Microsoft, Google, Intel, and IBM. Long the hub of several public-sector research and development operations related to the defense, aviation, aerospace, and electronics industries, Bangalore currently is the third richest city in India. It is also one of the fastest growing in the nation.[27] Neighborhoods such as the literally named Software Technology Parks of India, the International Tech Park Bangalore, and Electronics City have seen record growth as transnational companies situate their headquarters in the sprawling office parks and strip malls on the edges of the ancient city.[28] Similarly, in Hyderabad, the Gachibowli and Hyderabad Information Technology and Engineering Consultancy City (known as HITECH City) neighborhoods have seen an explosion of gated housing communities cropping up close to new technology parks.

These communities have made an indelible mark on urban India, as new services and industries have grown to meet the demands of their residents.[29] While returnees are increasingly taking up jobs at Indian salaries and enrolling their children in local schools, returnees see themselves as different from the local population, due in great part to their experiences living in the US. In Bangalore and Hyderabad, returnees' desire for US-style houses and amenities has led to the boom in real estate prices and speculation, and also is shaping the local economy and social relationships. I focused on one gated community, which was situated about fifteen miles from Bangalore city center in the neighborhood of White Field. I call this neighborhood "Lake View," and though it is but one example, many similar communities have grown in the area.[30] Through the women I met at Lake View, I connected with returnees living in a similar housing colony in Hyderabad, which I call "Mountain Meadows."

NEW RETURNEE COMMUNITIES

The first time I traveled to Lake View, I was struck by how the housing complex resembled US suburban neighborhoods, but it was also an enclave away from the pressures wrought by rapid urbanization and development. The main road leading into Lake View was paved and filled with chauffeured cars, while the several kilometers of road between the neighborhood and the city center were flanked by gutters of sewage and heaps of broken stones.

Since Lake View was a relatively underdeveloped part of town, the area was less congested than older parts of the city, and the contrast between the worlds on either side of the gated walls was stark. After I entered the neighborhood and was cleared by security, I started to walk through the tree-lined paved streets of the subdivision. Despite the neighborhood being about ten years old, the sidewalks were neatly maintained, with only few cracks or signs of disrepair. I arrived midmorning and found that the activity of the day was well under way, as I began to pass maid after maid busily watering the verdant, well-manicured lawns and moving briskly between houses. Considering that I was in Bangalore during the beginning of the summer season, and a long way from the rains of the monsoon, I was immediately overwhelmed by the greenness of the lawns. It soon became obvious that those houses closest to the high-traffic areas by the security gate and entrance were smaller and less expensive. With each house I passed, the lots grew larger and the area of visible grass stretched further away from the public space of the sidewalk. The red-tiled roofs and bay windows, coupled with the immaculately maintained foliage, gave the appearance of being in a wealthy neighborhood in California. Meanwhile, the ornate ironwork of the rooftop terraces, elegant statues of Ganesha or Buddha flanking front doors, and the polished pillars supporting the sweeping front porches lent a distinctly Eastern vibe to the villas.

As I wove my way through the development, I quickly realized that my pedestrian strolling was drawing attention, as I was the only woman walking through the streets at the time who was not dressed in the brightly colored polyester saris favored by domestic workers in the area. I was one of very few pedestrians on the roads at all, as residents zipped by me in their climate-controlled cars, safely ensconced from the dust billowing from the few plots where new houses were still under construction. I passed a large fitness complex, complete with a swimming pool, tennis courts, an entertainment space, and a clubhouse. In addition, Lake View offered privately maintained water treatment plants, generator stations, grounds and road crews, and security guards. Shareen, a five-year resident of Lake View, related: "You don't need to worry about anything here—no blackouts, no dirty water. A company brings in tanks of clean water every week. Every house has its own generator. You have your own car, driver, maids. That's the only way we could do it." It was clear that the community did not rely on the state for the provision of basic services, such as water, electricity, or education. In their survey of urban Indian residents, Julian Sagebiel and Kai Rommel argue that there is a strong preference for state-provided utilities in Indian cities regardless of socioeconomic status, but in private communities such as Lake View, there is a keen distrust of the state's ability to regularly meet the needs of individual consumers.[31] While the ability to secure private services has long been a hallmark of the upper and middle classes in India, this was a key feature of returnee communities that could ensure uninterrupted electricity to keep air-conditioning, electric washers and dryers, and wi-fi services running. As a result, seemingly "sovereign republics" have cropped up that are dislocated from the crumbling infrastructure of the larger nation-state, where individual households can procure utilities for themselves.[32]

Along with the desire to escape the bureaucratic cycles of visa renewals, immigration applications, and the lack of job mobility, the chance to live in a community such as Lake View entices transmigrants to return, as they are able to maintain or improve upon the amenities they associate with life in the US. That these communities are filled with other returnees makes the transition smoother, as most prefer to live among others who have experienced life outside of India. Sheila, who had been born in Bangalore but lived in the US for about eight years before returning, noted, "I think it's more people who have been out, their mind-set has changed, your worldview has changed moving out from India and then coming back." Sita was more blunt when talking about her desire to live in a returnee community: "I realized that we are like oil and water. We are US citizens. We are different. We are not accepted. Even when I enrolled my daughter in one of the best local schools in Bangalore—I have been told to my face that, you know what, this is a local school, if you want better facilities, go to an international school." Sheila, Sita, and almost all of the other returnees I met, were eager to explore life in India, but only from within specific parameters that allowed them to stay connected to the identities and lifestyles they had cultivated while living abroad. As a result, they sought out friends who had lived in the US, enrolled their children in new schools with international curricula that model US, rather than Indian (or British) standards, and purchased or sent away for US-style foods and consumer goods.

GENDERED RESPONSIBILITIES AND EXPECTATIONS

Even as returnees enjoyed luxurious accommodations and lifestyles, the return to India has had gendered effects. Return is almost inevitably accompanied by an increased burden of domestic responsibility, despite the availability of household help, and the consolidation of traditional gender roles for women. In my study, men worked full-time whether in the US or India, whereas restrictions for women who migrated on H-4 family reunification visas, a lack of jobs in the same geographical area as their husbands, or the burden of childcare and household management meant that married women were likely to move in and out of the labor force while they were living abroad. Even for the women who wanted to move back to India in order to pursue careers that were put on hold in the US, the decision was ultimately driven by men's opportunities for work. Many women hoped that, once back, they would eventually start working absent visa constraints. Of the twenty-five women I met in Bangalore and Hyderabad, eighteen had degrees in technical fields like engineering or computer science and had been employed using those skills for some period (though this was often before or after long periods of unemployment while on H-4 visas). The majority thought they would work after returning. However, with some key exceptions, few women were able to fully launch their careers in India or prioritize their work in comparison to their husband's jobs. They found it difficult to work full-time while attempting the daily management of their homes and the coordination of their children's schooling and extracurricular activities. Others had been out of the workforce too long and had difficulty competing with younger workers. In most cases, they made the choice to focus on the family and continue in their roles as housewives, which was a fairly common trend among others in their peer groups.

For example, Vimi had been on an H-4 when she initially lived in Seattle, but was able to transition to an H-1B, which helped her launch a successful career alongside her husband in IT. She and her husband both split household chores and childcare, as they worked to balance their work and life priorities. But, like many other returnee women in Lake View, after returning to India, she left the workforce and became the primary caregiver and housekeeper. She noted:

> I don't think it's about career as much as it's about understanding what family life is [about]. One person has to be there for the family. When we were just the two of us, both of us could have worked and it would have been fine. Since the kids came in the picture, it was important that they had the strong foundation of what a family is all about. They should be able to come any time to us—it shouldn't feel like mom or dad is busy. Maybe that is the Indian roots, but both of us felt that way. So he always told me, "If you want to work, that's fine. But then we have to juggle our career life and the family." If I had kept working, I wouldn't have made as much money as him. So it automatically boils down to that: I needed to sacrifice in that area.

In her narrative, Vimi paints her decision as economic (i.e., her lower salary, which was compounded by years of cycling in and out of the workforce). She also reiterates the gendered expectations to which professional Indian women must still subscribe, despite their training and experience, to prioritize their family's needs over their own. Smitha Radhakrishnan argues that even for women who are active participants in IT as workers, "the 'option' to stay at home and take care of husband, children, and in-laws is always the invisible norm that women relate themselves to—it is the form of gendered cultural capital that will most readily be valued."[33] Of course, the ability to leave the workforce is a privilege open to middle-class and elite women, and the ability to have a wife *not* working at home is often a sign of high status itself, as in the case of H-1B workers in the US who assert that it is men's responsibility to earn for the family. But this expectation that women should stay home is reinforced after returning to India, where it is often easier for a couple to rely on one spouse's salary, and having a wife stay at home is a marker of a family's economic success. While some women do continue working after returning, they often move into lower-prestige or flexible positions.

Like many of the women I met, "R2I-ed Blogger," the author of a blog chronicling her family's return to India over several years, decided to stop working in order to support her husband's job opportunity in India. After having a child, she wanted to be closer to family and expose her daughter to life in India. In a post titled "Ladies Special," R2I-ed Blogger noted, "To maintain sanity and peace, I decided to take it easy and stay at home . . .Definitely, I have much more time at hand than I did in the US even when I was a stay at home mom there. But, I still get completely stressed out here."[34] While R2I-ed Blogger had worked intermittently while living abroad, after returning to India, she became fully dedicated to the household. Even though she insisted that she had more free time from chores, she was now in charge of hiring and supervising domestic workers. Her husband's work with a US multinational corporation meant that he had to work long hours in the evenings, and she did not have additional family nearby in the city where they settled. As a result, her domestic duties did not necessarily abate with the return, but shifted, as she became a household manager and now was responsible for overseeing paid laborers, who took over the cooking, cleaning, and caretaking required for her family. For almost all of the returnee women that I encountered, moving to India opened some doors in terms of access to a higher-status lifestyle, but it also created barriers to personal career growth and turned them from housewives into household managers.

MANAGERS AND EMPLOYEES

Though the gendered responsibility of caring for the household overall did not substantially abate for returnee women, their reliance on domestic labor did help alleviate the burden for performing domestic work for some. By employing other (mostly lower class and caste) women for those reproductive tasks, returnee women were able to pursue new interests. Anya had worked for Intel as a market research consultant and had a background as a graphic designer. After moving back to Bangalore, she stopped working formally, while her husband continued at Intel's India branch office. However, once she hired a reliable nanny and housekeeper, she began to develop her talents as a nature photographer. Unlike the women who completely exited the workforce after moving to India, Anya was able to use domestic labor to start a new career path:

> I was able to convert that into a career and I can take these amazing trips. I've shot for *National Geographic*, major newspapers in India and the US. Just yesterday, I was doing this portrait session with some friends. It took a long time, like four to five hours to set it up, have the right location, and so on. I have the freedom to do that. I'm not sitting around having to cook or pick up my kid. And that freedom of, you know, being exposed to the arts and culture and you know, may be your passion, to be involved in some NGO, for example, doing social work. There is so much you can do here. It just opens so many doors, just the time you have.

Anya launched a successful career that required a fair amount of traveling, primarily because she was able to outsource much of the day-to-day running of her household to a staff of workers. Such reliance on domestic labor is common across India, where a wide range of households employ various workers to help with daily childcare, transportation, and cleaning, as well as coordinating shopping and food preparation. These workers do the most onerous and intimate reproductive labor. This "caring labor" blurs the line between public and private spheres of work and turns the household into a transactional space that allows more affluent women to relinquish the domestic tasks for which they are normally held accountable.

At the same time, the availability of cheap domestic labor creates new layers of household management. Domestic servitude has a long history in India, and the colonial-era *bhadramahila* has long been the model for respectable femininity in many parts of the country.[35] In these traditional households, rigid caste, class, and gender hierarchies create distance between employers and the domestic workers who perform unseemly household tasks. At the same time, there is a long-standing "culture of servitude" in India that relies on the "rhetoric of love" and familial obligation to maintain unequal relationships between employers and domestic workers.[36] In comparison, returnees prefer to manage their households like the workplaces where they have been or their husbands are employed, and do not view their domestic staff as servants per se, but rather as workers. As employers, women desire to have an intimate relationship with their domestic workers for some kinds of affective work, like childcare or caring for aging parents; however, for other kinds of labor, they prefer to maintain a more contractual and distancing model of management. This desire to run an Indian household like a Western company is further complicated by returnees' lack of experience with hiring and managing domestic staff in India. Many left India as students or young adults and, therefore, their household management experience was almost entirely based on living in the US without domestic help. As a result, in each interview I conducted at Lake View and Mountain Meadows, the conversation circled back to the elements required to maintain and run a household in India that is reminiscent of their former US lifestyle (such as using modern convenience appliances like dishwashers and washing machines or preparing Western-style food), all while dealing with the realities of relying on Indian domestic workers who do not have exposure to the same products, machines, or food preferences as returnees.

In order to manage these households, returnee housewives turn to transnational discourses of employee empowerment and loyalty that draw on their own experiences of working or living in global corporate cultures. Though most Indians refer to their domestic workers as "servants," or by the specific job they perform (i.e., cook, maid, driver), my informants emphasized their own roles as modern employers who were responsible for shaping workers' skills and personal attributes.[37] For example, Sita found the task of running the household to be more difficult than expected and saw herself as a manager who must create systems and workflows:

> It's still harder to run the house here. You manage these people also, right? The intelligence level is also at that point: they are not that smart. So everything has to be spelled out. You create a system. And that system has to work like clockwork. Like, for example, now all the grocery stores are giving out a directive that if you want to use plastic bags, you will be charged. So now we carry cloth bags. So the cloth bags come home, we have to know

that they are emptied and put back in the car. So you spend a lot of energy teaching them to do that.

Though she interpolated her domestic workers through class- and caste-based distinctions ("they are not that smart"), she aimed to train her staff to keep up certain standards without her constant supervision. Reinforcing caste and class hierarchies to set herself apart from her household workers, the social reproduction of Sita's household transcended the performance of daily tasks and was tied to notions of quality control and workflow management. She wanted to be able to see her "team" work independently so she could pursue her own interests outside of the home rather than oversee the daily tasks and remain wedded to the house.

Other returnees, such as Shirin, viewed herself as responsible both for shaping the labor of her live-in nanny and also for uplifting and caring for her maid as a conscientious employer. She used her husband's IT employer as her model for employee governance:

> My maid [Lalita] has equal rights in my house and I put her through computer classes. She's a very good masseuse, so I'm trying to hone that skill of hers and get her into a job because I don't see her with my family for her whole life. But I want her to be committed to me, because I need her really! I think I'm trying to follow the same principle that Microsoft did with my husband with this girl at home. I always remind myself of that, the way this company has taken care of us, I need to take care of this girl. I know she will be loyal. I see my husband's loyalty to this company. He's so loyal. He would not leave the company! I think if I do the same, she'll be loyal to me, which she is. And there's a certain . . . you know? It's like a symbiotic relationship. She needs me, I need her.

Shirin sought to apply what she saw as IT companies' models for extracting equally high levels of performance to her domestic workers. Shirin offered to pay for her maid's computer classes and massage school, just as a corporation might do through an employee development program. At the same time, these were calculated moves intended to ensure the loyalty of a domestic worker who might then feel obligated to remain with an employer who invested in her personal growth. By offering such "perks," the rational self-interest of Shirin to maintain a reliable labor pool was reworked as benevolence that would inspire "company loyalty." Her evocation of "equal rights" in the household pointed to an imagining of the master-servant relationship along democratic lines, where Shirin and Lalita were both free agents coming together to meet each other's needs—Shirin's need for quality and reliable childcare and Lalita's need for economic security and work. However, such discourses obscure the obvious class differences that kept Lalita in a subservient position and the ways in which her labor could never lead to the kinds of economic or social rewards that working in IT could. Nonetheless, the fetishization of IT has led to the notion that the expertise engendered through working in technology industries can be applied to all arenas; as Simanti Dasgupta argues, this "expertise is not limited to one's knowledge, say in IT, but can be borrowed from IT and implemented and implanted in the social domain," which is exemplified by Shirin's discourse about personal empowerment, company loyalty, and team unity.[38] At the same time, by relying on Lalita's labor, Shirin was able to restart her career and move back into the paid workforce (making much more than Lalita could), which she admittedly enjoyed much more than staying at home and caring for the house and kids full-time. In contrast to most women who return to India and put their careers on pause, the return to India actually enabled Shirin to launch her own design company and begin working as an instructor in a prestigious fashion institute, but only by shifting her domestic responsibilities away.

While the focus on "equal rights" might signal a sense of worker justice, it also points to the lengths that employers must go to find and keep workers who possess the attributes that returnees desire: the ability to communicate well (preferably in English), to maintain certain levels of hygiene and dress, to learn how to use modern products and appliances, and to come to work on time and work hard, all while remaining in the background of daily family life. These qualities stand in contrast to older criteria for domestic workers, such as possessing specific caste, community, or religious backgrounds. Many returnees employed workers from different faiths or communities than their own, and they were more concerned with the other "soft" qualities that their workers displayed. In order to retain such a worker, Shirin was compelled to provide benefits in part because of the perceived scarcity of this form of labor. In India, historically, procuring household workers usually happens through personal referrals and social networks. However, to find domestic servants that met their criteria, several returnees mentioned seeking out agencies or placement services that screened and recommended workers based on employer needs. Writing about the formalization of the market for domestic labor in Los Angeles, Pierrette Hondagneu-Sotelo notes that such placement agencies invest more time in screening women to work as "higher-end" domestic workers for wealthy families and raise the cost of labor overall.[39] These agencies not only evaluate and market the skills of domestic workers, but also ensure that their behavior, dress, education level, and demeanor meet the standards of discerning employers. Yan Hairong has described the development of these appropriate attributes in urban China as *suzhi*, or the "somewhat ephemeral qualities of civility, self-discipline, and modernity," that allow lower-status women to fashion themselves as modern working subjects.[40] The ability to demonstrate these qualities is what makes such domestic workers highly sought-after in India and informed Sita's decision to use an agency when she and her family relocated to Bangalore:

> The agencies hire maids, servants and drivers and then train them. Because it's not just Indians here—it's people from all over the world. So they need to know how to behave with them, take care of their kids, cook their kind of food. Because they are used to the local food, so the agencies have trained them to do these things. How to talk to them, how to behave, how to dress up.

Sita preferred to pay more to use an agency that would screen and select servants with particular traits and training, including speaking English, because her US-raised children did not speak much of her native language of Gujarati, the local Kannada, or even widely used Hindi. She saw her ability to converse with her maids as a benefit to the workers, too: "For them trying to talk in English is a big deal. They know that they can put it on their résumé!" Here, learning English is seen as a transformative skill that helps domestic workers beyond their immediate occupation and ties back into returnees' desire to see themselves not just as mistresses of the household but as conscientious employers who are concerned with uplifting and developing their employees. While Sita's decision to use an agency derived in part from her inability to access the same referral networks as local Bangalore residents, hiring from an agency also symbolically set her apart as a transmigrant returnee who had distinct needs and desires that tied her to the West.

Moreover, the focus on finding workers who transcend the markers of caste and class serves to discipline the otherwise unruly subaltern body and to ease the discomfort of the returnee, who must confront the very unequal terms on which India's cheap labor pool is sustained. In this way, Sita's desire to hire English-speaking maids and professionalized domestic workers allows her to feel as though she is empowering her lower-status workers by exposing them to new skills and sensibilities, and by creating a contractual relationship that formalizes the otherwise intimate relationships of care-workers and receivers. Anjali, who moved to Bangalore three years prior to our interview upon her husband's work transfer to the Indian branch of a California-based microchip processing company, underscored this reframed relationship when discussing her maid:

> We try to bend over backwards to help her raise [her three] kids. I don't know how it is in the rest of India, but in Bangalore, it's very hard to find good help. Her daughter recently was bit by a rabid dog, last week or the week before. I immediately took her to the best hospital in town. The next day I was paying her salary and she asked me to cut the medical expenses. I explained to her, "No, the way we do it is that I'm your employer and I'm responsible for your health care. I'm not going to cut it, I'm just going to pay."

By taking on the social functions of the state to provide basic services (i.e., health care) for her employees, Anjali was not simply reenacting the feudal relationship of servitude; instead, she perceived her responsibility to her maid as a matter of contract. She proceeded to remark: "I am responsible for her health care, just like in the US. So when something happens to her or her children, they can come to me. It's like when I was working at my job in Seattle." Anjali drew upon her experience working for a US multinational corporation, where she received regular health benefits, as the model for dealing with her maid's crisis. Though what Anjali offers is actually much less expensive than a long-term insurance plan, she reasserted her role as a socially conscious employer who moved beyond the established conventions of Indian domestic labor system. It was not a matter of love for Anjali, or seeing her domestic workers as "part of the family," that motivated her, but rather her responsibility as an employer who should provide such services. What was left unsaid is that, on her current wages, her maid does not have access to adequate health care, and must rely on her employer to mitigate an emergency situation. Anjali casts the fundamentally unequal position of her maid in the language of privatization, where the well-being of individuals is the responsibility of the private sector, not the state. At the same time, for women who employ domestic workers, the language of contract, rather than caste or class distinction, becomes a way for them to maintain distance between themselves and the economically disadvantaged women who perform the reproductive labor of their households.

Returnee transmigrants not only frame their relationships with domestic workers in neoliberal terms, but also see their employment of subaltern men and women as a form of uplift that goes beyond the sphere of the household.[41] Using the language of empowerment, returnees view their engagement with domestic workers as a version of the volunteer work they may have participated in while living abroad. In that vein, the returnee household, rather than state programs, becomes a site where the Indian underclasses experience a trickle-down version of development. Mina, who moved to Bangalore from Seattle in 2007 when her husband took up a job with a major online services provider, spoke about her responsibility to help her domestic workers become modern subjects as part of her service to the nation. Mina explicitly saw her role as both an employer and a counselor who had a chance to change her employees' behaviors and to help them cultivate the appropriate social capital that would facilitate their advancement beyond their employment as domestic workers:

> Our help is not only direct but I think we also influence the way they think. Like my maid, she's eighteen years old. Her family would've gotten her married two years ago. So I explained to her, that as a woman, your body is not developed yet. You should not even be getting into this. Now to her older sister who got married last year, I said, "Do not have children for the next three years. You're only nineteen." You know, a little bit, we influence the way they think. I really like that.

Mina's evocation of the contemporary women's empowerment rhetoric prevalent in postcolonial Indian development projects echoes historical state-led initiatives extolling the virtues of a "small family, happy family," as well as recent campaigns focusing on girls' empowerment to reduce fertility rates.[42] Beyond presuming that lower fertility will inevitably lead to lower poverty rates, there has rarely been a corresponding effort to increase the standard of living or introduce sustainable livelihoods to improve the actual conditions in which lower-class women and men live. As Aradhana Sharma argues in her assessment of the turn to NGOs or the private sector for executing Indian development projects, this logic of self-control over economic empowerment works to "produce self-governing and self-caring social actors, orient them toward the free market, direct their behaviors toward entrepreneurial ends, and attach them to the project of rule."[43] However, there are limits to this form of neoliberal self-improvement. When subaltern subjects begin to demand higher wages, access to consumer goods, educational opportunities, and other rights that would actually help them transcend their status, class and caste hierarchies are reiterated. While Mina wanted to help her young maids break with historical patterns, she was also concerned: "At the same time, we also do some damage because what happens, if we start giving them so much, is that they don't get accepted in their own community. So that risk is there." Thus, Mina can encourage her maid to take personal responsibility for her actions, but only within appropriate boundaries that do not fundamentally reshape the social order.

Bindu, who came to the US as a graduate student and went on to work in California for ten years before moving to Bangalore, expressed more ambivalence about her role in empowering her workers. Like Anjali, who offered "benefits" to her maid by paying for her daughter's medical expenses, Bindu provided more than wages to improve the lives of her employees. At the same time, she was wary of overextending her responsibility as an employer. She noted:

> That's the down side of having the household help. Everyone cries about problems. To a certain extent, you feel sorry for them. They can't help it if one of their family members is sick and needs medical attention. For them, it means their entire month's livelihood goes into one person's medical care. That's a hit for them. But like I said, the more you help them, the more they get used to that. They begin to use it as a crutch. It's dangerous for them and you.

Bindu's reading of her servants' financial woes is not only couched in the language of irresponsibility, but also in terms of danger. This danger arises from becoming too entangled in servants' lives and also from a fear of being exploited, which was a common issue for returnees who expressed frustration with being treated differently from other Indians when negotiating daily life in India. She proceeded to draw on her own experience by arguing, "We all have been through a credit card debt situation. Everyone does that when you achieve financial independence, you don't know how to handle it. We've all lived beyond our means and realized it's no good. But we scale down. They don't. They just think someone's going to bail them out." Rather than viewing the economic insecurity that traps the working classes into a cycle of debt and borrowing as problematic, Bindu saw her workers' lack of education as the problem, or even more sinisterly, as a deliberate deception and character flaw of the underclasses. Bindu presented her ability to move past her previous debt as a matter of personal responsibility and fiscal restraint, rather than of historical advantage, cultural capital, and educational opportunity. Bindu decided that instead of providing additional monetary support, she would give donations toward her domestic workers' children in times of need:

> I ask them: how will you, with 4,000 to 5,000 rupees a month, how are you going to make ends meet? You have to learn to live on your salary! I had a conversation with my neighbor about how she is influencing her driver to get insurance because he has two small children. And even the guy that does our ironing—he comes with the school bill and he shows it to me. He has two boys and they go to a very nice school. He shows it to me and he says, "Out of this, whatever you can pay, you pay me. Just donation." So I'll pay for the books or I'll pay for the uniform. It's like 1,000 rupees or something like that. For us it's nothing.

By encouraging their maids and drivers to control their family size, improve their money management skills, or purchase certain consumer goods, returnees articulate *middle-class-ness* as an aspirational subjectivity that is open to all. They see their emphasis on self-governance as a way to offer the Indian lower classes, through modifications in their behavior, a pathway out of class and caste stratifications. In this way, the possibility of class mobility is imagined through the elevation and emulation of the transnational middle classes, whose "correct" habitus can be spread through the lower classes.

Returnees view this desire to lift up their lower-class compatriots as tied to their experiences of living abroad. Like the H-1B workers who attributed their time away from India to their newfound interest in Indian development issues, returnees reference their association with the West as the motivator for their nationalist interventions. Bindu argued that her time in the US shaped her thinking about equality, and she wanted to expose her domestic workers to the same transnational flows of people, ideas, and consumption goods that she enjoyed:

> The maids who work here are now used to the kind of income they get here. So their lives have picked up. My maid has shopped at the Benetton

outlet. She's bought the same clothes that I bought my son. They all know what comes from America. The last time I went to the US, my maid asked me to get her a bottle of Johnson's [baby] lotion. She was using it on my son and she asked me to get one for her nephew. So they know what comes from the US but they also have learned to expect more and more in their lives because of the income. Inadvertently, subconsciously, they are comparing their lifestyle to yours.

For these returnee housewives, seeing their maids and drivers participate in the same neoliberal consumption practices allows for at least a symbolic inclusion of the working classes into the middle class.[44] This emphasis on consumption marks a break with the old Indian middle class, as Leela Fernandes argues, that was characterized by moderation, thrift, and a nationalistic sense of sacrifice and hard work.[45] Sheena, another friend of Mina's, noted,

I think the servants are better off now . . . when you look at society, definitely they know they want their children to go to an English medium school, they want them to learn. They want niceties in life. You know, they want to take a vacation. They want to go out, even if it's for a day. So they want to see a movie on a Sunday. They want that day off, you know. I don't think they expected that before they started seeing people like us—and that we give it to them!

The emphasis on the returnee as the model for neoliberal success—measured by disposable income, leisure time, and a global sensibility—reinforces the turn away from the state for providing access to basic welfare or livelihood, and instead prioritizes private solutions that do little to address the structural causes of poverty. Instead, the transnational household, and the activism of the transnational housewife who exhorts underclass women and men to work harder, save money, and reduce their fertility rates, becomes a site that has the potential to transform unruly subjects into a disciplined modern citizenry.

In the same vein, returnees see themselves as catalysts for other kinds of development issues, such as fighting pollution and environmental restoration. Mina discussed changes that she and others who previously lived in the US instituted in Lake View, such as collecting rainwater for gardening purposes and working to beautify public spaces in nearby parks. She observed, "The government's role is just pathetic. I think private citizens are making a lot of change. But publicly, we are not getting a lot of support." She described a small group of other returnees who have taken on the task of making small improvements in their neighborhood through the website and Facebook community *The Ugly Indian*. The Ugly Indian project encourages individuals to take responsibility for their communities: "It's time we admitted that many of India's problems are because many of us are Ugly Indians. . . . this is not about money, knowhow, or systems. This is about attitudes. And a rooted cultural behavior."[46] With almost half a million "likes" and regular posts, The Ugly Indian reinforces the neoliberal notion that real change cannot come from the government or public sector, but must be sought through individualized solutions and behavior. As Mina noted, "We have done some of these cleanups and it's all the NRIs there . . . because we feel we can make contributions in this way. You take up the cause yourself. If you have a problem with something, fix it yourself. Don't expect the government to do it for you." Like the transmigrant workers who see their location in the US as a vital link between IT cultures of entrepreneurialism, privatization, and Indian development, returnees transplant that ethos back to India, and they see the cultivation of the necessary "attitudes" as the key to pushing for change in India. Though they are not long-distance nationals anymore, they still draw on transnational circuits as the basis for their engagement locally.

CONCLUSION

The desire to return to India and simultaneously maintain a transnational life creates dissonances and opportunities for former H-1B and H-4 visa holders. After spending years in limbo waiting to secure their residency or citizenship status, the transmigrant's decision to return to India is often driven by a combination of career and personal factors. For the majority in this study, the return became more appealing only after obtaining citizenship or a green card in the US. In that way, they may be moving back to India, but just as their time in the US was couched in the veneer of "temporariness," often the return was also seen as a stage, rather than a permanent move. For men who are working in IT, moving to India can be a chance to build their careers outside of the US market, while women hope that the availability of cheap domestic labor will free their time for other uses. Once again, circulation becomes the modality through which transmigrants claim citizenship across national locations, rather than affiliation to one state or another.

For many, return provides a welcome homecoming. Others must reinvent themselves as returnees who are unaccustomed to living as adults in India. For women who previously were on the H-4 visa, the return to India sometimes means liberation from the struggle to find a job or the day-to-day living as a dependent spouse in a foreign country. The reliance on domestic workers in India can also relieve women of some of their domestic responsibilities, freeing them to seek out new career or leisure pursuits. At the same time, it also creates new problems, as they must now learn how to manage a household in India without the same level of independence they experienced in the US and contend with increased public and family pressures. Moreover, women face challenges starting or maintaining new careers outside the home, as men work long hours and children and household needs still demand their attention. As a result, for many returnee women, their roles as housewives actually are reinforced rather than diminished in the return to India, despite the hope that many harbor to the contrary.

Returnees manage this discomfort by imagining their household as a site for technical management where they can use their experience of living in the US as the reference point for overseeing labor within their India-based households. In this way, they are once again positioned as transnational housewives who attempt to bridge "US" and "Indian" lifestyles. Rather than focus just on their own empowerment and caring for their families, as documented earlier in this study, many turn their attention (both deliberately and out of perceived necessity) to empowering the working classes they employ. This occurs in part as returnees shift their desires for national development, engendered through their US-based volunteer work, to their engagements with their domestic workers. However, rather than seek transformative change, returnees intertwine the discourses of neoliberal empowerment with the scripts of global capital by emphasizing skill acquisition, self-development, sexual restraint, fiscal responsibility, and consumption as goals for their domestic workers to achieve. These domestic worker-returnee relationships mark a break from the rhetoric of love or familialism that has characterized the culture of servitude in some parts of India, but are reconstituted through the logics of neoliberal empowerment and a disavowal of the state.

In part, because the process of return is complicated by the experience of negotiating patriarchal gender roles, managing complex households, and dealing with reverse culture shock, returnees strive to maintain a strong connection to their US experience and to ensure that their children are exposed to lifestyles similar to those they experienced while living abroad. As I show in the next chapter, this dislocation is not easily resolved for all returnees, and many decide to re-return to the US. This re-migration further adds to the perpetual dislocation that constitutes transmigration and has implications for how circulating citizenship and settlement are imagined and experienced.

5 Re-migrants

Challenges, Repatriation, and Future Migrations

WHEN WE MET IN 2015, VIMI WAS PACKING UP HER VILLA IN LAKE View and getting ready to move back to Seattle. When she first arrived in Bangalore, she thought she would live there forever. She had grown up in Mumbai, but moved to the United States soon after marrying. She and her husband began discussions about moving back to India after living abroad for almost a decade and decided to take the plunge after her husband was able to obtain a company transfer. She reflected, "With the whole thing about global citizenship and all, this was our chance to do something for our kids where they could go to a new country." After enduring the long green card process and obtaining US citizenship, she and her husband went so far as to sell their home in Seattle so that they would no longer have a reason to return to the US. Eager to share her love of Indian food, holidays, and music with her two young sons, Vimi jumped into the vibrant social life of her returnee community. However, after having resided for ten years in the greater Seattle area, she found herself struggling to reestablish roots in the country she had left as a young woman. It was even harder for her US-born and -raised children to adapt to the educational and cultural systems of their new home in India: "For them, everything is the US. The way I feel for India, they don't really feel for India because they had never lived here." She, too, had been altered by her experience abroad and found that, as a returnee, she no longer felt as though she fit snugly into the friendship circles that were locally grounded. Ultimately, Vimi and her husband decided to reverse their return. Sitting among the boxes in the spacious living room of her soon to be for-sale home in Bangalore, she sighed: "I know that I would like to stay on here, but it's just not good for my family. But in the end, your family is the most important thing and you have to be willing to adjust and make sacrifices to ensure they are happy and secure. So we will be going back."

Like many of the participants in this study, Vimi was unmoored from both India and the US as she attempted to live as a global and flexible subject who was able to traverse national borders as the need arose. While circulating citizenship may be the goal for transmigrants, such regular movement can carry a high cost. Migration had been a constant in her life, a factor that did not seem to end with conventional markers such as obtaining citizenship or starting a family. Instead, her migrations were heavily influenced by the needs of others, such as her husband's career in IT and her children's personal preferences. Even though she had enjoyed living in India and expressed satisfaction with some elements of living in her homeland, the return was not as seamless as she had hoped. Between these competing pulls, where, then, is home for transmigrants such as Vimi? Where most analyses of professional migration presume that workers move according to the ebbs and flows of capital's need for labor or for their own economic gain, the case studies outlined here and throughout this book have demonstrated how mobility is also predicated on considerations that go beyond the economic. Vimi and other transmigrants spend their early adult lives laying down the foundation for greater mobility so that they may create multiple homes. But in practice, those decisions set in motion circulations that exceed their expectations and can keep them from truly feeling at home anywhere.

FROM R2I TO RE-MIGRATION: MAKING THE JOURNEY AGAIN

For many transmigrants, return does not necessarily result in reintegration. Even when they choose to return and are generally happy, they must also contend with reverse culture shock, regressive gender norms, work challenges, family obligations, and the maladjustment of their children, all of which can lead to additional displacements.[1] A great deal of transmigration scholarship has focused on the repeated border crossings of laborers, domestic and other low-wage workers, or on the shuttling of the elite, who can manipulate passports and citizenship to seek out the best locations for capital investment.[2] But, there is less written about the repeated movement of middle-class households, particularly after they have returned to their homelands. This is not an insignificant population. Among transmigrants who have returned to India, one in four believes they are likely to return to the US in the future: "When asked how they would respond to the offer of a suitable U.S. job and a permanent resident visa, 23% of Indians and 17% of Chinese said they would return to the U.S., and an additional 40% of Indians and 54% of Chinese said they would consider the offer seriously."[3] In my study, migration is no longer couched in terms of choosing to live in one place over another. Instead, transmigrants must weigh the value they place on living in one location over another at a given moment in time, as they often choose circulation over linear settlement, and as they seek to maximize opportunities for themselves and their children.

REVERSE CULTURE SHOCK

While often exciting, the return to India also is plagued with unanticipated emotional challenges and cultural adjustments. Many IT workers experience culture shock when they initially go abroad, but also find the return to India equally difficult, as they must readjust to the pace of work in India, social norms and expectations, and cultural idiosyncrasies.[4] Those who move to a new part of the country are sometimes unable to acclimate to regional differences. Many who returned to their home states or cities experience lingering ambivalence, primarily because life in India no longer resembles their fond memories. Mina noted: "We are so surprised at how much India has changed. We hardly recognize it. When you go to a department store, you get all the American brands!" But, as she also observed, the presence of returnees also has increased the price of goods and services and altered local modes of commerce. She remarked:

> The local people are not very happy because we drive the prices up. We feel sorry for the maids and all that. We are not so desensitized about poverty, so we don't mind shelling out 200 to 300 rupees more . . . so the local people feel that we've driven up the prices of everything. I have a certain supermarket and I only shop there. They do well because of people like me.

The demand created by returnees has led to a greater availability of Western-style stores, products, and services, which eases the transition for returnees. For example, the demand for organic food has led to a greater variety of produce options in Bangalore, and it has also helped grocery chains that conduct business with foreign suppliers to thrive.[5] However, the higher prices and the shift in goods and services available can also generate resentment between returnees and the older populations, who now find it difficult to purchase both basic and luxury items.

Returnees, too, are often at a loss when they try to establish themselves in India, which can lead them to feel perpetually unsettled. After living in the Pacific Northwest, Anita moved with her husband and two young children when he accepted a company transfer to Bangalore. Even though she was born in the US, she spent many of her childhood years traveling to and from India. Her husband was born and raised in South India, and they visited Bangalore and Hyderabad several times before deciding to return for good. Even though she was fluent in Telegu and proficient in Kannada, she found the experience overwhelming:

> The funny thing is, I figured if there was anybody who was ever ready to move to India, it was me. But it was still difficult. The first few days, you find yourself in tears of frustration. Trying to set up a household was not like coming on a three-month visit and staying with friends or family. My husband had never lived in India as an adult. He left for grad school and had never been back to live. He wasn't any help. And trying to adjust to life with a maid and driver, it was very difficult and frustrating . . . the pace of things, trying to adjust to people making promises and not keeping them. It was a big adjustment.

Similarly, Richa moved to Bangalore after her husband took a new job with a major search engine provider. She was new to the city, having grown up in North India and resided in Seattle for sixteen years. Richa never thought she would actually take the opportunity to move back: "I would never say that I would want to move back to India. Because you look at the life over here [in India], and feel like, oh my gosh, I could never live in a place like this." However, over subsequent trips back to visit her family, she noticed rapid changes that ranged from the mundane (i.e., shopping in malls and air-conditioned shops, as opposed to street vendors) to the profound (i.e., the explosion of entertainment outlets, financial services, housing communities, and schools catering to the middle classes). For these reasons, she pushed her husband to apply for jobs in Bangalore. He was subsequently offered a job, but at an Indian salary:

> Financially, it absolutely didn't make sense to move to India. Why would you take a pay cut? Why would you want to live the life here where things are not the way that you are used to? And we worked out all the numbers. Even for our kids' sake—one was going to do middle school and the other one was already in [an advanced placement program] and doing well and was going to be in fourth grade. We didn't see any reason why we should do this. But suddenly, [it] just worked out.

Even though the decision to return was not entirely financially sound, Richa and her husband decided to sell their house and relocate to Bangalore. They had both grown up in India, but neither was from the southern state of Karnataka, where Bangalore is located. As a result, upon arrival, they faced substantial cultural and language barriers, especially as they tried to hire domestic workers and drivers to staff their home. Richa found life in the city to be a far cry from what she had imagined:

> The thing about Bangalore is that nothing seems to be settled. Everyone is going in different directions. To do anything as a family, forget about it. We don't have the energy by then. And really in Bangalore, you feel there's nothing much you can do outdoors. All you can do is go to the mall, or watch movies, go shopping. If somebody comes, you really have to go an hour or two away, to take them anywhere.

Tired of commuting long distances through heavy traffic or relying on a driver to chauffeur her almost everywhere, Richa longed for the sense of freedom she had experienced in the US, where she could set her own schedule and control her mobility. Moreover, she felt frustrated by her inability to do business or get basic services. She, like almost every returnee I interviewed, described feeling ill-equipped to deal with complicated bureaucracies, bribes, inefficient government systems, inconsistency in private-service providers, poor roads, and water and electric shortages—in sum, all of the shortcomings of the developing nation she imagined she had left behind. By choosing to live in gated enclaves, she and others assumed they were purchasing their way out of such inconveniences. However, even private communities did not offer enough amenities to completely insulate them from the challenges of day-to-day living.

Even the returnees who had been raised in the cities to which they returned encountered difficulties when attempting to reacclimatize to Indian life. When we met in 2015, six years after her arrival in Bangalore, Rekha was living in a high-rise complex just outside of Whitefield. Although she longed to move back to India while she was in the US, after returning she felt trapped by her role as a homemaker and stifled by the expectations of her nearby extended family. She was shocked by how difficult she found parenting and running her household. She noted,

> We're just used to taking things for granted in the US because everything's just available to us in an easy and neat form. When you see

something or call a company to get work done, it actually gets done. Here, it doesn't. You have to call every five minutes and even then, it takes a month to get something done. That whole culture change itself was hard to get used to. You're just sitting there, micromanaging everything. That's just one job—think about having ten jobs like that! The whole day, all you are doing is just calling these people and trying to argue. You're always at the receiving end here—whether you have money or not. It is not fun.

The redundancies and work slowdowns that characterized life in Bangalore deeply frustrated Rekha, having grown accustomed to what she called "customer service." She admitted: "I don't think we knew the tactics of handling it. The moment you get frustrated here, people just say, 'Okay, go do it yourself. So what?'" Likewise, other returnees expressed that their much-anticipated homecoming was disappointing, primarily because they were incapable of deploying the appropriate codes that would facilitate their ability to obtain the services they sought. Sheena lamented, "The work ethics are not the same. You know you can get services from people, make them sit in a room and you tell them this is exactly what you do. But when you have to innovate and when you have to create—that's where it breaks down." In some ways, Sheena internalized the same critiques that are leveled against Indian technologists by Western workers—that they are good at simple, routine tasks, but not higher-level thinking. Even when they paid a premium for work and services, Sheena observed, there was no guarantee that the services received would be of high quality or completed according to their expectations.

The issue of cost-effectiveness resurfaced in many of my conversations with returnees. While many decided to move to India because they presumed they would enjoy a higher standard of living in India while taking advantage of cheaper labor and housing prices, the costs associated with maintaining the lifestyle they had envisioned prior to returning often surprised them. For example, when I visited her in 2015, Sita observed that even though she lived in relative luxury compared to her life in the US, in absolute terms, the personal and economic cost was very high. "We are saving nothing," she noted. "And look at the way we live, we live so lavishly. I have three maids; we travel all the time. I don't think we'd live like that in the US. But things are so expensive here too now. So the value for our money isn't there." Whereas many once regarded the cost of living in India as a bargain, maintaining a global middle-class lifestyle often proved too great a financial strain. Sita admitted, "What I'm not liking about my life in India now is that it is changing me. I am becoming part of the system. And that is becoming a struggle. Can we keep struggling to remain who we used to be?" As with other transmigrants, this desire to *not* become "part of the system" in India often is enough to motivate some to return to the US, especially as they strive to position themselves as global subjects who can fit in multiple locations.

Beyond annoyance with services, many women returnees lament that they must contend daily with gender discrimination upon returning. "When we were talking to real estate agents . . . If I ask them a question, they'll look at my husband and answer," Mina recalled. "I don't like that. So you are not treated equally for sure. Nobody takes you seriously as a woman," she noted. Though it is likely that returnee women face the dual effects of gender and race discrimination while living in the West, they are not prepared to deal with how gender discrimination would encumber their autonomy in India on a day-to-day basis. The issue of gender parity and safety is a serious issue, especially as spectacular acts of violence in public spaces against women have grown across India.[6] In 2009, for example, a right-wing Hindu group attacked a gathering of young women in a Mangalore pub. The vigilantes claimed that they were punishing the women for behaving immodestly, given that they were drinking, smoking, and consorting publicly in mixed company. Even more horrifying, in 2012, the world's attention turned to an outlying neighborhood of New Delhi, after the brutal gang rape and subsequent death of Jyoti Singh, a twenty-three-year-old female physiotherapy intern who was traveling with her male friend on a bus.[7] The case became a flashpoint of controversy over the dangers that women face in urban India, particularly as they increasingly move through public spaces. The attack on Jyoti Singh became emblematic of the clash between a progressive, modern version of Indian urbanity and a regressive masculinity rooted in cultural backwardness and gender-based discrimination. Another returnee named Banu described how difficult she found it to travel alone as a woman. Comparing her experience in the US, she noted, "It's very safe for ladies in Seattle. I could literally do what I want all alone by myself. If I wanted to drive to Oregon by myself with my kids, I don't have to depend on anyone. I can't do the same thing in India." Even though Banu was initially hamstrung as a H-4 visa holder, once she transitioned to her green card and adapted to life in the US, she found that she had a great deal of relative autonomy. However, once back in India, the gendered expectation that women should be sheltered from public spaces inhibited her ability to drive on her own or travel unaccompanied. Thus, for women who are accustomed to a high degree of independence in the US, the return to India requires a reframing of their status and power vis-à-vis gender and cultural norms.

CHALLENGES IN THE WORKPLACE

Amid daily frustrations, men found it challenging to acclimate to working in India, as those who had previously worked in the US often have difficulty adjusting to the emphasis on hierarchies, working late hours to accommodate Western offices, and the feeling of being on call constantly. A longtime scholar of the IT sector in India, Carol Upadhya notes that despite the emphasis on flexibility in IT, Indian companies still adhere to a rigid model for managing work and staff.[8] Projects often are broken into segments, and teams are often unaware of or unincorporated into the larger planning and execution of product development. As a result, individual workers are isolated from one another and other sections of the company. For companies that have Western offices, this feeling is amplified by the sense that the Indian team operates as an auxiliary unit to the main operation of the business.

Moreover, among midlevel employees there is a strong desire to maintain control over their individual contributions. After transitioning to an Indian team, many US-trained IT professionals find the emphasis on hierarchy and the distance between managers and workers less desirable than the relatively flat team structures to which they grew accustomed in the US. For instance, having worked for Microsoft in the US, Sheena's husband moved to assume a new role within the same company. The transition was not seamless, however, even though he was working for the same firm with ostensibly the same corporate culture: "I think that it has taken a big toll on us as a family and terribly on him, moving here. I mean he is so stressed and I guess you know after living in Seattle—he was there, I think, close to eighteen to nineteen years before we moved back—and he was a manager there." After having spent so much time and developing his career in the US, he was ill-prepared for what work would be like in India: "When you leave, you forget what it was like here, and India has changed a lot. You think you know it, but you don't," Sheena remarked of her husband's experience. He found that his Indian counterparts were often enmeshed in what he viewed as petty disputes or unnecessary displays of power and control, and he felt unwilling to relinquish his sense of autonomy and conform to a more hierarchical environment.

This disjuncture is compounded by the fact that almost all returnees had spent the majority of their working lives in the US. In fact, many had only ever worked in the States. As a result, they exhausted a great deal of time trying to fit into US workplaces as a way of justifying company sponsorship for permanent residency or promotion. For those who successfully adjusted, returning to India made them feel "as if they have come to another 'foreign' country."[9] This proved true even for returnees who wound up working for the same multinational corporations or who found themselves occupying roles that were similar to those they had in the US, much like Sheena's husband: "I think work-wise, my husband feels that the opportunities are better [in the US], in the sense that there's a lot of politics here." Though workplace politics exist everywhere, she argued that such issues in India are worse because of a lack of cultural conditioning. "He feels that people are more ethical there. You know, when somebody says let's have a meeting at this time, they'll actually show up. In India you can't trust anybody." While Indian technologists may not have the same professional opportunities as they find in India for advancement, many see their work in the US as offering other kinds of tangible benefits. It was only after returning, however, that they were able to recognize how much they had changed and adapted to the West.

At the same time, because they feel insecure in their relationships with upper-division managers, many workers feel as though they must prove their value by working long hours or by making themselves available to their bosses at all times. Many workers fear that if they are not constantly in the office, they will be seen as uncommitted, and this could inhibit their chances for promotion. Banu also related that her husband's work obligations caused stress by pulling him away from the household: "You can't come home at 7:00 p.m. or 6:00 p.m. like you do in the US. It's an issue. I think the hierarchy in India is tough—you are expected to be a manager and lead even if you have been an engineer for a long time." For transmigrants, this sort of insecurity, coupled with a shift in roles, often leads workers to complete ten- to twelve-hour days and, in many cases, to work beyond office hours even while at home. In Indian workplaces, such demands are even worse for women, who must confront gendered stereotypes alongside the pressures of a hierarchical work culture.[10]

The disconnect that US-trained and US-experienced workers feel with Indian management styles and company cultures plays a significant role in whether returnees are likely to remain in India. Some of my respondents found more support for their entrepreneurial ventures in India, primarily because the cost of hiring developers is cheaper than in the US technology sector. However, many who transitioned into similar (or even better) roles in India soon were disappointed. They were unable to relinquish their sense that the US was still the epicenter of the technology industry, a perspective they adopted in order to endure the long and uncertain process of obtaining a visa, permanent residency, and, for some, citizenship. As a result, return-ees often internalized the idea that working in Indian companies or branch offices was subordinate to US-based work and less likely to result in pro-gressive career development. Moreover, considering that instability in the job market was a leading factor that compelled transmigrants to return to India initially, they were more likely to consider re-migration once when the economy abroad grew stronger.[11]

FRUSTRATIONS WITH FAMILY LIFE

For transmigrants, the burdens created by workplace expectations can also have a negative impact on family life and childrearing. Upon her return to Bangalore from Seattle, where she resided for eleven years, Mina noticed a shift in her husband's behavior toward his responsibilities at home. When they lived in the US, he contributed equally to the care of their young daugh-ters. While she still bore a greater share of the total household burden, she and her husband each attended to domestic tasks: "He was totally hands on. And that's the thing about Indian men. When they go to the US, they become so hands on. Otherwise, in India, they don't lift a finger. That is a huge change actually." In transmigrant households where both parents are employed, men and women are more likely to share reproductive tasks, particularly tasks that are related to children and the household. Yet many behave like Mina's husband, who, upon returning to India and taking a job in Bangalore, retreated from this sort of work. As a result, the couple fell into a more traditional division of labor, as Mina related: "He seems to be working a lot more than he used to. I don't know what it is about India, but I have seen that in a lot of cases. For some reason, the men seem to be having longer hours. Things don't happen quickly, right? So it takes longer to do anything. So he's not as available for his children as he used to be." Mina lamented the change in her status from equal partner to primary caregiver, but also attributed this to a broader cultural milieu in India, where men are not expected to participate in household-related matters. Her husband's demanding job played a part, but so, too, did the cultural expectation that men are supposed to avoid domestic tasks. This feeling was heightened among their peer group in India, where almost all women were house-wives and primary caregivers. Since Mina wasn't working, her husband was even less likely to contribute at home. One of Mina's friends, Anita, pointed specifically to cultural stereotypes about men and women's roles in the family. She noted: "It's definitely been worse. Less attention to family time, less importance on work and family balance. Like there's just not even the concept that a dad might have responsibilities at home. It's just assumed that you're the working partner, so you're available to the company twenty-four/seven." For many couples, this division has negative impacts on relationships between spouses as well as between parents and children. Taking her marriage as an example, Sita remarked that this pattern of long working hours created tension between her partner and herself. Though she enjoyed the domestic workers at her disposal, her social life, and other luxuries of life in India, she was displeased with how the return had changed her relationship with her husband. When discussing her husband's work obligations, she noted, "I am not happy [about this]. My husband comes home at 8:00 at night, but he still works. Yesterday, he was on a call late—actually, the last three days actually he was on a call. I would say five out of seven nights, I go to sleep without knowing where he is, literally. So that's not very good for us as a couple." Of course, such work-life balance issues exist in other locations; however, the time difference between India and the US, which requires employees to be available around the clock, amplifies the patriarchal divisions of labor and the disruption of family life.

Additionally, the impact on quality time for families often leads returnees to question their decision to relocate back to India, even though the desire for a better family life is what initially motivated many transmigrants to return. Between the expectation for men to work late and the intensification of social obligations, many returnees long for the kind of lifestyle and family activities in which they engaged while living abroad. As Madhu noted,

> When you are living in the US and you're a family of four, you only see the four of you. Here we tend to party more, we go out on a lot of dinners or whatever. Even in the middle of the week. We don't take the kids with us. So they don't see us as much. There, we work together as a family unit. We unloaded the dishwasher, we did the laundry, we'd sit together for dinner, we'd cook things together, we took classes together, and we'd go out to a park and do a picnic. We don't do that here.

The returnees I interviewed had significantly more social obligations as well as more domestic assistance in India, but they found that they were less likely to spend time with their children. The Indian school day was longer than in the US, particularly for secondary students, and extracurricular activities and private tutorials after school often lengthened their schedules. Commuting times also increased, as traffic congestion in Bangalore had grown worse as a result of more families opting to use private cars as opposed to public transport, auto-rickshaws, or company vans to commute.[12] Ironically, although drivers and domestic workers were seen as conveniences, relying on them also signaled a corresponding decrease in family time. Nearly everyone I interviewed noted that there was a better sense of family-work balance in the US, and they longed for that aspect of life abroad. Observing US managers who left work early to pick up kids or deal with other issues at home left a strong impression on transmigrants. With positive role models at work, they were able to maintain a healthier balance in the US, which translated into better family and household management.

Along with dealing with family issues in the household after having been away for several years, some returnees were surprised by how distant they felt from relatives. Even though she lived in closer proximity to her relatives and she was generally happy with the friends she made after returning to India, Sita found that her relationship with her family was not as strong as she had anticipated. She noted that her family was unwilling to rearrange schedules or make accommodations to visit them in a different city. Sita attributed this disconnect to changing familial obligations in India: "I have seen that change, that girls are becoming more vocal about what they want. And I think not just the bride I'm talking about even the mother-in-law. She has her own social thing and parties and she needs her space too." This is evident across India, not just in my interviews. Many families still live jointly, but there is also growing acceptance of nuclear households, particularly as younger couples demand more space and privacy from their parents.[13] Yet, in Sita's case, after her husband was diagnosed with a serious illness, she was especially disappointed that she did not experience the sort of immediate support that she had anticipated. While she enjoyed the returnee parties and lifestyle in her neighborhood, she was still seen as a foreigner who had lived away from her community for a long time. "And honestly, you know, we came back for the family, right? Who was there when my husband was sick? Nobody was there," Sita remarked. At the same time, familial obligations actually encroached on their personal space as returnees felt pressure to visit relatives frequently or go to all manner of social functions. Sita noted, "My uncle called me for his daughter's engagement. That was enough for me to be like, 'OK, they really want me to be there, I should go.' I spent 10,000 rupees to go take a one-day flight." Although she was willing to make an effort to visit her family on short notice, she remained uncertain about whether they would do the same for her: "I've been here for seven years and they have never come to my house." Sita initially assumed that she would feel more connected to the extended kin she had missed while living abroad. However, she soon found that her time abroad, living in a different part of India and shifts in the way Indian society regarding familial expectations meant that those networks were harder to reestablish than she had imagined.

Even as returnees seek to be closer to some family members, it can mean that they also must leave other members of their families behind in the US. Social networks and extended family ties, even those considered "weak," such as between cousins or friends of friends, have a strong impact on migration and return.[14] In my interviews, Indian transmigrants who relocated to the US for school or work generally already had some ties there, even if they were not geographically close to friends or family. After years of living in the US, those ties deepened and expanded, as workers could sponsor other family members (after becoming citizens themselves) or help new arrivals settle into US life. As more relatives migrated, their kinship networks widened. For example, Talal and his wife moved back to India to be closer to his parents, but his wife's siblings subsequently relocated to the US, which created new challenges concerning which location their family would prioritize in the long term. "Would we would want to go back to the US at some point in time? It seems very likely. Would we go back in the next couple of years? I don't know at this point in time. But it is hard; we miss our family there. For my wife, many of her relatives are there and she misses the independence there," Talal remarked. Almost all returnees reported enjoying the social life in India, and some felt more connected with friends and family. Yet, overall, the issue of how to continue to maintain relationships transnationally remained unresolved.

THE (MAL)ADJUSTMENT OF CHILDREN

Finally, in my interviews, it became apparent that transmigrants were most likely to return to the US out of regard to their children's well-being and educational opportunities. Vimi said that her children's future schooling (secondary and beyond) and their dissatisfaction with living in India ultimately pushed their decision to re-migrate: "They absolutely do not think that this was worth it. They don't know why we did this. Why are we here?" Vimi's young sons entered into the Indian educational system in elementary school and found that the pressure of performing at a more rigorous

educational standard, coupled with the hardships brought on by the alienation they experienced as cultural outsiders, was just too much to manage.
The boys, who were four and six when they moved, were often teased for
having American accents and for their lack of familiarity with Indian games
and television shows. They also experienced a series of health problems;
after they moved to Bangalore, Vimi's younger son's asthma became particularly acute, since Bangalore suffers from significantly worse air quality
than Seattle. Since her sons were US citizens, she felt that it was ultimately to
their benefit to continue their high school and college education in Seattle,
rather than prolong their stay in India.

Additionally, Sita noted that she was unhappy with the quality of education her children received in India. Ironically, many returnees initially cited
better educational opportunities, or at least cheaper private schools, as a
major factor for their decisions to return to India. However, those who had
personally attended undergraduate or graduate schools in the US found it
difficult to adjust to the Indian systems, as did their children. Citing the
difference between her daughter's education in the US and her private
school in India, Sita offered the following:

> For example, my daughter drew a perfectly nice picture and her art
> teacher says, "This is not art." And she is a very beautiful artist, but this
> woman says, "This is not art." My daughter is so deep into art that she
> learned about a particular artist and then actually went to a park and
> painted a whole wall based on this artist. And when she produced a pic-
> ture similar to that same artist and shows it to her teacher, her teacher
> says, "No, I want you to draw flowers, and leaves and this and that." So
> my daughter is now confused. There is no creative expression here! No
> room to think.

Sita's complaints regarding her daughter's education echo Western technologists' critiques about Indian IT workers: those trained in Indian systems are good at memorization and routine work, but they are unable to
tackle the creative, high-level systemic thinking required to move up in
Western work environments. Likewise, Sita believed the education system
in India reinforced negative behaviors, such as obedience to form without
care for expression or content. She feared that this trend would only become
more acute as her children moved into secondary schooling and the emphasis on memorization needed for standardized tests and college entry exams
increased.

Currently in India, only one in five, or about 20 percent, of the general population enters higher education.[15] Nevertheless, the education sector is growing rapidly. While engineering is the number-one ranked course of study, India has also witnessed an explosion in the numbers of colleges and universities catering to other fields.[16] In 1991, for example, there were 190 universities and 7,364 colleges. By 2013, there were 700 universities and 35,500 colleges. Though there has been a rapid proliferation of schools as new institutions attempt to draw students interested in diverse fields, the quality and standardization of curriculum, as well as infrastructure, teachers, and material presented in these new schools are highly variable.[17] These discrepancies are also evident within the more expensive schools with international curriculums, where most returnees preferred to send their children. Moreover, returnees reported concerns about the "reservation system" in higher education, which is a form of affirmative action whereby schools allot seats for underrepresented caste and religious minorities. Many returnees believed that this system could make it more difficult for their caste- and class-privileged children to secure a spot at a high-caliber university. The anxieties over quotas, in addition to concerns about government policies, internal corruption, and bureaucracy, influenced the negative perceptions held by many transmigrants about the education system in India.[18]

As a result, traveling abroad for education has long been a facet of elite and upper-class Indian experiences, and about 200,000 of India's elite class travel abroad annually to study, with the majority migrating to the US.[19] This trend has a long history. Ross Bassett found that some US institutions, such as the Massachusetts Institute of Technology, have enrolled Indian students since 1882.[20] In the contemporary moment, even middle-class Indian families regard studying abroad as a long-term investment in the future of their children and as a primary way to expose them to global job opportunities. As students, H-1B workers, and returnees, transmigrants value education in the US, and they credit the networks and exposure they developed through their study abroad with their professional mobility. As Rekha noted:

> If you really want to raise kids over here in India, it's a great environment. The amount of social interaction they get is great. But the kinds of mannerisms they pick up, the kinds of schools that are available, and for the kind of fee you can afford, the schools are not nearly a match to what you get in the US. I still think that an individual develops a much better personality over in the US versus here. See, I did my bachelor's over there.

Then, when I moved over to Sacramento, I met a lot of people that did master's. I saw a huge difference even between those people with the bachelor's from the US and just the grad students. The bachelor's life teaches you a whole lot more.

Because of her own experience, Rekha preferred to send her children to the US, not just for graduate school, but for undergraduate degrees, as well. Through the decisions they make about schooling for their kids across international borders, transmigrants are ensuring both their own ability to circulate and their children's academic success. This means planning for admission early on and navigating in-state residency requirements for public universities. Rekha noted, "Most families who move back plan to go when the kids are entering eighth or ninth grade. That's the calculation—you have to live in the same state for like five years to get the in-state tuition fees so that's the right amount of time." Children of transmigrants are able to mobilize their naturalization/citizenship status to maintain or reestablish connections in the US.

In other transmigrant communities, children can be a mobilizing force for families as they pursue living in multiple locations. This phenomenon has been prevalent among wealthy and elite migrants from mainland China, Hong Kong, and Taiwan, as Aihwa Ong, Min Zhou, and Ken Sun have shown.[21] Thus, the practice of sending children on their own to the US for education, or leaving them with relatives in the US, allows parents to shuttle between Asia and the US to manage their various businesses. Estimating that more than 40,000 children come to the US as "parachute kids," Zhou argues that many families pursue foreign education for children as a means of establishing residency abroad for other family members. She notes that "even as they pursue economic opportunities at home, wealthy Chinese entrepreneurs want an 'insurance policy' abroad," which in turn serves as "a practical way of investing in the future."[22] In this way, middle-class Indian families also seek out citizenship strategies that allow them to enable future migrations, either for themselves or for their children. When it came time to advance their children's educational opportunities, their children, at the very least, are able to travel more easily across borders. The desire to use formal and informal transnational links to further their children's education mirrors the experiences of East Asian families; however, rather than send children abroad on their own, the entire family unit is likely to circulate. In this way, citizenship becomes a key driver in circulation and ensures mobility for the future.

CONCLUSION

As Indian IT workers and their spouses seek to balance their careers and family demands, several factors converge to blur the line between their positions as migrants and returnees, such as the desire for self-actualization, family obligations, their children's well-being, gender norms, and national conditions. As transmigrants, they must navigate a bureaucracy of visas, immigration policy, and national boundary-keeping. Some decide to move back to India in order to resolve their insecure status in the US and pursue opportunities to which they would not have had access otherwise. However, the transition back to India does not always proceed as planned: returnees must navigate difficult relationships with family members, work colleagues and supervisors, and, more generally, learn how to live in a country that no longer feels familiar. As a result, some of those migrants-turned-returnees turn into re-migrants, heading back to the US.

At each stage of these movements, returnees view migration as an act of disjuncture, but also as a way to lay the groundwork for the next link in their circulation chain. In large part, this cross-border movement becomes normalized, intergenerational, and foundational to the circulating citizenship that they seek. Far from being a radical break, the cases profiled here demonstrate how transmigration is ongoing, procedural, and a without predictable conclusion. Indian IT workers and their families make decisions about migration that are not purely motivated by economic reasons, but rather influenced by events along their life courses. They are also careful to maintain a foothold in host nations through their or their children's citizenship status, even as they move across borders. Though deeply attached to their Indian identities, the transmigrants profiled here trade in geographic grounding for a version of citizenship that is predicated on circulation instead of settlement. This circulating citizenship is still tied to specific nation-state formations, but is deployed flexibly and with the intention of easing the process of movement. While debates over visas, immigration policies, and the nature of work shape the conditions for these migrations, the stories profiled here show us how important intimate, as well as structural, factors are for transmigrants as they claim multiple spaces as "home."

CONCLUSION

Circulations

"I THINK GLOBAL MOVEMENT IS JUST A REALITY AT THIS POINT in time. It's kind of hard to grow up in one place and stay there all your life," Talal noted, reflecting on the many border crossings that have punctuated his personal and professional life. While migration has become an expectation rather than exception for some, this book does not tell a story of borderless worlds or inevitable globalization. Instead, it shows how the process of crafting a transnational life requires a series of long-term strategic acts that are as dependent on global flows and juridical openings as they are on the intimate practices contained in the household. Transmigrants mobilize both work opportunities in the IT industry and family reunification policies to pursue personal goals and career aspirations. At the same time, the complicated and contingent immigration process that brings workers to the US leaves them in a liminal state, as they endure long delays while transferring from temporary visas to permanent residency. Many remain partial citizen-subjects for half a decade or more as a result of a process that reshapes their identities, marriage, family formation choices, and their ability (or desire) to settle in one location or another.

GENDERING TRANSMIGRATION
Whereas transmigration is usually couched in economic terms, the application of gender as an analytic to understand how transmigration is actually lived, embodied, and practiced is at the core of this study. While cross-border movement is predicated on temporary worker programs that over-whelmingly create the conditions for men's migration, women become intractably linked to transnational circuits of labor as spouses and, in lesser numbers, as workers themselves. As Rajni Palriwala and Patricia Uberoi argue in the introduction to their anthology on the sociology of marriage and migration, migration as a result of marriage is often one of the most socially acceptable and efficient pathways available for women to achieve social or economic mobility.[1] For technically-trained and educated women

in my study who migrated after marriage, many, indeed, hoped that trans-migration would lead to opportunities for work abroad. In reality, the H-4 visa limited their job prospects and future chances as they were subse-quently displaced from the workforce and found reentry difficult or even impossible. For the much smaller pool of women who were able to obtain H-1Bs, transmigration sometimes impacted their partnerships. After hav-ing experienced the autonomy and independence of living and working on their own terms, they became unwilling to strike the patriarchal bargains often required in transmigrant households. While there were certainly examples where both partners successfully obtained H-1B visas, or where women were able to launch careers after obtaining work authorization, the majority of women who were linked to temporary worker programs remained trapped in a state of dependency that reduced their roles to the domestic and reproductive sphere.

I have argued that these legal barriers to women's employment position many Indian transmigrant women as transnational housewives whose gen-dered labor and cultural transmission plays a vital role in bridging the mul-tiple worlds that transmigrants inhabit. While the decision to migrate is often willingly undertaken, it can come at high personal cost. Key to being a transnational housewife is meeting the needs of the immediate family unit and engaging in place-making activities that can be continued across bor-ders. Though many of the transmigrant women I profiled throughout this book generally embraced their roles as mothers and wives and regarded their time at home as necessary and good for their families, it often meant relinquishing their own self-interest. In fact, many actively chose to have children while living in the US to ensure that their progeny would have the benefit of citizenship. Others felt trapped by having children while stuck in a place of economic dependency. Ultimately, caring for children offered a potential claim to social and national belonging, but also became a factor that blunted women's career aspirations and opportunities.

As immigration constraints are compounded by cultural norms tied to sacrificial Indian womanhood, some transmigrants consider the "R2I," or the return to India, as a way to avail themselves of new opportunities. Though the decision to return is usually driven, once again, by men's career choices, many women also hope that returning will allow them to launch their own careers, or at least pursue projects outside of the home. They anticipate that once they are free of the US immigration system and can rely on paid domestic labor, they will be free to pursue new opportunities. In actuality, many women experience an intensification of their household responsibilities, even if their actual reproductive labor is eased by the purchase of cooking, cleaning, driving, and childcare services. While men work long hours away from the home, women spend their time supervising households and managing children's schooling, activities, and running daily household tasks. This gendered division of labor is socially reinforced by the communities in which they live, where women are expected to devote their energies to "homely" tasks. Their labor is amplified by the expectation that the households they run can be transported back to the US if needed.

Though many envision their return to India as the end of their journey, it often turns out to be a stopgap along the way to the next stage of migration. The frustrations they experience while living in India, including difficulties associated with adjusting to domestic conditions, social expectations, and concerns about their children's health and education, influence their decision to leave. Of the returnees who are able to establish permanent residency or become US citizens, some actually reverse the "R2I" and go back to the United States. Again, by delaying or relinquishing their own desires, women facilitate this transition process by prioritizing their children's future schooling and their husbands' opportunities in the US. We are just beginning to see this next phase of Indian IT transmigration unfolding, so it is unclear how the patterns will play out among future generations—whether they will stay in the US or, once again, return to India as they age. It is clear, however, that the gendered labor and sacrifices of women will play a vital role in enabling the next loop of this circulation to progress.

Throughout this book, I have centered gendered narratives in order to illustrate the intimate and personal ways in which transmigrants navigate the social, political, and cultural codes that structure transnationalism and adapt them to their circumstances. Transmigration may amplify gendered divisions of labor and family norms; however, Indian women still actively try to resist their presumed dependency. At the very least, many recode their positioning as beneficial for the family unit, and therefore, themselves. In particular, I highlighted the ways in which women use the time away from the formal workforce to develop new skills or occupations, as well as for self-discovery, social development, and entrepreneurialism. At the same time, women's retreat from the full-time labor force reinforces the perception that women's work is auxiliary to men's and exists as surplus labor, rather than foundational to the persistence of capitalism. While ideal transnational workers are envisioned as divorced from the social realm and free to move around the globe as needed, the stories in this book show how all members of the household must demonstrate flexibility and mobility. In some ways, the grounded-ness and traditional expectations of the household are antithetical to the notion of the unfettered transnational worker, but in actuality, it is the site that underpins and facilitates workers' ability to move and assume jobs around the world.

CIRCUITS OF CITIZENSHIP

The cultural processes and practices that I have examined in this study shed light on how transnationalism is lived and tied to contemporary forms of capitalism, and they also reorient discussions about the material and symbolic value of citizenship. The transmigrants in this study utilize citizenship to initiate circuits that are closely tied to the ability to move between specific nation-states. To that end, I have shown how transmigration has resulted in the cultivation of circulating citizenship, or the development of a set of practices (including, though not exclusive to, obtaining formal US citizenship) that allow transmigrants to transverse certain borders and territories without necessarily seeking settlement. Contrary to the accounts of citizenship that view it as a way to claim belonging within a national entity, or as a utilitarian mechanism to ease cross-border investment and movement, circulating citizenship is dedicated to creating lives in multiple locations, and feeling at home across them.

Movement between locations improves the long-term career options and boosts the economic position of transmigrants. It also allows for a stair-step approach to migration that sets in motion future chains that allow children and other family members to move. Using matrimonial and reproductive strategies to gain access to citizenship or permanent residency also allows transmigrants to secure a foothold abroad, even if they may not live permanently in one location. Specifically, by having children in the US, transmigrants view citizenship as a sort of safeguard should they decide to return to India, and as a way to ease the future re-migration of their families. These movements also inform identity formation and understandings of "Indianness." Transmigrants are attached to their national and cultural identities regardless of their citizenship status and act as bridge builders between locations. Nevertheless, it becomes clear that the meaning of this identification shifts depending on social and political stratifications. While living abroad, transmigrants are defined by their foreign status and lack of formal integration into the workplace and social spheres. However, once back in their home countries, they are returnees who may feel as though they no longer fit into the communities or cities in which they have come to reside. Since they already have experienced migration to and are familiar with the US context, re-migration becomes a way to resolve the disconnection they feel in India. This option is not available to all returnees, and generally only those with US citizenship can actually re-migrate as a family unit, which makes naturalization even more valuable. In this way, migration is long-term strategy for accessing the resources of multiple nation-states, even if it is couched in temporary or contingent terms. It is for this potential reward that so many transmigrants still seek to come to the US and pursue their "American dreams," even as it transforms their Indian identity.

Thus, the cases in this book actively disrupt the line between movement and settlement, migrant and citizen. "Circulation" becomes the most apt descriptor for both these patterns of migration and the methodology of this study. As my fieldwork moved between the US and India, I found myself traveling the same routes as my study participants. Though suburban Seattle and metropolitan Bangalore, and Hyderabad are spatially and culturally separated by thousands of miles, the distances between them are made smaller through the networks generated and sustained by those living partially in various sites. For many transmigrants, digital communities facilitate their connection with others who are in similar situations, as well as the transfer of information about how to best sustain a circulating lifestyle and household. At the same time, even though transmigrants are part of a mobile and geographically unbounded community, their connections and networks are surprisingly situated. For instance, I found that several of my informants in Bangalore and Hyderabad were connected on Facebook to other informants (including some of my own friends) and social community in Seattle, even though the links never emerged during our interviews or in other interactions. So, even though they are not always co-located, personal relationships, desires for opportunities in multiple locations, and the needs of various family members are all key factors in facilitating global flows and shape how transmigration is actually put into practice.

EXECUTIVE ORDERS AND FUTURE DIRECTIONS

During the time that I have been completing this book, as part of a dramatic political swing in the US toward isolationism, right-wing nationalism, and the closing of borders, the H-1B program has come under a fresh wave of criticism. The election of Donald Trump in 2016 as the forty-fifth president of the US has ushered in virulent strains of xenophobia and anti-immigrant activism that are likely to have profound effects on US immigration policy

and how foreign visitors, workers, and students view the country for generations to come. Although this book has been nearly ten years in the making,
from the time that I began data collection in 2008 through publication,
never in that time has the H-1B program come under such direct attack as
it is now. It is viewed as a conduit for nonwhite, non-Western immigrants
to displace US workers, and most unsettling to detractors, a backdoor to US
citizenship for "unassimilable" foreigners. In other words, transmigrants
have become symbolic of the problems that neo-nativists see as plaguing
the US as a result of globalization.

With Trump's penchant for executive orders, immigration policy, regulations, and enforcement have been in a state of flux almost weekly since
his inauguration in January 2017. While the majority of his executive actions
regarding immigration have been aimed at fulfilling campaign promises,
such as initiating the "Muslim travel ban," eliminating the entry of refugees,
and the building of a "border wall" between the US and Mexico, he has also
expressed the desire to curtail severely or eliminate altogether the H-1B
program. As this book goes to press, Trump has signed two major orders.
The first temporarily suspends the premium processing of H-1B visas, which
previously allowed companies or institutions to pay a fee to accelerate the
review of certain applications.[2] This means that applicants will potentially
wait up to six or nine months for their petitions to be reviewed, rather than
go through the expedited process previously in place.

Second, Trump signed the "Buy American, Hire American" executive
order, which states that "in order to create higher wages and employment
rates for workers in the United States, and to protect their economic interests, it shall be the policy of the executive branch to rigorously enforce
and administer the laws governing entry into the United States of workers
from abroad."[3] With specific regard to the hiring of H-1B workers, the executive order calls for reforms that are intended to ensure that H-1Bs go to
"the most-skilled or highest-paid petition beneficiaries." Under the guise of
immigration enforcement, the executive order attempts to stop the use of
H-1B visas for lower-skilled jobs and, in many cases, to pay foreign workers
less than US workers. It also mandates stronger requirements for companies
to prove that they could not find suitable US workers before turning to the
H-1B. Though there are no details about how the program will be reformed
to meet these criteria, there will likely be rule changes about the fees for the
visa, a crackdown on outsourcing firms that supply H-1B workers, or perhaps requirements that applicants have a graduate degree. Actual changes

to the operation of the program will still require congressional approval and be subject to intense national debate. While some large technology companies would absorb the costs of paying top dollar to hire foreign workers, the call to increase salaries and look first at domestic labor pools would hurt smaller start-ups and the overwhelmingly Indian-owned and -operated contracting firms that currently win the majority of H-1B visas.

Set against this juridical jockeying, there has been a spate of hate crimes directed at Indians, as well as mounting evidence that the veneer of welcome that tech transmigrants have experienced in the past three decades is peeling away. As detailed earlier, the 2017 murder of Srinivas Kuchibhotla and the shooting of Alok Madasani in Kansas thrust the threats facing H-1B workers into the spotlight. While these sorts of attacks are neither new nor isolated to the professional Indian class, as the shooting of Deep Rai in the state of Washington and the arson of an Indian-own grocery store in Florida in 2017 suggest, these trends are creating new uncertainties and divisions across South Asian communities.[4] Universities have already reported a drop in Indian applications for undergraduate and graduate programs, and H-1B petition approvals are dropping, as transmigrants experience heightened scrutiny with each border crossing, while fearing for their safety once arrived.

Despite these efforts to halt globalization, the effects of transmigration cannot be undone easily. Those who maintain cross-border affiliations are not likely to stop, even in the face of hostile US policy, and future generations with US citizens will continue to travel between locations. However, the immigration regimes that regulate the flow of people do have a significant impact on the quality of the lives transmigrants lead and the conditions under which they labor. Beyond the worker, the needs of other members of the household will continue to influence how flexible labor truly is and how it will be impacted by the opportunities and constraints posed through migration. While technology transmigrants are in a relatively privileged position and often regarded by many as "a model minority," there is a real need to craft alliances with other immigrant communities that are being systematically disenfranchised. For instance, as the migrant children of H-1B visa holders (who are also on H-4 visas) begin to age out of the program after turning twenty-one, new questions arise about what possible paths to legal residency or citizenship might be available to them. One way to begin building common ground is by recognizing the roles that the household and the family play in creating the very workers and citizens that nation-states desire. Immigration advocacy must start by prioritizing the needs of all workers and dependents, as the fates of foreigners are linked in the US through the immigration system, regardless of their status or national origin. As this book has sought to underscore, we cannot imagine global movement without grasping the embodied and often intimate effects it produces, and without understanding how people strive to create homes amid its many disjunctures, nonetheless.

Notes

Introduction

1   This study focuses on individuals born in India, though I also use the terms *South Asian* and *Asian Indian*, the latter of which is a term used by the US Census Bureau and includes those born abroad as well as US-born and naturalized "Indians." I use *South Asian* as a politically expansive category that includes populations from India, Pakistan, Bangladesh, Nepal, Sri Lanka, Bhutan, and the Maldives.

2   I use the term *knowledge worker* here to refer to individuals who work in fields devoted to creating, managing, and disseminating information. Technology workers are considered knowledge workers, as are professionals in education, finance, science, the law, and other fields. Peter Drucker is widely credited with coining the term in his *America's Next Twenty Years* (New York: Harper, 1957).

3   Though there are several excellent accounts of women migrants throughout the world, much of that literature focuses on women's employment in caregiving or other precarious sectors. For examples, see Barbara Ehrenreich and Arlie Russell Hochschild, *Global Woman: Nannies, Maids, and Sex Workers in the New Economy* (New York: Metropolitan Books, 2003). Most examinations of professional migration networks have focused on men's experiences. This study bridges that gap by bringing a gendered focus to the experience of professional migration between the Global South and the West.

4   According to the United Nations, "The percentage of women among all migrants declined from 46 in 1990 to 43 per cent in 2013 in the developing regions. In the Global North during the same period, however, the share of women among all international migrants increased slightly, from 51 per cent to 52 per cent." United Nations, "International Migration Report 2013" (New York: Department of Economic and Social Affairs, Population Division, 2013), 7, www.un.org/en/development/desa/population/publications /migration/migration-report-2013.shtml.

5   Joan Jensen, *Passage from India: Asian Indian Immigrants in North America* (New Haven, CT: Yale University Press, 1988), Karen Isaksen Leonard, *Making Ethnic Choices: California's Punjabi Mexican Americans* (Philadelphia: Temple University Press, 1992), Vivek Bald, *Bengali Harlem and the Lost Histories of South Asian America* (Cambridge, MA: Harvard University Press, 2013), and several other scholars have documented the long history of Indian immigration to the US starting from the 1880s. This flow accelerated after the passage of the 1965 Immigration and Nationality Act. In the contemporary era, the United Nations' "International Migration Report 2013" states that migration between India and the US made up the third largest global movement

block between 1990 and 2000. That figure dropped to the sixth largest in the 2010s, but the US still has the second largest group of Indians living overseas as of 2016.

6   For a historical account of the collusion of technical education and government development initiatives in India, see Aparna Basu, *The Growth of Education and Political Development in India, 1898–1920* (Delhi: Oxford University Press, 1974).

7   Ross Knox Bassett, in *The Technological Indian* (Cambridge, MA: Harvard University Press, 2016), traces the history of Indians who came to study abroad at Massachusetts Institute of Technology starting from the 1880s and the impact that those students had on technical education in India. For broader accounts of Indian emigration, see Sunil Amrith, *Migration and Diaspora in Modern Asia* (Cambridge: Cambridge University Press, 2011); B. Singh Bolaria and Rosemary von Elling Bolaria, *International Labour Migrations* (Oxford: Oxford University Press, 1997); Brij V. Lal, Peter Reeves, and Rajesh Rai, *The Encyclopedia of the Indian Diaspora* (Honolulu: University of Hawaii Press, 2006); Parvati Raghuram, Ajaya Kumar Sahoo, Brij Maharaj, and Dave Sangha, *Tracing an Indian Diaspora: Contexts, Memories, Representations* (New York: Sage, 2008).

8   The passage of the landmark Immigration and Nationality Act of 1965 (known also as the Hart-Celler Act) opened new pathways for South Asian immigration. American universities increased admissions for international students in this period, and the "space race" of the 1960s with the former Soviet Union coincided with the repeal of national origin quotas in place since 1921. The Hart-Celler Act established skills, labor needs, and family reunification as central to American immigration policy. At the same time in India, universities established to train new generations of technocrats were producing graduates faster than jobs could be created for them, leading to a surplus of workers. Many graduates left to pursue further study or employment abroad. The openings in the US immigration system, along with restrictions in traditional host countries in Europe, made the US an attractive landing spot for Indians trained in technology, science, and engineering.

9   The H-1B guest worker program was an outcrop of the Bracero Program, which allowed temporary workers from Mexico to migrate starting in the early 1940s. The Bracero Program was modified by Public Law 78, which was passed as part of congressional efforts to formalize contract labor migration between the US and Mexico; this had the effect of bringing in nearly half a million workers at the height of the program. For a longer history of the program and law, see Richard B. Craig, *The Bracero Program: Interest Groups and Foreign Policy* (Austin: University of Texas Press, 1971), and Sharmila Rudrappa, "Braceros and Techno-braceros: Guest Workers in the United States and the Commodification of Low-Wage and High-Wage Labour," in *Transnational South Asians: The Making of a Neo-diaspora*, ed. Susan Koshy and R. Radhakrishnan, 291–324 (New York: Oxford University Press, 2008). Since the program was reformed in 1990, the H-1B program has expanded the numbers of professional workers in the technology sector as it allows companies to recruit "workers in a specialty occupation" who meet the following criteria: that the applicant holds a bachelor's or higher degree or its equivalent; "that the degree requirement for the job is common to the industry or the job is so complex or unique that it can be performed only by an individual with a degree"; and that "the nature of the specific duties is so specialized

and complex that the knowledge required to perform the duties is usually associated with the attainment of a bachelor's or higher degree." US Citizenship and Immigration Services, "H-1B Specialty Occupations, DOD Cooperative Research and Development Project Workers, and Fashion Models," US Department of Homeland Security, April 3, 2017, accessed July 20, 2017, www.uscis.gov/working-united-states/temporary-workers/h-1b-specialty-occupations-dod-cooperative-research-and-development-project-workers-and-fashion-models.

10 The number of Indian H-1B workers in the US grew by 113 percent between 1990 and 2000, making Indians the second fastest growing immigrant population nationally. By 2010, there were an estimated 3.2 million people of Indian origin living in the US, making Indians the third largest Asian group numerically after the Chinese and Filipinos. Elizabeth M. Hoeffel, Sonya Rastogi, Myoung Ouk Kim, and Hasan Shahid, "The Asian Population: 2010," US Bureau of the Census, 2012, www.census.gov/library/publications/2012/dec/c2010br-11.html. In 2017, 197,129 new and renewed H-1B visas were issued, but the USCIS received 336,107 petitions, of which an estimated 74 percent came from Indian nationals. Chinese nationals received the second largest proportion of visas, with 10 percent of approved petitions. See USCIS, "Number of H-1B Filings," 2017, https://www.uscis.gov/sites/default/files/USCIS/Resources/Reports%20and%20Studies/Immigration%20Forms%20Data/BAHA/h-1b-2007-2017-trend-tables.pdf.

11 Reporting on the US Census Bureau's 2011 American Community Survey, Jie Zong and Jeanne Batalova note that "the top three occupations that employed Indian-born men ages 16 and older were information technology (29 percent of all 717,000 Indian male workers); management, business, and finance (21 percent); and sales (11 percent)." "Indian Immigrants in the United States" (Washington, DC: Migration Policy Institute, 2015), www.migrationpolicy.org/article/indian-immigrants-united-states.

12 Indian immigration to the US has been male driven; for counterpoint, see Sheba George, *When Women Come First: Gender and Class in Transnational Migration* (Berkeley: University of California Press, 2005), and Sujani Reddy, *Nursing and Empire: Gendered Labor and Migration from India to the United States* (Chapel Hill: University of North Carolina, 2015). However, among technology workers, nearly 233,000 H-1B applications were filed for a combined 85,000 visas in 2015, of which 78 percent were issued to men, whereas only 22 percent went to women; see Nicole Kreisberg, "H-1B Jobs: Filling the Skills Gap," research brief (Great Barrington, MA: American Institute for Economic Research, 2014), www.aier.org/research/h1b-jobs-filling-skill-gap.

13 The H-1B program is capped at issuing 65,000 visas plus an additional 20,000 for those who obtain graduate degrees in the US.

14 As part of the H-1B program, the H-4 visa can be used to sponsor spouses and children under the age of twenty-one to migrate to the US. If the primary H-1B visa holder were to lose his job or leave the country, H-4 visa holders would lose their immigration standing and would also have to leave or be deported. According to data released by the US Department of State, in 2016, 84 percent of H-4 visas were issued to Indian citizens. "Report of the Visa Office 2016" (Washington, DC: US Department of State, Bureau of Security and Consular Affairs, 2016), *https://travel.state.gov/content/visas/en/law-and-policy/statistics/annual-reports/report-of-the-visa-office-2016.html*. Though

the gender breakdown of this figure is not available, it can reasonably be deduced that these are issued overwhelmingly to women.

15 Among the twenty-two temporary worker visas categories delineated by the US Citizenship and Immigration Services (USCIS), only a handful allow dependents to work while on family reunification visas. The majority, including the H-1B, do not.

16 As Anu Kõu and Ajay Bailey argue, transnational migration must be traced along the life course, which offers a broader perspective on how migration decisions and behaviors are situated amid social and political structures. Life events such as studying abroad, getting married, having children, caring for elderly parents, and changing jobs are important benchmarks around which the transnational migration profiled in this study occurs. Anu Kõu and Ajay Bailey, "'Movement Is a Constant Feature in My Life': Contextualising Migration Processes of Highly Skilled Indians," *Geoforum* 52 (2014): 113–22.

17 Deborah A. Boehm, *Intimate Migrations: Gender, Family, and Illegality among Transnational Mexicans* (New York: New York University Press, 2012), 6.

18 For a longer analysis of the role of the transnational worker in the formation of the contemporary global IT industry, see Paula Chakravartty, "Weak Winners of Globalization: Indian H-1B Workers in the American Information Economy," *AAPI Nexus* 3, no. 2 (2005): 59–84.

19 David Harvey, "Globalization in Question," *Rethinking Marxism* 8, no 4. (1995): 1–17.

20 Payal Banerjee, "Indian Information Technology Workers in the United States: The H-1B Visa, Flexible Production, and the Racialization of Labor," *Critical Sociology* 32, no. 2/3 (2006): 425–45, and Paula Chakravartty, "Symbolic Analysts or Indentured Servants? Indian High-Tech Migrants in America's Information Economy," *Knowledge, Technology, and Policy* 19, no. 3 (2006): 27–43, highlight the challenges faced by H-1B workers, while AnnaLee Saxenian's extensive body of scholarship argues that Asian workers experience cultural and regional advantage that has led to significant Indian (and Chinese) advancement in Silicon Valley. Similarly, Vivek Wadhwa, "An Outflow of Talent: Nativism and the US Reverse Brain Drain," *Harvard International Review* 31, no. 1 (2009): 76–80, and A. Aneesh, "Rethinking Migration: High-Skilled Labor Flows from India to the United States," CCIS Working Paper 18 (Center for Comparative Immigration Studies, University of California, San Diego, 2001), argue that Indian IT workers play a pivotal role in US industries, but are not sufficiently appreciated despite their adding value to these global economies.

21 The following studies examine the phenomenon of women remaining in home countries while men venture out as transmigrants: Michiel Baas, "The IT Caste: Love and Arranged Marriages in the IT Industry of Bangalore," *South Asia: Journal of South Asian Studies* 32, no. 2 (2009): 285–307; Xiang Biao, *Global "Body Shopping": An Indian Labor System in the Information Technology Industry* (Princeton, NJ: Princeton University Press, 2007); Jamie McEvoy, Peggy Petrzelka, Claudia Radel, and Birgit Schmook, "Gendered Mobility and Morality in a South-Eastern Mexican Community: Impacts of Male Labour Migration on the Women Left Behind," *Mobilities* 7, no. 3 (2012): 369–88; Rebecca M. Torres and Lindsey Carte, "Migration and Development? The Gendered Costs of Migration on Mexico's Rural 'Left Behind,'" *Geographical Review* 106, no. 3 (2016): 399–420.

22 Smitha Radhakrishnan, *Appropriately Indian: Gender and Culture in a New Transnational Class* (Durham, NC: Duke University Press, 2011).

23 See Jyoti Puri, *Woman, Body, Desire in Post-Colonial India: Narratives of Gender and Sexuality* (New York: Routledge, 1999); Nilanjana Chatterjee and Nancy Riley, "Planning an Indian Modernity: The Gendered Politics of Fertility Control," *Signs* 26, no. 3 (2001): 811–46; and Rajeswari Sunder Rajan, *Real and Imagined Women: Gender, Culture, and Postcolonialism* (New York: Routledge, 1993). For a longer discussion about the figure of the "new Indian woman," see Susie Tharu and Tejaswini Niranjana, "Problems for a Contemporary Theory of Gender," *Subaltern Studies* 9 (1996): 232–60.

24 Gillian J. Hewitson, "Domestic Labor and Gender Identity: Are All Women Careers?" in *Toward a Feminist Philosophy of Economics*, ed. Drucilla K. Barker and Edith Kuiper (New York: Routledge, 2003), 266. For broader articulations of how women's unpaid reproductive work subsidizes the costs and conditions of the paid labor force see also Lydia Sargent, *Women and Revolution: A Discussion of the Unhappy Marriage of Marxism and Feminism* (Boston: South End Press, 1981); Heidi Hartmann, "The Family as the Locus of Gender, Class, and Political Struggle: The Example of Housework," *Signs* 6, no. 3 (1981): 366–94; Rosemary Hennessy, *Profit and Pleasure: Sexual Identities in Late Capitalism* (New York: Routledge, 2000); Arlie Hochschild, "Global Care Chains and Emotional Surplus Value," in *Global Capitalism*, ed. Will Hutton and Anthony Giddens, 130–46 (New York: New Press, 2000); Susan Okin, *Justice, Gender, and the Family* (New York: Basic Books, 1989); and S. Charusheela, "'Empowering Work'? Bargaining Models Reconsidered," in *Toward a Feminist Philosophy of Economics*, ed. Drucilla K. Barker and Edith Kuiper, 287–303 (New York: Routledge, 2003).

25 Maria Mies, *Patriarchy and Accumulation on a World Scale: Women in the International Division of Labour* (Atlantic Highlands, NJ: Zed Books, 1986).

26 The H-1B and H-4 visas are considered non-immigrant "dual-intent" visas, which allow holders to apply for permanent residency and citizenship. Other visas, such as the F category student visa, do not allow for permanent residency. Holders of such visas have to obtain another type of visa before applying for residency or they must be legally sponsored by a US entity with legal standing.

27 Theoretical conceptions of citizenship are too numerous to recount here; my analysis is informed by literatures on citizenship as they intersect with gender, such as Seyla Benhabib and Judith Resnik, *Migrations and Mobilities: Citizenship, Borders, and Gender* (New York: New York University Press, 2009); race and ethnicity, such as Lisa Lowe, *Immigrant Acts: on Asian American Cultural Politics* (Durham, NC: Duke University Press, 1996), and Aihwa Ong, "Cultural Citizenship as Subject-Making: Immigrants Negotiate Racial and Cultural Boundaries in the United States," *Current Anthropology* 37, no. 5 (1996): 737–62; and diaspora politics, such as Daniel Naujoks, *Migration, Citizenship, and Development: Diasporic Membership Policies and Overseas Indians in the United States* (London: Oxford University Press, 2013).

28 In her ethnographic text, Aihwa Ong examines the experiences of wealthy Hong Kong entrepreneurs and elites who amass resources and passports from multiple locations in order to claim belonging in two or more nations. They do so by using ideas about Asian culture and "family values" to manipulate citizenship regimes transnationally and "to respond fluidly and opportunistically to changing political-economic conditions."

Aihwa Ong, *Flexible Citizenship: The Cultural Logics of Transnationality* (Durham, NC: Duke University Press, 1999), 6.

29 Ong's sample focuses on business elites who are able to obtain US green cards through special programs that admit individuals planning to invest between $500,000 and $1 million in "targeted employment areas" or planning to create or preserve jobs for US citizens. In contrast, the IT transmigrants in this study almost exclusively came through student visas or H-1B visas and are generally not part of this "investor class."

30 After successfully completing the I-140 "Immigrant Petition for Alien Worker," H-1B holders enter into the permanent residency ("green card") application process. Currently, the US Citizenship and Immigration Service is backlogged with green card applications submitted more than half a decade ago. Thus, many individuals are in limbo for several years as they await the processing and approval of their application. Even after receiving permanent residency, they must wait additional years before they can apply for citizenship.

31 From Lisong Liu, I borrow the term *selective citizenship* to describe the practices of "ordinary" international students and professionals who must manipulate "complex immigration laws and citizenship requirements to gain their transnational mobility." *Chinese Student Migration and Selective Citizenship: Mobility, Community and Identity between China and the United States* (New York: Routledge, 2015), 36.

32 On hybrid identities, see Elizabeth Chacko, "Hybrid Sensibilities: Highly Skilled Asian Indians Negotiating Identity in Private and Public Spaces of Washington, DC," *Journal of Cultural Geography* 32, no. 1 (2015): 115–28; and Koen Van Laer and Maddy Janssens, "Between the Devil and the Deep Blue Sea: Exploring the Hybrid Identity Narratives of Ethnic Minority Professionals," *Scandinavian Journal of Management* 30 (2014): 186–96. On transcultural identities, see Tina Kin Ng, Tina Rochelle, Steven Shardlow, and Sik Hung Ng, "A Transnational Bicultural Place Model of Cultural Selves and Psychological Citizenship: The Case of Chinese Immigrants in Britain," *Journal of Environmental Psychology* 40 (2014): 440–50. On hyphenated identities, see Yuching Julia Cheng, "Bridging Immigration Research and Racial Formation Theory to Examine Contemporary Immigrant Identities," *Sociology Compass* 8, no. 6 (2014): 745–54.

33 Julie Y. Chu, *Cosmologies of Credit: Transnational Mobility and the Politics of Destination in China* (Durham, NC: Duke University Press, 2010), 11.

34 I draw on the notion of transmigrants as bridge builders from Margarita Sanchez-Mazas and Olivier Klein, "Social Identity and Citizenship: Introduction to the Special Issue," *Psychologica Belgica* 43, no. 1/2 (2003): 1–8.

35 For historical and contemporary accounts of South Asian settlement and work in Silicon Valley and Northern California, see Anuradha Basu and Meghna Virick, "Silicon Valley's Indian Diaspora: Networking and Entrepreneurial Success," *South Asian Journal of Global Business Research* 4, no. 2 (2015): 190; Monica Rao Biradavolu, *Indian Entrepreneurs in Silicon Valley: The Making of a Transnational Techno-capitalist Class* (Amherst, NY: Cambria Press, 2008); Smitha Radhakrishnan, "Examining the 'Global' Indian Middle Class: Gender and Culture in the Silicon Valley/Bangalore Circuit," *Journal of Intercultural Studies* 29, no. 1 (2008): 7–20. For historical and contemporary accounts of South Asian settlement and work in Silicon Valley and Northern California,

see AnnaLee Saxenian, "Silicon Valley's New Immigrant High-Growth Entrepreneurs," *Economic Development Quarterly* 16, no. 1 (2002): 20–31; and AnnaLee Saxenian, *The New Argonauts: Regional Advantage in a Global Economy* (Cambridge, MA: Harvard University Press, 2006).

36 Zong and Batalova, in "Indian Immigrants in the United States," have documented the growth of Asian populations nationally.

37 For example, in 1981, Microsoft hired its twenty-ninth employee, Rao Remala, who was the first Indian to join the company. Remala had been part of Hindustan Computers Ltd. and was directly recruited by Bill Gates and Paul Allen. After he was hired, Remala was instrumental in making connections with such universities. Amy Bhatt and Nalini Iyer, *Roots and Reflections: South Asians in the Pacific Northwest* (Seattle: University of Washington Press, 2013).

38 As of 2015, Boeing employed 81,919 workers and Microsoft employed 43,031. Economic Development Council of Seattle and King County, "King County Economy," accessed July 20, 2017, www.edc-seaking.org/service/economic-data/economic-basics.

39 The US government does not release gender-disaggregated data on H-1B visa applications or approved petitions. The most frequently cited figures come from the 2013 testimony of Karen Panetta at a US Senate Judiciary Committee hearing on immigration reform. US Congress, Senate, Committee on the Judiciary United States Senate, *Testimony of Karen Panetta on How Comprehensive Immigration Reform Should Address the Needs of Women and Families*, 113th Congress, 1st sess., March 18, 2013.

40 I have used aliases throughout this book to protect the anonymity of participants. Though I did not conduct face-to-face interviews in the five years intervening between my two periods of fieldwork, I maintained close connections to many of my participants through social media and my analysis is grounded in informal and formal conversations with over one hundred Indian transmigrants in the US.

41 Anthropologists Christopher Fuller and Haripriya Narasimhan, "Companionate Marriage in India: The Changing Marriage System in a Middle-Class Brahman Subcaste," *Journal of the Royal Anthropological Institute* 14, no. 4 (2008): 736–54, have written in depth about the consolidation of caste and class hierarchies in the "IT caste." This endogamy is heightened by marriage practices that reinforce inter-caste unions. Taking a sociological approach, Carol Upadhya and Aninhalli R. Vasavi, "Work, Culture, and Sociality in the Indian IT Industry: A Sociological Study" (Bangalore: National Institute of Advanced Studies, August 2006), have also shown how participation in the IT sector reinforces caste and class segmentation. My study further demonstrates how this demographic homogenization persists through the IT sector as it is formulated abroad. While my study does include Muslim and Christian Indian participants, individuals from these groups remain minorities among the vast Hindu majorities in US-based IT companies. The lack of representation in the IT industry is reflected in this book.

42 Because of the high profile of gated communities in Bangalore and Hyderabad, I use pseudonyms for the neighborhoods.

43 Nicholas Hookway, "'Entering the Blogosphere': Some Strategies for Using Blogs in Social Research," *Qualitative Research* 8, no. 1 (2008): 91–113, argues that the narrative, first-person accounts available through blogs can be used to triangulate data derived from traditional ethnographic methods.

1. Transmigrants

1   According to the National Association of Software and Services Companies (NASS-COM), an India-based technology research advocacy agency, H-1B workers pay nearly $1 billion annually into Social Security, which they cannot access unless they become permanent residents or citizens in the US.

2   Payal Banerjee, "Transnational Subcontracting, Indian IT Workers, and the U.S. Visa System," *Women's Studies Quarterly* 38, no. 1/2 (2010): 97.

3   David Conradson and Alan Latham, "Transnational Urbanism: Attending to Everyday Practices and Mobilities," *Journal of Ethnic and Migration Studies* 31, no. 2 (2005): 227–33, argue that "middling" forms of transnationalism encompass a greater number of migrants beyond transnational elites or the working-class subjects of the Global South. As part of the middle classes, a substantial flow of professional migrants moves along employment streams around the world. However, they are underrepresented in studies of transnationalism even though they act as important liaisons between nation-states and are in many cases the backbone of transnational exchange. The authors' call for greater attention to the "everyday practices" of such transmigrants informs my analysis and nuances our understanding of how class is mobilized to support migration.

4   In addition to expanding H-1B, H-2, and L category visas, the 1990 act created five new categories for employment-based visas that include "priority workers" with exceptional ability or managerial positions; members of professions holding advanced degrees; skilled workers; and foreign nationals who invest between $500,000 and $1 million in the US.

5   They can also look for a new employer to sponsor them or marry a US citizen or permanent resident in order to enter into the green card process.

6   The annual cap was raised to 195,000 between 2001 and 2003. In 2004, the L-1 Visa and H-1B Visa Reform Act of 2004 returned the overall H-1B cap to 65,000 visas annually, with 20,000 additional visas available for foreign degree holders from US graduate programs. The 2004 law also raised the fees associated with obtaining the visa and allowed those funds to be used for domestic worker retraining programs.

7   In 2017, the last year for which data on approvals was available at the time of this book's publication, the USCIS approved 197,129 H-1B petitions and renewals, though in 2016, they approved 348,162. USCIS, "Number of H-1B Petition Filings," 2017, accessed October 13, 2017, https://www.uscis.gov/sites/default/files/USCIS/Resources/Reports%20and%20Studies/Immigration%20Forms%20Data/BAHA/h-1b-2007-2017-trend-tables.pdf.

8   In 2014, President Obama issued a series of executive orders and actions, including the "Immigration Accountability Executive Action: Notices," 79 *Federal Register* 249 (December 30, 2014), pp. 78458–60, as a way to jumpstart the stymied congressional conversation around immigration reform. These executive actions address a wide swath of issues, such as offering relief from deportation for some undocumented migrants and their children, hastening the processing of permanent residency applications, and increasing opportunities for skilled transmigrants to apply for visas. While the actions related to undocumented immigrants have garnered the most media attention, a secondary set of provisions meant to ease regulations on "foreign investors, researchers,

inventors and skilled foreign workers" has also created waves in the technology industries. In particular, President Obama's action allowed workers to change jobs while on
temporary visas and lifted work restrictions for H-4 visa holders. If H-1B workers had
been working in the US on the H-1B for six or more years and successfully completed
the I-140 section of the green card application, their spouses would be eligible to apply
for the EAD (Employment Authorization Document), which granted them work authorization. Though the fate of Obama's immigration-related executive orders is in danger
under the Trump administration's anticipated revisions to the H-1B program, it has
been a lifeline for women who have been unable to obtain an H-1B visa of their own or
who are stuck waiting for their permanent residency applications to be processed.

9   US Citizenship and Immigration Service, "DHS Extends Eligibility for Employment
    Authorization to Certain H-4 Dependent Spouses of H-1B Nonimmigrants Seeking
    Employment-Based Lawful Permanent Residence, 2015," accessed July 21, 2017, www
    .uscis.gov/news/dhs-extends-eligibility-employment-authorization-certain-h-4
    -dependent-spouses-h-1b-nonimmigrants-seeking-employment-based-lawful
    -permanent-residence.

10 An example of legislation intended to expand the H-1B program, the Immigration
    Innovation Act, or the "I-squared" bill, would have increased the cap on H-1B visas
    issued annually to 115,000. It would also have created a "market-based H-1B escalator"
    that adjusts the cap based on demand up to 195,000 annually, and would have
    exempted foreign graduates of American universities with advanced degrees from the
    cap altogether. The bill also would have made it easier for H-1B visa holders to switch
    employers, remove restrictions on the spouses of H-1B visas from working, and fun-
    damentally change how green cards are issued. The 1965 Immigration and Nationality
    Act stipulated that no more than 7 percent of green cards can be issued to citizens from
    any one country each year. Expanding this limit would have helped Indian nationals,
    as they make up the third largest national-origin group seeking green cards, after
    Mexicans and Filipinos.

11 In contrast to the "I-squared" bill, the H-1B and L-1 Reform Act of 2017 focused on
    penalizing employers who do not demonstrate a good-faith effort to find US workers
    to fill positions and seeks limits on the number of visas issued annually. Several ver-
    sions of this bill have been introduced in previous sessions, but have not passed.

12 While there has been a drop in approved applications from previous years, 2017 still
    saw more than 336,000 petitions.

13 The Optional Training Program allows graduates from science, technology, engineer-
    ing, and math (STEM) fields to stay in the US for up to twenty-seven months, whereas
    graduates from other degree programs have only twelve months to obtain an employ-
    ment visa.

14 B. Venkatesh Kumar, David L. Finegold, Anne-Laure Winkler, and Vikas Argod, "Will
    They Return? The Willingness of Potential Faculty to Return to India and the Key
    Factors Affecting Their Decision" (paper, Institute of Social Sciences, Penn State, and
    Rutgers School of Management and Labor Relations, 2011).

15 Lisong Liu, "Return Migration and Selective Citizenship: A Study of Returning Chi-
    nese Professional Migrants from the United States," *Journal of Asian American Studies*
    15, no. 1 (2012): 35–68.

16 Xiang Biao, *Global "Body Shopping": An Indian Labor System in the Information Technology Industry* (Princeton, NJ: Princeton University Press, 2007).

17 Smitha Radhakrishnan, *Appropriately Indian: Gender and Culture in a New Transnational Class* (Durham, NC: Duke University Press, 2011), 3.

18 Christine Oh and Nadia Y. Kim argue that historically migrants from Asia have been characterized as either as unassimilable or as model minorities whose economic success stands in contrast to the supposed cultural deficiencies of marginalized US populations. In either case, Asians are flattened into a homogenous category that is seen as auxiliary or outside the nation. "Success Is Relative," *Sociological Perspectives* 59, no. 2 (2016): 270–95.

19 For a longer history of Indian labor migration, see Radhika Chopra, *Militant and Migrant: The Politics and Social History of Punjab* (New York: Routledge, 2011).

20 Madeline Y. Hsu and Ellen D. Wu, "'Smoke and Mirrors': Conditional Inclusion, Model Minorities, and the Pre-1965 Dismantling of Asian Exclusion," *Journal of American Ethnic History* 34, no. 4 (2015): 51.

21 Sareeta Bipin Amrute, *Encoding Class, Encoding Race: Indian IT Workers in Berlin* (Durham, NC: Duke University Press, 2016).

22 See Sangeeta Kamat, Ali Mir, and Biju Mathew for a longer demonstration of the vital role that state immigration and labor policies have played in the creation of South Asian communities in the West. "Producing Hi-Tech: Globalization, the State and Migrant Subjects," *Globalisation, Societies and Education* 2, no. 1 (2004): 5–23.

23 Carol Upadhya and Aninhalli R. Vasavi use the term *new economy subject* to describe the imbrication of caste and class in the production of IT workers. "Work, Culture, and Sociality in the Indian IT Industry: A Sociological Study" (Bangalore: National Institute of Advanced Studies, 2006), 112.

24 Carol Upadhya, "Software and the 'New' Middle Class in the 'New India,'" in *Elite and Everyman: The Cultural Politics of the Indian Middle Class*, ed. Amita Baviskar and Raka Ray, 167–92 (New Delhi: Routledge, 2011).

25 Elaine Lynn-Ee Ho, "Identity Politics and Cultural Asymmetries: Singaporean Transmigrants 'Fashioning' Cosmopolitanism," *Journal of Ethnic and Migration Studies* 37, no. 5 (2011): 731.

26 Ascend, "The Illusion of Asian Success: Scant Progress for Minorities in Cracking the Glass Ceiling from 2007-2015," Report, 2017: 3. http://c.ymcdn.com/sites/www.ascend leadership.org/resource/resmgr/research/TheIllusionofAsianSuccess.pdf.

27 Parvati Raghuram, "The Difference That Skills Make: Gender, Family Migration Strategies and Regulated Labour Markets," *Journal of Ethnic and Migration Studies* 30, no. 2 (2004): 303–21.

28 Nina Glick Schiller, Linda G. Basch, and Cristina Blanc-Szanton, *Nations Unbound: Transnational Projects, Postcolonial Predicaments, and Deterritorialized Nation-States* (New York: Routledge, 1994).

29 Shobhita Jain, "Transmigrant Women's Agency and Indian Diaspora," *South Asian Diaspora* 2 no. 2 (2010): 185–200; Gita Rajan and Shailja Sharma, *New Cosmopolitanisms: South Asians in the US* (Stanford, CA: Stanford University Press, 2006).

30 Prakash Khanal, "Diasporic Shrines: Transnational Networks Linking South Asia through Pilgrimage and Welfare Development," in *Diaspora Engagement and Develop-*

ment in South Asia, ed. Tan Tai Yong and Mizanur Rahman, 176–93 (Hampshire: Palgrave Macmillan, 2013).

31 Tan Tai Yong and Mizanur Rahman, *Diaspora Engagement and Development in South Asia*, (Hampshire: Palgrave Macmillan, 2013).

32 I draw on Margarita Sanchez-Mazas and Olivier Klein's articulation of the transmigrant as bridge builder across national locations. Margarita Sanchez-Mazas and Olivier Klein, "Social Identity and Citizenship: Introduction to the Special Issue," *Psychologica Belgica* 43 no. 1/2 (2003): 1–8.

33 Children's Rights and You Cry America, "About CRY," accessed June 15, 2017, http://america.cry.org/site/about-cry.html.

34 Teresa Amabile and Steven Kramer argue that IT industries have blurred the line between work and personal life through the deliberate construction of office spaces. IT campuses collapse the space between public and private life by reinvigorating the notion of early twentieth-century "company towns" that tied workers to companies through housing, food rations, and credit. "Do Happier People Work Harder?" *New York Times*, September 3, 2011.

35 Jay Yarow, "A Tour of Microsoft's Truly Gigantic, Sprawling Headquarters," *Business Insider*, August 2, 2013, accessed July 23, 2017, www.businessinsider.com/a-tour-of-microsofts-truly-gigantic-sprawling-headquarters-2013-7.

36 Sandro Cattacin and Dagmar Domenig, "Why Do Transnationally Mobile People Volunteer? Insights from a Swiss Case Study," *Voluntas: International Journal of Voluntary and Nonprofit Organizations* 25, no. 3 (2014): 726.

37 Latha Varadarajan, *The Domestic Abroad: Diasporas in International Relations* (New York: Oxford University Press, 2010).

38 The following studies exemplify this point: Leela Fernandes, *India's New Middle Class: Democratic Politics in an Era of Economic Reform* (Minneapolis: University of Minnesota Press, 2006); Paula Chakravartty, "Flexible Citizens and the Internet: The Global Politics of Local High-Tech Development in India," *Emergences: Journal for the Study of Media and Composite Cultures* 11, no. 1 (2001): 69–88; Rohit Chopra, "Global Primordialities: Virtual Identity Politics in Online Hindutva and Online Dalit Discourse," *New Media and Society* 8, no. 2 (2006): 187–206.

39 Writing about the emergence of modern Indian nationalism, Srirupa Roy notes, "Both the domestic and the external arenas are of equivalent importance in any discussion of nationalism, with the actual project of nation formation best understood as a mediation between these two domains." "'A Symbol of Freedom': The Indian Flag and the Transformations of Nationalism, 1906–2002," *Journal of Asian Studies* 65, no. 3 (2006): 496–97.

40 The Person of Indian Origin (PIO) scheme (program) issues an identity card to individuals holding passports from foreign nations, excluding Afghanistan, Bangladesh, Bhutan, China, Nepal, Pakistan, and Sri Lanka. In 2005, the Citizenship Act was further amended to allow a PIO living overseas to register as an Overseas Citizen of India (OCI), which would create a sort of dual citizenship, but without the right to vote, hold some public positions, or take a government appointment. While the OCI falls short of full citizenship, it extends rights to PIOs, including a lifelong visa for visiting India, exemption from local police registration when in the country, and parity with nonresident

Indians (in this case, meaning those who still retain Indian citizenship) with respect to most economic, financial, and education fields.

41 The India Shining campaign, initiated by the Bharatiya Janata Party, included TV, print, and multimedia advertisements pronouncing the success of globalization and the technology sectors in India. Millions of Indians felt left out of the purported national successes, which contributed to the BJP defeat in the 2004 elections.

42 Indo-Asian News Service, "Manmohan Singh's Address at Pravasi Bharatiya Divas," *India Forums*, January 8, 2008, accessed February 16, 2017. www.india-forums.com/news/diaspora/68227-manmohan-singh-address-at-pravasi-bharatiya-divas.htm.

43 Ibid.

44 Anita N. Jain, "Imaginary Diasporas," *South Asian Diaspora* 8, no. 1 (2016): 7.

45 The phrase "unity in diversity" is often attributed to the first Indian prime minister, Jawaharlal Nehru, who was tasked with bringing the nascent Indian nation into its postcolonial existence and suturing together the wounds wrought by Partition. Jawaharlal Nehru, Sarvepalli Gopal, and Uma Iyengar, *The Essential Writings of Jawaharlal Nehru* (New Delhi: Oxford University Press, 2003).

46 For an in-depth analysis of the conservative political orientations of Indian technology transmigrants, see Paula Chakravartty, "White-Collar Nationalisms," *Social Semiotics* 16, no. 1 (2006): 39–55; and Chopra, "Global Primordialities."

47 See Joyojeet Pal, Priyank Chandra, and V. G. Vinod Vidyaswaran, "Twitter and the Re-branding of Narendra Modi," *Economic and Political Weekly* 51, no. 8 (2016): 52–60, for a history of sectarian violence perpetuated by the BJP and its contemporary incarnations.

48 Modi is among the top 100 global Twitter users with the highest numbers of followers.

49 Nilanjana Bhowmick, "India's Opposition Leader Takes on Congress and Corruption," *Time Magazine*, January 20, 2014, accessed February 1, 2017, http://world.time.com/2014/01/20/indias-opposition-leader-takes-on-congress-and-corruption.

50 Saskia Sassen, "The Repositioning of Citizenship: Emergent Subjects and Spaces for Politics," *CR: The New Centennial Review* 3, no. 2 (2003): 41–66.

2. Engineer Brides and H-1B Grooms

1   Parvati Raghuram, "Migration, Gender, and the IT Sector: Intersecting Debates," *Women's Studies International Forum* 27, no. 2 (2004): 165.

2   Roli Varma's studies of women computer science and engineering students show how attitudes differ across cultures; women in the US are less likely to pursue STEM degrees or occupations than Indian women. See "Exposure, Training, and Environment: Women's Participation in Computing Education in the United States and India," *Journal of Women and Minorities in Science and Engineering* 15, no. 3 (2009): 205–22; and "Why So Few Women Enroll in Computing? Gender and Ethnic Differences in Students' Perception," *Computer Science Education* 20, no. 4 (2010): 301–16.

3   Namrata Gupta, "Indian Women in Doctoral Education in Science and Engineering: A Study of Informal Milieu at the Reputed Indian Institutes of Technology," *Science, Technology and Human Values* 32, no. 5 (2007): 511.

4   See Lorraine G. Kisselburgh, Brenda L. Berkelaar, and Patrice M. Buzzanell's study for an in-depth perspective on women's attitudes toward and motivations for pursuing STEM degrees. "Discourse, Gender, and the Meaning of Work: Rearticulating Science, Technology, and Engineering Careers through Communicative Lenses," *Communication Yearbook* 33 (2009): 259–300. Also see Debalina Dutta, "Negotiations of Cultural Identities by Indian Women Engineering Students in US Engineering Programmes," *Journal of Intercultural Communication Research* 45, no. 3 (2016): 177–95.

5   Gupta, "Indian Women in Doctoral Education in Science and Engineering," 510.

6   Harry Stevens reports that "between 1990 and 2005, the percentage of working-age Indian women in the workforce rose from 35 percent to 37 percent. In the last decade, however, the country has reversed course, with female labour participation declining to just 27 percent by 2014. That's tied for 16th-lowest in the world." "Indian Women Are Rapidly Leaving the Workplace," *Hindustan Times,* June 29, 2016.

7   Xiang Biao, "Gender, Dowry and the Migration System of Indian Information Technology Professionals," *Indian Journal of Gender Studies* 12, no. 2/3 (2005): 358.

8   US Congress, Senate, Committee on the Judiciary United States Senate, *Testimony of Karen Panetta on How Comprehensive Immigration Reform Should Address the Needs of Women and Families,* 113th Congress, 1st sess., March 18, 2013.

9   See B. Venkatesh Kumar, David L Finegold, Anne-Laure Winkler, and Vikas Argod, "Will They Return? The Willingness of Potential Faculty to Return to India and the Key Factors Affecting Their Decision" (Institute of Social Sciences, Penn State, and Rutgers School of Management and Labor Relations, 2011), for an analysis of the factors that drive Indian return migration.

10 Historically, marriage has been a vital part of Indian cultural life, and continues to be so. In 1991, only 2.5 percent of Indian men and .7 percent of women between the ages of forty-five and fifty-four had never married, according to Bishnupriya Gupta, "Where Have All the Brides Gone? Son Preference and Marriage in India over the Twentieth Century," *Economic History Review* 67, no. 1 (2014): 20.

11 Elena Gabor, "Career as Sensemaking for Immigrant Women Engineers," *Journal of Ethnographic and Qualitative Research* 8, no. 2 (2014): 113–28, also finds that a broader group of immigrant women engineers encounter a sense of urgency and competition to prove themselves as successful engineers in the workplace.

12 Dutta, "Negotiations of Cultural Identities by Indian Women Engineering Students in US Engineering Programmes," 187.

13 Center for Studies of Developing Societies–Konrad Adenaur Stiftung, "Key Highlights from the CSDS-KAS Report 'Attitudes, Anxieties and Aspirations of India's Youth: Changing Patterns,'" New Delhi: CSDS-KAS, April 3, 2017, accessed July 24, 2017, www.kas.de/wf/en/33.48472.

14 Smitha Radhakrishnan, *Appropriately Indian: Gender and Culture in a New Transnational Class* (Durham, NC: Duke University Press, 2011).

15 Christopher Fuller and Haripriya Narasimhan, "Marriage, Education, and Employment among Tamil Brahman Women in South India, 1891–2010," *Modern Asian Studies* 47, no. 1 (2013): 53–84.

16 Carol Upadhya and Aninhalli R. Vasavi, "Work, Culture, and Sociality in the Indian IT Industry: A Sociological Study" (Bangalore: National Institute of Advanced Studies, 2006).

17 Michiel Baas, "The IT Caste: Love and Arranged Marriages in the IT Industry of Bangalore," *South Asia: Journal of South Asian Studies* 32, no. 2 (2009): 286.

18 Marisa D'Mello, "Gendered Selves and Identities of Information Technology Professionals in Global Software Organizations in India," *Information Technology for Development* 12, no. 2 (2006): 137.

19 For a longer discussion of the development of the "new Indian woman" see Nilanjana Chatterjee and Nancy Riley, "Planning an Indian Modernity: The Gendered Politics of Fertility Control," *Signs* 26, no. 3 (2001): 811–45; Jyoti Puri, *Woman, Body, Desire in Post-colonial India: Narratives of Gender and Sexuality* (New York: Routledge, 1999); Smitha Radhakrishnan, "Professional Women, Good Families: Respectable Femininity and the Cultural Politics of a 'New' India," *Qualitative Sociology* 32, no. 2 (2009): 195–212; Susie Tharu and Tejaswini Niranjana, "Problems for a Contemporary Theory of Gender," *Subaltern Studies* 9 (1996): 232–60.

20 Upadhya and Vasavi, "Work, Culture, and Sociality in the Indian IT Industry," 113.

21 Center for Studies of Developing Societies–Konrad Adeneur Stiftung, "Key Highlights."

22 Raghuram, "Migration, Gender, and the IT Sector," 170.

23 Deborah A. Boehm shows how Mexican men, who often migrate before getting married, quickly figure out how to cook simple dishes and handle household cleaning and chores, including grocery shopping. However, after marriage, their reproductive labor significantly diminishes. "'Now I Am a Man and a Woman!' Gendered Moves and Migrations in a Transnational Mexican Community," *Latin American Perspectives* 35, no. 1 (2008): 16–30.

24 Anastasia Ustinova, "Indian Women Isolated in Silicon Valley," *San Francisco Chronicle*, March 9, 2008.

25 Katherine Culliton-González, "Born in the Americas: Birthright Citizenship and Human Rights," *Harvard Human Rights Journal* 25, no. 1 (2012): 127–82.

26 See Margaret Franz, "Will to Love, Will to Fear: The Emotional Politics of Illegality and Citizenship in the Campaign against Birthright Citizenship in the US," *Social Identities* 21, no. 2 (2015): 184–98.

27 See Kate Pickert, "Dispelling 'Anchor Baby' Myths," *Time Magazine*, August 11, 2010, http://swampland.time.com/2010/08/11/dispelling-anchor-baby-myths; and Jeffrey Passel and Paul Taylor, *Unauthorized Immigrants and Their U.S.-Born Children*, Pew Hispanic Center, August 11, 2010, accessed July 24, 2017, www.pewhispanic.org/2010/08/11/unauthorized-immigrants-and-their-us-born-children.

28 Edwin Rubenstein, "Legal Immigration: The Bigger Problem," *Social Contract* 17, no. 4 (2007): 259.

29 Tierney Sneed, "Why Ending Birthright Citizenship Would Be Terrible for Silicon Valley," *Talking Points Memo*, August 25, 2015, accessed August 5, 2016. http://talkingpointsmemo.com/dc/birthright-citizenship-techcommunity.

30 Ibid.

31 Aihwa Ong, "Cultural Citizenship as Subject-Making: Immigrants Negotiate Racial and Cultural Boundaries in the United States," *Current Anthropology* 37, no. 5 (1996): 737–62.

32 Ibid., 749.

33 Caroline Bledsoe, "Reproduction at the Margins: Migration and Legitimacy in the New Europe," *Demographic Research* 3, no. 4 (2004): 88.

34 Ibid.

35 For examples of second-generation and transnational parenting issues, see Rubén G. Rumbaut and Alejandro Portes, eds., *Ethnicities: Children of Immigrants in America* (Berkeley: University of California Press, 2001); Sunaina Maira, *Desis in the House: Indian American Youth Culture in New York City* (Philadelphia: Temple University Press, 2002); Gina J. Grillo, *Between Cultures: Children of Immigrants in America* (Chicago: University of Chicago Press, 2004); and Bandana Purkayastha, *Negotiating Ethnicity: Second-Generation South Asian Americans Traverse a Transnational World* (New Brunswick, NJ: Rutgers University Press, 2005). These studies all give detailed accounts of intergenerational conflict as it intersects with racial and gender identity formation in the US.

36 Denise Spitzer, Anne Neufeld, Margaret Harrison, Karen Hughes, and Miriam Stewart, "Caregiving in Transnational Context: 'My Wings Have Been Cut; Where Can I Fly?'" In *Global Dimensions of Gender and Carework*, ed. Mary K. Zimmerman, Jacquelyn S. Litt, and Christine E. Bose (Stanford, CA: Stanford University Press, 2006), 176.

37 Swapan Dasgupta, "How the Non-Resident Indian Has Fallen from Grace," *Times of India*, August 16, 2009.

38 "Expat Indian Men's Marriage Prospects Hit by Global Slowdown," *Economic Times*.

39 Shalini Singh, "Reverse Marriage Drain," *Hindustan Times*, January 23, 2012.

40 Nimisha Jaiswal, "After Kansas, Indians Fear for the Safety of Their Loved Ones in Trump's America," *Public Radio International*, March 3, 2017, accessed March 20, 2017, www.pri.org/stories/2017-03-03/after-kansas-indians-fear-safety-their-loved-ones-trumps-america.

41 Biao, "Gender, Dowry and the Migration System of Indian Information Technology Professionals," 368.

3. Transnational Housewives

1 Meghna Damani, *Hearts Suspended,* dir. Meghna Damani (Jersey City, NJ: Treasure Tower Films, 2007).

2 A number of news media accounts have portrayed the struggles that H-4 visa holders face around the country. For example: Raheel Dhattiwala," Housewives on H-4 Visa Get Desperate on Chat Sites," *Times of India*, October 2, 2006; Elsa Mathews, "Life's a Full Stop for Women with H-4 US Visas," *NewsBlaze,* June 24, 2009, http://newsblaze.com/world/south-asia/lifes-a-full-stop-for-women-with-h-4-us-visas_9686; Kalita S. Mitra, "Immigrant Wives' Visa Status Keeps Them out of Workplace," *Washington Post*, October 3, 2005; and Lynn Thompson, "Identity Crisis: Wives of Immigrant Tech Workers Struggle to Find Purpose," *Seattle Times Pacific NW Magazine*, August 28, 2015, www.seattletimes.com/pacific-nw-magazine/while-their-husbands-work-immigrant-wives-often-struggle-in-this-new-land.

3 Numerous scholarly accounts have considered how H-4 visa holders fare in the US after migration. My analysis adds to this discussion by examining the personal narratives

of H-4 visa holders and how they are victimized by immigration policies but also how they resist this classification. See, for example, Sharmila Lodhia, "Brides without Borders: New Topographies of Violence and the Future of Law in an Era of Transnational Citizen-Subjects," *Columbia Journal of Gender and Law* 19, no. 3 (2010): 703–46; Sabrina Balgamwall, "Bride and Prejudice: How U.S. Immigration Law Discriminates against Spousal Visa Holders," *Berkeley Journal of Gender, Law and Justice* 29, no. 1 (2014): 25–71; Magdalena Bragun, "The Golden Cage: How Immigration Law Turns Foreign Women into Involuntary Housewives," *Seattle University Law Review* 31, no. 4 (2008): 937–72; Stewart Chang, "Dreams of My Father, Prison for My Mother: The H-4 Nonimmigrant Visa Dilemma and the Need for an 'Immigration-Status Spousal Support,'" *Asian Pacific American Law Journal* 19, no. 1 (2013): 1–28; Chien-Juh Gu, "Women's Status in the Context of International Migration," *Sociology Compass* 6, no. 6 (2012): 458–71; Shivali Shah, "Middle Class, Documented, and Helpless: The H-4 Visa Bind," in *Body Evidence: Intimate Violence against South Asian Women in America*, ed. Shamita Das Dasgupta, 195–210 (New Brunswick, NJ: Rutgers University Press, 2007).

4   Claire Bergeron, *Going to the Back of the Line: A Primer on Lines, Visa Categories and Wait Times* (Washington, DC: Migration Policy Institute, 2013), accessed July 25, 2017, www.migrationpolicy.org/research/going-back-line-primer-lines-visa-categories -and-wait-times.

5   Historical and contemporary accounts of migration confirm the significant role that family reunification has played in the evolution of US immigrant populations and how it is the largest stream of immigration. See, for example, Catherine Lee, "Family Reunification and the Limits of Immigration Reform: Impact and Legacy of the 1965 Immigration Act," *Sociological Forum* 30 (2015): 528–48; Ramah McKay, "Migration Information Source–Family Reunification," last modified May 1, 2003, www.migration policy.org/article/family-reunification; James Monger and Randall Yankay, "U.S. Legal Permanent Residents: 2011" (Washington, D.C. US Department of Homeland Security, Office of Immigration Statistics, 2012), www.dhs.gov/xlibrary/assets/statistics/publica tions/lpr_fr_2011.pdf.

6   Kerry Abrams, "What Makes the Family Special?" *University of Chicago Law Review* 80, no. 1 (2013): 7–28.

7   For a longer analysis of the race and gender implications of early US immigration policies, see Amy Bhatt and Nalini Iyer, *Roots and Reflections: South Asians in the Pacific Northwest* (Seattle: University of Washington Press, 2013); Susan Koshy and Rajago- palan Radhakrishnan, *Transnational South Asians: The Making of a Neo-Diaspora* (New York: Oxford University Press, 2008); Ronald T. Takaki, *Strangers from a Different Shore: A History of Asian Americans* (Boston: Little, Brown, 1989); Deenesh Sohoni, "Unsuitable Suitors: Anti-Miscegenation Laws, Naturalization Laws, and the Construction of Asian Identities," *Law and Society Review* 41, no. 3 (2007): 587–618.

8   Abrams, "What Makes the Family Special?" 10.

9   United Nations General Assembly, "International Covenant on Economic, Social and Cultural Rights," December 16, 1966, www.ohchr.org/EN/ProfessionalInterest/Pages /CESCR.aspx.

10   Immigration Act of 1990, Public Law 101-649, *U.S. Statutes at Large* 104 (1992): 4978.

11 Though not ratified by the US, the International Convention on the Protection of the Rights of All Migrant Workers and Members of Their Families was adopted by the United Nations General Assembly in 1990; it recognizes the rights of family members who accompany migrant workers also to migrate. Setting forth a set of principles and rights, the Convention sought to secure fair treatment for non-immigrants and their relatives. See Torsten Heinemann, Ursula Naue, and Anna-Maria Tapaninen, "Verifying the Family? A Comparison of DNA Analysis for Family Reunification in Three European Countries (Austria, Finland and Germany)," *European Journal of Migration and Law* 15, no. 2 (2013): 183–202.

12 See María Enchautegui and Cecilia Menjívar, "Paradoxes of Family Immigration Policy: Separation, Reorganization, and Reunification of Families under Current Immigration Laws," *Law and Policy* 37, no. 1/2 (2015): 32–60; Dong-Hoon Seol and John D. Skrentny, "Why Is There So Little Migrant Settlement in East Asia?" *International Migration Review* 43, no. 3 (2009): 578–620; Marta Moskal, "Transnationalism and the Role of Family and Children in Intra-European Labour Migration," *European Societies* 13, no. 1 (2011): 29–50; Laura Zanfrini, "Family Migration: Fulfilling the Gap between Law and Social Processes," *Societies* 2, no. 3 (2012): 63–74.

13 While many congressional supporters of the 1990 Immigration Act hoped that the changes in the law would significantly increase the numbers of immigrants entering to align with US labor priorities, the effect has been less dramatic than anticipated. As Muzaffar Chishti and Stephen Yale-Loehr report, "While the employment-based component of newly admitted immigrants has increased from 9 percent in 1990 to 15 percent today, more than half of employment-based immigrant visas are issued to workers' family members, making the share of actual workers admitted on the basis of their skill close to 7 percent." Thus, while there has been an upswing in foreign-born workers, the much greater demographic impact of employer-based visa programs has come from the rising numbers of family members who also migrate. "The Immigration Act of 1990: Unfinished Business a Quarter-Century Later" (Washington, DC: Migration Policy Institute, 2016), 10.

14 With the expansion of border control after 9/11 and the harsh mandate levied by recent White House administrations, US Immigration and Customs Enforcement has increased the detention and deportation of undocumented immigrants, regardless of whether they have family ties. In 2013, nearly 72,000 parents of US-born children were deported, leaving many minors behind in the US. See Elise Foley, "Deportation Separated Thousands of U.S.-Born Children from Parents in 2013," *Huffington Post*, June 25, 2014, www.huffing tonpost.com/2014/06/25/parents-deportation_n_5531552.html. Since the ascendency of Trump, the number of deportations has dropped, but arrests of undocumented immigrants have risen substantially. See Aria Bendix, "Immigrant Arrests Are Up, but Deportation Is Down, *Atlantic,* May 17, 2017, www.theatlantic.com/news/archive/2017/05 /under-trump-immigrants-arrests-are-up-but-deportation-is-down/527103/.

15 Melanie Cline, "Equal Rights? Not for 100,000+ American H-4 Visa Holders," *Equal Opportunities International* 22, no. 1 (2003): 46–49.

16 Damani, *Hearts Suspended.*

17 Kalita S. Mitra, *Suburban Sahib: Three Immigrant Families and Their Passage from India to America* (New Brunswick, NJ: Rutgers University Press, 2003).

18 Wei Li offers an excellent account of how Chinese American communities have reshaped California's San Gabriel Valley into an "ethnoburb" that links ethnicity, space, and suburban development outside of more traditional immigration settlement frameworks that have focused on urban ethnic enclaves historically. *Ethnoburb: The New Ethnic Community in Urban America* (Honolulu: University of Hawaii Press, 2009). More recent scholarship on "techno-burbs" points to the specific rise of wealthy Asian suburbs adjacent to US technology centers as a result of Indian and Chinese IT migration. See Wei Li and Lucia Lo, "New Geographies of Migration: A Canada-U.S. Comparison of Highly Skilled Chinese and Indian Migration," *Journal of Asian American Studies* 15, no. 1 (2012): 1–34. Relatedly, Willow Lung-Amam argues that high-status symbols like Asian malls or homeownership in ethnic communities in the suburbs solidify ethnic community formation and offer modalities of belonging to new immigrants. "Malls of Meaning: Building Asian America in Silicon Valley Suburbia," *Journal of American Ethnic History* 34, no. 2 (2015): 18–53. See also Eric J. Pido, "The Performance of Property: Suburban Homeownership as a Claim to Citizenship for Filipinos in Daly City," *Journal of Asian American Studies* 15, no. 1 (2012): 69–104.

19 See the following studies for examples of H-4 visa holders' experiences with domestic violence: Sabrina Balgamwalla, "Bride and Prejudice: How U.S. Immigration Law Discriminates against Spousal Visa Holders," *Berkeley Journal of Gender, Law and Justice* 29, no. 1 (2014): 25–71; Anannya Bhattacharjee, "Immigrant Dreams and Nightmares: South Asian Domestic Workers in North America in a Time of Global Mobility," in *Trans-status Subjects: Gender in the Globalization of South and Southeast Asia*, eds. Sonita Sarker and Esha Niyogi De, 289–308 (Durham, NC: Duke University Press, 2002); Rupaleem Bhuyan, "Navigating Immigration, Gender, and Domestic Violence: Domestic Violence Advocacy with Work Visa Holders," in *Body Evidence: Intimate Violence against South Asian Women in America*, ed. Shamita Das Dasgupta, 229–42 (New Brunswick, NJ: Rutgers University Press, 2007); Rupaleem Bhuyan, "Reconstructing Citizenship in a Global Economy: How Restricting Immigrants from Welfare Undermines Social Rights for U.S. Citizens," *Journal of Sociology and Social Welfare* 37 (2010): 63; Shivali Shah, "Middle Class, Documented, and Helpless: The H-4 Visa Bind," in *Body Evidence: Intimate Violence against South Asian Women in America*, ed. Shamita Das Dasgupta, 195–210 (New Brunswick, NJ: Rutgers University Press, 2007).

20 Sharmila Rudrappa, "Law's Culture and Cultural Difference," In *Body Evidence: Intimate Violence against South Asian Women in America*, ed. Shamita Das Dasgupta, 181–94 (New Brunswick, NJ: Rutgers University Press, 2007), 188.

21 US Consulate General Chennai, "Child and Family Matters," accessed May 2, 2010, http://chennai.usconsulate.gov/childfamily.html.

22 See Vic Satzewich, "Canadian Visa Officers and the Social Construction of 'Real' Spousal Relationship," *Canadian Review of Sociology* 51, no. 1 (2014): 1–21.

23 Sherene Razack, *Looking White People in the Eye: Gender, Race, and Culture in Courtrooms and Classrooms* (Toronto: University of Toronto Press, 1998).

24 For an analysis of how the US immigration system reinforces heterosexist assumptions of the immigrant family while also acting as a "savior" of Third World marginalized

subjects through refugee and asylum policies, see Chandan Reddy, "Asian Diasporas, Neoliberalism, and Family: Reviewing the Case for Homosexual Asylum in the Context of Family Rights," *Social Text* 23, no. 3/4 (2005): 101–20.

25 For de-skilling, see Guida C. Man, "Gender, Work and Migration: Deskilling Chinese Immigrant Women in Canada," *Women's Studies International Forum* 27 (2004): 135–48; for re-domestication, see Brenda Yeoh, S. A. Yoeh, and Katie Willis, "Singaporeans in China: Transnational Women Elites and the Negotiation of Gendered Identities," *Geoforum* 36, no. 2 (2005): 211–22; for cumulative disadvantage, see Bandana Purkayastha, "Skilled Migration and Cumulative Disadvantage: The Case of Highly Qualified Asian Indian Immigrant Women in the US," *Geoforum* 36, no. 2 (2005): 181–96.

26 Carina Meares, "A Fine Balance: Women, Work and Skilled Migration," *Women's Studies International Forum* 33 (2010): 474.

27 Asmita Bhattacharyya and Bhola Nath Ghosh, "Women in Indian Information Technology (IT) Sector: A Sociological Analysis," *Journal of Humanities and Social Science* 3, no. 6 (2012): 49.

28 Sandra G. Harding has argued that the division of "women's issues," such as the family, from the "objective" inquiries of the public domain reduces concerns about intimate life to "the irrational, the incomprehensible and to the unintelligible," rather than a vital component of how society, politics, or the economy is constituted and organized. Sandra G. Harding, *Sciences from Below: Feminisms, Postcolonialities, and Modernities* (Durham, NC: Duke University Press, 2008), 8. See also Susan Himmelweit, "An Evolutionary Approach to Feminist Economics: Two Different Models of Caring," in *Toward a Feminist Philosophy of Economics*, eds. Drucilla K. Barker and Edith Kuiper, 247–65 (New York: Routledge, 2003); and Nancy Folbre and Michael Bittman, *Family Time: The Social Organization of Care* (New York: Routledge, 2004).

29 Pamela Stone, *Opting Out? Why Women Really Quit Careers and Head Home* (Berkeley: University of California Press, 2007).

30 Ibid.

31 Ann Bagchi has stressed the importance of networking and volunteering for professional immigrants, particularly when formal employment avenues are closed to them. *Making Connections: A Study of Networking among Immigrant Professionals* (New York: LFB Scholarly Publishing, 2001).

32 Ann Vogel and Iain Lang, "Working in the Age of Flexibility: The 'Crisis of Work' and the Meaning of Volunteering" (paper presented at the American Sociological Association 101th Annual Conference, Montreal, Canada, 2006).

33 Society for Human Resources Management, "Internships," November 6, 2013, www .shrm.org/hr-today/trends-and-forecasting/research-and-surveys/pages/shrm-2013 -internships.aspx.

34 Vogel and Lang, "Working in the Age of Flexibility," 1.

35 Even among economically and socially privileged women who take on unpaid positions to further their knowledge of a specific field, there is still the strong desire to be paid for one's work as a signal of their personal worth. See Leslie Shade and Jenna Jacobson, "Hungry for the Job: Gender, Unpaid Internships, and the Creative Industries," *Sociological Review* 63, no. 1 (2015): 188–205.

36 Lawrence M. Berger and Jane Waldfogel, "Maternity Leave and the Employment of New Mothers in the United States," *Journal of Population Economics* 17, no. 2 (2004): 331–49.

37 Caren A. Arbeit and John Robert Warren, "Labor Market Penalties for Foreign Degrees among College Educated Immigrants," *Social Science Research* 42 (2013): 852–71.

38 Shibao Guo, "Immigrants as Active Citizens: Exploring the Volunteering Experience of Chinese Immigrants in Vancouver," *Globalisation, Societies and Education* 12, no. 1 (2014): 51–70; Young-joo Lee and Seong-Gin Moon, "Mainstream and Ethnic Volunteering by Korean Immigrants in the United States," *Voluntas: International Journal of Voluntary and Nonprofit Organizations* 22, no. 4 (2011): 811–30.

39 Stacey Wilson-Forsberg and Bharati Sethi, "The Volunteering Dogma and Canadian Work Experience: Do Recent Immigrants Volunteer Voluntarily?" *Canadian Ethnic Studies Journal*, no. 3 (2015): 91–110.

40 See Aparna Rayaprol, *Negotiating Identities: Women in the Indian Diaspora* (New York: Oxford University Press, 1997).

41 See Meeta Mehrotra and Toni M. Calasanti, "The Family as a Site for Gendered Ethnic Identity Work among Asian Indian Immigrants," *Journal of Family Issues* 31 no. 6 (2010): 778–807.

42 Namita N. Manohar, "Mothering for Class and Ethnicity: The Case of Indian Professional Immigrants in the United States," *Advances in Gender Research* 17 (2013): 159–85.

43 Miabi Chatterji, "Putting 'the Family' to Work: Managerial Discourses of Control in the Immigrant Service Sector," in *The Sun Never Sets: South Asian Migrants in an Age of US Power*, eds. Vivek Bald, Miabi Chatterji, Sujani Reddy, and Manu Vimalassery, 127–55 (New York: New York University Press, 2013).

44 Sandya Hewamanne, "Threading Meaningful Lives: Respectability, Home Businesses and Identity Negotiations among Newly Immigrant South Asian Women," *Identities* 19, no. 3 (2012): 320–38.

45 Chase M. Billingham and Shelley McDonough Kimelberg, "Middle-Class Parents, Urban Schooling, and the Shift from Consumption to Production of Urban Space," *Sociological Forum* 28, no. 1 (2013): 85–108.

46 Sharon Hays, *The Cultural Contradictions of Motherhood* (New Haven, CT: Yale University Press, 1996).

47 Lynn Thompson, "Bellevue Schools Engage Influx of Tech-Sector Immigrants' Children," *Seattle Times*, February 16, 2015.

48 Anastasia Ustinova, "Indian Women Isolated in Silicon Valley," *San Francisco Chronicle*, March 9, 2008.

49 Namita N. Manohar and Erika Busse-Cárdenas, "Valuing 'Good' Motherhood in Migration," *Journal of the Motherhood Initiative for Research and Community Involvement* 2, no. 2 (2011): 175–95.

50 Mehrotra and Calasanti, "The Family as a Site for Gendered Ethnic Identity Work among Asian Indian Immigrants."

51 Namita N. Manohar, "Mothering for Class and Ethnicity: The Case of Indian Professional Immigrants in the United States," *Advances in Gender Research* 17 (2013): 159–85.

52 Paul Adams and Rina Ghose, "India.com: The Construction of a Space Between," *Progress in Human Geography* 27 no. 4 (2003): 414–37.

53 Arjun Appadurai, *Modernity at Large: Cultural Dimensions of Globalization* (Minneapolis: University of Minnesota Press, 1996).

54 Microsoft Corporation, Microsoft Family Immigration Network, accessed March 1, 2010, http://msimmigrationfamily.com/Home/tabid/36/%20Default.aspx.

55 Rashi Bhatnagar, H-4 Visa: A Curse, accessed August 1, 2017, www.facebook.com/H4 visaacurse/info/?entry_point=page_nav_about_item&tab=page_info.

56 Summer Harlow and Dustin Harp, "Collective Action on the Web: A Cross-Cultural Study of Social Networking Sites and Online and Offline Activism in the United States and Latin America," *Information, Communication and Society* 15, no. 2 (2012): 196–216.

57 Paul C. Adams and Emily Skop, "The Gendering of Asian Indian Transnationalism on the Internet," *Journal of Cultural Geography* 25, no. 2 (2008): 121.

58 *The Involuntary Housewife: Trapped!!* Accessed July 20, 2017, https://trappedinh4mess.wordpress.com.

59 Ibid.

60 Lori Kido Lopez, "The Radical Act of 'Mommy Blogging': Redefining Motherhood through the Blogosphere," *New Media and Society* 11, no. 5 (2009): 729–47.

61 Radha S. Hegde, "Food Blogs and the Digital Reimagination of South Asian Diasporic Publics," *South Asian Diaspora* 6, no. 1 (2014): 89–103.

62 Ibid., 100.

63 Sharmila Lodhia, "Constructing an Imperfect Citizen-Subject: Globalization, National 'Security,' and Violence against South Asian Women," *Women's Studies Quarterly* 38, no. 1/2 (2010): 167.

64 Hegde, "Food Blogs and the Digital Reimagination of South Asian Diasporic Publics," 91.

4. Returnees

1   See the following accounts of return migration among professional transmigrants: Williams S. Harvey, "British and Indian Scientists in Boston Considering Returning to their Home Countries," *Population Space and Place* 15, no. 6 (2009): 493–508; Russell King and Anastasia Christou, "Second-Generation 'Return' to Greece: New Dynamics of Transnationalism and Integration," *International Migration* 52, no. 6 (2014): 85–99; Stefanie Konzett-Smoliner, "Return Migration as a 'Family Project': Exploring the Relationship between Family Life and the Readjustment Experiences of Highly Skilled Austrians," *Journal of Ethnic and Migration Studies* 42, no. 7 (2016): 1094–1114; and John Percival, *Return Migration in Later Life* (Chicago: University of Chicago Press, 2013).

2   For a longer and comparative account of the reasons transmigrants return to their home countries, see Elizabeth Chacko, "From Brain Drain to Brain Gain: Reverse Migration to Bangalore and Hyderabad, India's Globalizing High Tech Cities," *GeoJournal* 68, no. 2/3 (2007): 131–40; and Evelyn Ravuri, "Return Migration Predictors for Undocumented Mexican Immigrants Living in Dallas," *Social Science Journal* 51 (2014): 35–43.

3   See Işık Kuşçu, "Ethnic Return Migration and Public Debate: The Case of Kazakhstan," *International Migration* 52, no. 2 (2014): 178–97; Vanya Ivanova, "The Return

Migration of Highly-Qualified Workers in Bulgaria and in Bosnia and Herzegovina: Policies and Returnees' Responses," *South East Europe Review* 18, no. 1 (2015): 93–111; John D. Skrentny, Stephanie Chan, Jon Fox, and Denis Kim, "Defining Nations in Asia and Europe: A Comparative Analysis of Ethnic Return Migration Policy," *International Migration Review* 41, no. 4 (2007): 793–825.

4   For deeper explorations of the factors that push transmigrants out of their host countries, see Amparo González-Ferrer et al., "Distance, Transnational Arrangements, and Return Decisions of Senegalese, Ghanaian, and Congolese Migrants," *International Migration Review* 48, no. 4 (2014): 939–71; Siew-Ean Khoo, "Attracting and Retaining Globally Mobile Skilled Migrants: Policy Challenges Based on Australian Research," *International Migration* 52, no. 2 (2014): 20–30; Claudia Masferrer and Bryan Roberts, "Going Back Home? Changing Demography and Geography of Mexican Return Migration," *Population Research and Policy Review* 31, no. 4 (2012): 465–96.

5   For a longer account of how the NRI has historically and contemporarily been hailed by the Indian government as part of development efforts, see Sareeta Bipin Amrute, "The 'New' Non-Residents of India: A Short History of the NRI," in *A New India? Critical Reflections in the Long Twentieth Century,* ed. Anthony P. D'Costa (New York: Anthem Press, 2010); Chandrashekhar Sastry, *The Non-resident Indian: From Nonbeing to Being* (Bangalore: Panther Publishers, 1991).

6   See Alaina Brenick and Rainer K. Silbereisen, "Leaving (for) Home: Understanding Return Migration from the Diaspora," *European Psychologist* 17, no. 2 (2012): 85–92; Deepanjana Varshney, "The Return of the Natives: Asian Diaspora Issues and Dilemmas; The Case of India," *African and Asian Studies* 12, no. 3 (2013): 290–321; Roli Varma and Deepak Kapur, "Comparative Analysis of Brain Drain, Brain Circulation and Brain Retain: A Case Study of Indian Institutes of Technology," *Journal of Comparative Policy Analysis* 15, no. 4 (2013): 315–30.

7   Starting in 1991, India underwent a series of structural adjustments tied to the acceptance of funds from the International Monetary Fund (IMF) and the World Bank, which are broadly referred to as "economic reforms." For a closer examination of the history and effects of economic reforms in India, see Waquar Ahmed, Amitabh Kundu, and Richard Peet, *India's New Economic Policy: A Critical Analysis* (London: Routledge, 2011); Giovanni Andrea Cornia and World Institute for Development Economics Research, *Inequality, Growth, and Poverty in an Era of Liberalization and Globalization* (New York: Oxford University Press, 2004); and Arvind Panagariya, *India: The Emerging Giant* (New York: Oxford University Press, 2008).

8   Neoliberalism in the Indian context has been characterized by such economic reforms, increases in disposable income, higher rates of consumerism, the opening of media and entertainment industries, and a convergence of state and middle-class interests "on a shared vision of modernity in India." Leela Fernandes, *India's New Middle Class: Democratic Politics in an Era of Economic Reform* (Minneapolis: University of Minnesota Press, 2006), 3.

9   National Association of Software and Service Companies, "India IT-BPM Overview," accessed June 30, 2017, www.nasscom.in/indian-itbpo-industry.

10 Theodore Davis, "High-Skill Return Migration in the Technology, Medical, and Academic Sectors: The Case of India and the USA," *Diaspora Studies* 9, no. 1 (2016): 15–27.

11 Ibid., 21.

12 See AnnaLee Saxenian, *The New Argonauts: Regional Advantage in a Global Economy* (Cambridge, MA: Harvard University Press, 2006).

13 For an in-depth account of the impact of economic liberalization in India, see Amita Baviskar and Raka Ray, *Elite and Everyman: The Cultural Politics of the Indian Middle Classes* (New York: Routledge, 2011).

14 Vivek Wadhwa, "A Reverse Brain Drain," *Issues in Science and Technology* 25, no. 3 (2009): 45–52.

15 Each year, 140,000 green cards are issued to employment-based visa holders. Since no single country can receive any more than 7 percent of these green cards and Indian recipients constitute 71 percent of the total H-1B visa holder pool, there is a major backlog in the processing of Indian green card applications. As a result, they can wait as long as fifteen years to get a green card.

16 See Sonali Jain, "For Love and Money: Second-Generation Indian-Americans 'Return' to India," *Ethnic and Racial Studies* 36, no. 5 (2013): 896–914.

17 Varma and Kapur, "Comparative Analysis of Brain Drain, Brain Circulation and Brain Retain," 327.

18 See Dina Bass, "America's Unwanted Ivy Leaguers Are Flocking to India," *Bloomberg News*, June 2, 2015, www.bloomberg.com/news/articles/2015-06-02/chasing-the-american -dream-in-india; and Jay Greene, "India Draws Tech Dreamers Back Home," *Seattle Times*, November 28, 2015.

19 Varshney, "The Return of the Natives."

20 Wadhwa, "A Reverse Brain Drain," 50.

21 The authors of the following studies report that the isolation faced by immigrants not only adds mental stress, but also can lead to poor health outcomes and long-term emotional instability: Hua-Yu Sebastian Cherng, "Social Isolation among Racial/ Ethnic Minority Immigrant Youth," *Sociology Compass* 9, no. 6 (2015): 509–18; Kristine J. Ajrouch, "Social Isolation and Loneliness among Arab American Elders: Cultural, Social, and Personal Factors," *Research in Human Development* 5, no. 1 (2008): 44–59; Alejandra Hurtado-de-Mendoza, Felisa Gonzales, Adriana Serrano, and Stacey Kaltman, "Social Isolation and Perceived Barriers to Establishing Social Networks among Latina Immigrants," *American Journal of Community Psychology* 53, no. 1/2 (2014): 73–82.

22 For a historical account of the factors leading to India's contemporary drops in birth rates, see Robert Cassen, *India: Population, Economy, Society* (London: Palgrave Macmillan, 1978).

23 See Bum Kim, Kristen Linton, and Wesley Lum, "Social Capital and Life Satisfaction among Chinese and Korean Elderly Immigrants," *Journal of Social Work* 15, no. 1 (2015): 87–100.

24 Jyotsna Kalavar and D. Jamuna, "Aging of Indian Women in India: The Experience of Older Women in Formal Care Homes," *Journal of Women and Aging* 23, no. 3 (2011): 203–15.

25 Carol Upadhya and Aninhalli R. Vasavi, "Work, Culture, and Sociality in the Indian IT Industry: A Sociological Study" (Bangalore: National Institute of Advanced Studies, 2006), accessed June 24, 2015, http://eprints.nias.res.in/107), 110.

26 This desire to expose children to "home" cultures has been documented across immigrant groups. See Alex Stepick, Carol Dutton Stepick, Emmanuel Eugene, Deborah Teed, and Yves Labissiere, "Shifting Identities and Intergenerational Conflict: Growing up Haitian in Miami," in *Ethnicities: Children of Immigrants in America*, eds. Rubén G. Rumbaut and Alejandro Portes, 229–66 (Berkeley: University of California Press, 2001); Yen Le Espiritu and Diane L. Wolf, "The Paradox of Assimilation: Children of Filipino Immigrants in San Diego," in *Ethnicities: Children of Immigrants in America*, ed. Rubén G. Rumbaut and Alejandro Portes, 157–86 (Berkeley: University of California Press, 2001); Min Zhou, "Straddling Different Worlds: The Acculturation of Vietnamese Refugee Children," in *Ethnicities: Children of Immigrants in America*, eds. Rubén G. Rumbaut and Alejandro Portes, 187–227 (Berkeley: University of California Press, 2001); Gina J. Grillo, *Between Cultures: Children of Immigrants in America* (Chicago: University of Chicago Press, 2004).

27 M. R. Narayana, "Globalization and Urban Economic Growth: Evidence for Bangalore, India," *International Journal of Urban and Regional Research* 35, no. 6 (2011): 1284–1301.

28 For an account of the rapid changes in Bangalore's real estate and technology sectors, see Christaine Brosius, "The Gated Romance of 'India Shining': Visualizing Urban Lifestyle in Advertisement of Residential Housing Development," in *Popular Culture in a Globalised India*, ed. K. Moti Gokulsing and Wimal Dissanayake, 174–91 (New York: Routledge, 2009); Elizabeth Chacko and Paul Varghese, "Identity and Representations of Gated Communities in Bangalore, India," *Open House International* 34, no. 3 (2009): 57–64; Christoph Dittrich, "Bangalore: Divided City under the Impact of Globalization," *Asian Journal of Water, Environment and Pollution* 2, no. 2 (2005): 23–30; Christoph Dittrich, "Bangalore: Globalisation and Fragmentation in India's Hightech-Capital," *Asien* 103 (2007): 45–48; and Solomon Benjamin, "Occupancy Urbanism: Radicalizing Politics and Economy beyond Policy and Programs," *International Journal of Urban and Regional Research* 32, no. 3: 719.

29 For a longer discussion about the changes in food procurement and the availability of new services to meet the demand created by India's rising middle classes and returnees, see Jayan Jose Thomas, "An Uneasy Coexistence: The New and the Old in Indian Industry and Services," in *A New India? Critical Reflections in the Long Twentieth Century*, ed. Anthony P. D'Costa, 71–98 (New York: Anthem Press, 2010); and Anthony D. King, "Speaking from the Margins: "Postmodernism," Transnationalism, and the Imagining of Contemporary Indian Urbanity," in *Globalization and the Margins*, ed. Richard Grant and John R. Short, 72–90 (London: Palgrave Macmillan, 2002).

30 The names of all individuals and housing communities have been changed to provide anonymity.

31 Julian Sagebiel and Kai Rommel, "Preferences for Electricity Supply Attributes in Emerging Megacities: Policy Implications from a Discrete Choice Experiment of Private Households in Hyderabad, India," *Energy for Sustainable Development* 21 (2014): 89–99.

32 In an article for the *Indian Express*, editor-in-chief Shekhar Gupta underscored this independence for the Indian state for the provision of basic services: "All of us learnt to become individual, sovereign republics. We send our children to private schools,

get treatment only in private hospitals, have our own security in gated communities, never need to use public transport, even own our own diesel gensets to produce power, and in many parts of the country, arrange our own water supply, either through our own borewells or tankers." Manu Joseph, "Fighting to Shut out the Real India," *New York Times*, April 6, 2011.

33 Smitha Radhakrishnan, "Professional Women, Good Families: Respectable Femininity and the Cultural Politics of a 'New' India," *Qualitative Sociology* 32, no. 2 (2009): 204.

34 R2I-ed Blogger, "Dirty, Sexy, Wealthy India" (2009), http://r2i-thestorysofar.blogspot .com/2009/09/dirty-sexy-wealthy-india.html.

35 *Bhadramahila* is a term used to refer to a "gentlewoman" or a respectable upper-middle-class woman who is educated and culturally aware, but not overtly westernized. She oversees the work of the household and is in charge of satisfying the needs of her family. Rather than do the work herself, she manages the domestic workers' labor, which helps middle-class families maintain appropriate class and caste hierarchies. For a longer history, see Swapna M. Banerjee, *Men, Women, and Domestics: Articulating Middle-Class Identity in Colonial Bengal* (New York: Oxford University Press, 2004).

36 Raka Ray and Seemin Qayum argue that the language of "love" and "family" are used rhetorically and deliberately by employers to cultivate a sense of obligation between domestic workers and the households they serve. *Cultures of Servitude: Modernity, Domesticity, and Class in India* (Stanford, CA: Stanford University Press, 2009).

37 The terms *maids* and *servants* are used interchangeably by my interview subjects and bloggers. *Maid* tends to refer to young women who perform "inside" household tasks like cleaning, cooking, and childcare. *Servant* refers to the overall household staff, including maids, but also drivers and nannies. I prefer to use *domestic worker* or *laborer* when possible to maintain an emphasis on the explicit relationship of exchange that binds together employers and workers. At times, I use the terms *maid* and *servant* for consistency with the language of my interview subjects and bloggers.

38 Simanti Dasgupta, "Success, Market, Ethics," *Cultural Dynamics* 20, no. 3 (2008): 238.

39 Pierrette Hondagneu-Sotelo, *Doméstica: Immigrant Workers Cleaning and Caring in the Shadows of Affluence* (Berkeley: University of California Press, 2001).

40 Yan Hairong, *New Masters, New Servants: Migration, Development, and Women Workers in China* (Durham, NC: Duke University Press, 2008), 113.

41 The confluence of domesticity and "uplift" carries within it complicated colonial and postcolonial legacies. White women who came to India as part of the expansion of the British Empire were deeply concerned with "domestic administration" and how to manage relationships with household servants. In the postcolonial era, the notion of uplift has moved out of the household alone into state-sponsored and NGO development projects aimed at improving the quality of life for subaltern subjects.

42 Posters produced by the India Ministry of Information and Broadcasting, the Directorate of Audio-Visual Publicity (DAVP), and the India Ministry of Health and Family Welfare from the 1970s through the late 1990s convey slogans such as "Healthy mother, healthy child; small family, happy family" and "Not when you're too young; Not in a hurry; Not too many; Not when you're too old: A small family begets happiness."

43 Aradhana Sharma, *Logics of Empowerment: Development, Gender, and Governance in Neoliberal India* (Minneapolis: University of Minnesota Press, 2008), xx.

44 Bhatt, Murty, and Ramamurthy, "Hegemonic Developments."

45 Leela Fernandes, *India's New Middle Class: Democratic Politics in an Era of Economic Reform* (Minneapolis: University of Minnesota Press, 2006).

46 The Ugly Indian (2010), accessed July 8, 2017, www.theuglyindian.com/intro1.html.

5. Re-migrants

1 Christian Dustmann, "Children and Return Migration," *Journal of Population Economics* 16, no. 4 (2003): 815–30.

2 See, for example, scholarship on Mexican laborers such as Roger Rouse, "Making Sense of Settlement: Class Transformation, Cultural Struggle, and Transnationalism among Mexican Migrants in the United States," in *Towards a Transnational Perspective on Migration: Race, Class, Ethnicity, and Nationalism Reconsidered*, ed. Nina Glick Schiller, Linda G. Basch, and Cristina Szanton Blanc, 25–52 (New York: New York Academy of Sciences, 1992). For Filipina domestic workers, see Rhacel Salazar Parreñas, *Servants of Globalization: Women, Migration and Domestic Work* (Stanford, CA: Stanford University Press, 2001). On low-wage Asian workers moving between Middle Eastern oil economies, see Pnina Werbner, "Global Pathways: Working Class Cosmopolitans and the Creation of Transnational Ethnic Worlds," *Social Anthropology* 7, no. 1 (1999): 17–35. On the other end of the economic spectrum, Aiwha Ong's study of transnational elites also shows the regularity with which specific populations travel transnationally in order to maximize circuits of capital and wages. "Boundary Crossings: Neoliberalism as a Mobile Technology," *Transactions of the Institute of British Geographers* 32, no. 1 (2007): 3–8.

3 Vivek Wadhwa, "An Outflow of Talent: Nativism and the US Reverse Brain Drain," *Harvard International Review,* 31, no. 1 (2009): 50.

4 P. Sreeleakha, "Managing Culture Shock and Reverse Culture Shock of Indian Citizenship Employees," *International Journal of Management Practice* 7, no. 3 (2014): 250–74.

5 See Christoph Dittrich, "The Changing Food Scenario and the Middle Classes in the Emerging Mega City of Hyderabad/India," in *The New Middle Classes: Globalizing Lifestyles, Consumerism, and Environmental Concern*, ed. H. Lange and L. Meier, 289–303 (Dordrecht: Springer, 2009); and Ravi Nandi, Wolfgang Bokelmann, Nithya Vishwanath Gowdru, and Gustavo Dias, "Consumer Motives and Purchase Preferences for Organic Food Products: Empirical Evidence from a Consumer Survey in Bangalore, South India," *Journal of International Food and Agribusiness Marketing* 28, no. 1 (2016): 74–99.

6 Public forms of violence against all women, but particularly low-caste and minority women, are not new in India. However, in recent years, there has been substantial attention paid to the attacks on middle-class women as they move through urban areas on their own for work or to socialize. See Rupsayar Das, "Representation of Violence against Women in Indian Print Media: A Comparative Analysis," *Global Media Journal* 3, no. 1 (2012): 1–24, for a closer examination of media responses to public attacks on middle-class and elite Indian women.

7   On December 16, 2012, Jyoti Singh was beaten and gang raped by six men, including the bus driver, in a private bus in South Delhi after traveling home from seeing a movie with her male companion. Singh died from her injuries two weeks after the brutal assault. See Sharmila Lodhia, "From 'Living Corpse' to India's Daughter: Exploring the Social, Political and Legal Landscape of the 2012 Delhi Gang Rape," *Women's Studies International Forum* 50 (2015): 89–101, for a genealogy of the social, political, and legal discourse around rape and violence against women that has structured the responses to this and other cases.

8   Carol Upadhya, "Controlling Offshore Knowledge Workers: Power and Agency in India's Software Outsourcing Industry," *NTW New Technology, Work, and Employment* 24, no. 1 (2009): 2–18.

9   Sreeleakha, "Managing Culture Shock and Reverse Culture Shock of Indian Citizenship Employees."

10 Amy B. Woszczynski, Pamila Dembla, and Humayun Zafar, "Gender-Based Differences in Culture in the Indian IT Workplace," *International Journal of Information Management* 36, no. 4 (2016): 507–19.

11 Deepanjana Varshney argues that return migrants are likely to try to go abroad again if they believe the economic conditions in the host country are better than what they face in their home country. "The Return of the Natives: Asian Diaspora Issues and Dilemmas: The Case of India," *African and Asian Studies* 12, no. 3 (2013): 290–321.

12 Ashish Verma, T. M. Rahul, and Malvika Dixit, "Sustainability Impact Assessment of Transportation Policies: A Case Study for Bangalore City," *Case Studies on Transport Policy* 3, no. 3 (2015): 321–30.

13 Cicilia Chettiar, "A Study of Need Satisfaction in Joint and Nuclear Families in Mumbai," *Journal of Psychosocial Research* 10, no. 1 (2015): 83–88.

14 Migration scholars have found that family relationships play a significant role in predicting cross-border migration across different ethnic and national groups. See Sigal Kaplan, Luise Grünwald, and Georg Hirte, "The Effect of Social Networks and Norms on the Inter-regional migration Intentions of Knowledge-Workers: The Case of Saxony, Germany," *Cities* 55 (2016): 61–69; Yolanda Garcia-Rodriguez, Antonio Mihi-Ramirez, and Margarita Navarro-Pabsdorf, "Highly-Skilled Migration, Migrant Networks and the Prestige of Academic Institutions," *Engineering Economics* 26, no. 5 (2015): 500–506; Mao-Mei Liu, "Migrant Networks and International Migration: Testing Weak Ties," *Demography* 50, no. 4 (2013): 1243–77.

15 Deepak Gopinath, "Characterizing Indian Students Pursuing Global Higher Education: A Conceptual Framework of Pathways to Internationalization," *Journal of Studies in International Education* 19, no. 3 (2015): 284.

16 Sona Kanungo," Growth of Higher Education in India: Problems and Solutions," *Global Management Review* 9, no. 3 (2015): 53–60.

17 Abdul Razak Honnutagi, Rajendra Sonar, and Subash Babu, "Quality Accreditation System for Indian Engineering Education Using Knowledge Management and System Dynamics," *International Journal of Quality Assurance in Engineering and Technology Education* 2, no. 3 (2012): 47–61.

18 Theodore Davis, "High-Skill Return Migration in the Technology, Medical, and Academic sectors: The Case of India and the USA," *Diaspora Studies* 9, no. 1 (2016): 22.

19 Gopinath, "Characterizing Indian Students Pursuing Global Higher Education."

20 Ross Knox Bassett, *The Technological Indian* (Cambridge, MA: Harvard University Press, 2016).

21 Aihwa Ong, "Cultural Citizenship as Subject-Making: Immigrants Negotiate Racial and Cultural Boundaries in the United States," *Current Anthropology* 37, no. 5 (1996): 737–62; Min Zhou, "'Parachute Kids' in Southern California: The Educational Experience of Chinese Children in Transnational Families," *Educational Administration Abstracts* 34 no. 2 (1999): 682–704; Ken Chih-Yan Sun, "Transnational Kinscription: A Case of Parachute Kids in the USA and Their Parents in Taiwan," *Journal of Ethnic and Migration Studies* 40 no. 9 (2013): 1431–49.

22 Zhou, "'Parachute Kids' in Southern California," 688–89.

Conclusion

1 Rajni Palriwala and Patricia Uberoi, eds., *Marriage, Migration and Gender* (New Delhi: Sage, 2008).

2 The premium processing service offered by USCIS allows employers to pay an additional $1,225 fee to ensure that USCIS will review the H-1B the petition within fifteen days.

3 See the full text of the executive order here: "Buy American and Hire American; Presidential Documents," 82 *Federal Register* 76 (April 21, 2017): 18837–39.

4 The atrocities aimed at the South Asian community are too many to name here. Early examples of South Asian scapegoating date back to the Bellingham riots of 1907, which led to the expulsion of a significant number of Indians from communities along the Pacific coast. After 9/11, the rising number of attacks on and murders of Sikhs and Muslim South Asians and the 2012 massacre at a Sikh temple in Oak Creek, Wisconsin, are stark reminders of the long history and contemporary examples of violence aimed at South Asians in the US.

Bibliography

Abrams, Kerry. "What Makes the Family Special?" *University of Chicago Law Review* 80, no. 1 (2013): 7–28.

Adams, Kathleen M., and Sara Dickey. *Home and Hegemony: Domestic Service and Identity Politics in South and Southeast Asia*. Ann Arbor: University of Michigan Press, 2000.

Adams, Paul C., and Rina Ghose. "India.com: The Construction of a Space Between." *Progress in Human Geography* 27, no. 4 (2003): 414–37.

Adams, Paul C., and Emily Skop. "The Gendering of Asian Indian Transnationalism on the Internet." *Journal of Cultural Geography* 25, no. 2 (2008): 115–36.

Ahmed, Waquar, Amitabh Kundu, and Richard Peet. *India's New Economic Policy: A Critical Analysis*. New York: Routledge, 2011.

Ajrouch, Kristine J. "Social Isolation and Loneliness among Arab American Elders: Cultural, Social, and Personal Factors." *Research in Human Development* 5, no. 1 (2008): 44–59.

Amabile, Teresa, and Steven Kramer. "Do Happier People Work Harder?" *New York Times*, September 3, 2011.

Amcoff, Jan, and Thomas Niedomysl. "Is the Tied Returnee Male or Female? The Trailing Spouse Thesis Reconsidered." *Population, Space and Place* 21, no. 8 (2015): 872–81.

Amrith, Sunil. *Migration and Diaspora in Modern Asia*. Cambridge: Cambridge University Press, 2011.

Amrute, Sareeta Bipin. *Encoding Class, Encoding Race: Indian IT Workers in Berlin*. Durham, NC: Duke University Press, 2016.

———. "Living and Praying in the Code: The Flexibility and Discipline of Indian Information Technology Workers (ITers) in a Global Economy." *Anthropological Quarterly* 83, no. 3 (2010): 519–50.

———. "The 'New' Non-Residents of India: A Short History of the NRI." In *A New India? Critical Reflections in the Long Twentieth Century*, edited by Anthony P. D'Costa, 127–50. New York: Anthem Press, 2010.

Aneesh, A. "Rethinking Migration: High-Skilled Labor Flows from India to the United States." CCIS Working Paper 18, Center for Comparative Immigration Studies, University of California, San Diego, 2001.

Appadurai, Arjun. *Modernity at Large: Cultural Dimensions of Globalization*. Minneapolis: University of Minnesota Press, 1996.

Arbeit, Caren, and John Robert Warren. "Labor Market Penalties for Foreign Degrees among College Educated Immigrants." *Social Science Research* 42 (2013): 852–71.

Ascend. "The Illusion of Asian Success: Scant Progress for Minorities in Cracking the Glass Ceiling from 2007–2015." Report, 2017: 3. http://c.ymcdn.com/sites/www.ascend leadership.org/resource/resmgr/research/TheIllusionofAsianSuccess.pdf.

Baas, Michiel. "The IT Caste: Love and Arranged Marriages in the IT Industry of Bangalore." *South Asia: Journal of South Asian Studies* 32, no. 2 (2009): 285–307.

Bagchi, Ann. *Making Connections: A Study of Networking among Immigrant Professionals.* New York: LFB Scholarly Publishing, 2001.

Bald, Vivek. *Bengali Harlem and the Lost Histories of South Asian America.* Cambridge, MA: Harvard University Press, 2013.

Baldassar, Loretta. "Transnational Families and Aged Care: The Mobility of Care and the Migrancy of Ageing." *Journal of Ethnic and Migration Studies* 33, no. 2 (2007): 275–97.

Balgamwalla, Sabrina. "Bride and Prejudice: How U.S. Immigration Law Discriminates against Spousal Visa Holders." *Berkeley Journal of Gender, Law and Justice* 29, no. 1 (2014): 25–71.

Balk, Gene. "A Spike in King County Foreign-Born Populations." *Seattle Times*, October 5, 2015.

Banerjee, Pallavi. "Paradoxes of Patriarchy: South Asian Women in Ethnic Labor Markets." In *Immigrant Women Workers in the Neoliberal Age*, edited by Nilda Flores-González, 96–116. Urbana: University of Illinois Press, 2013.

Banerjee, Payal. "Indian Information Technology Workers in the United States: The H-1B Visa, Flexible Production, and the Racialization of Labor." *Critical Sociology* 32, no. 2/3 (2006): 425–45.

———. "Transnational Subcontracting, Indian IT Workers, and the U.S. Visa System." *Women's Studies Quarterly* 38, no. 1/2 (2010): 89–110.

Banerjee, Swapna M. *Men, Women, and Domestics: Articulating Middle-Class Identity in Colonial Bengal.* New York: Oxford University Press, 2004.

Bass, Dina. "America's Unwanted Ivy Leaguers Are Flocking to India." *Bloomberg News*, June 2, 2015. www.bloomberg.com/news/articles/2015-06-02/chasing-the-american -dream-in-india.

Bassett, Ross Knox. *The Technological Indian.* Cambridge, MA: Harvard University Press, 2016.

Basu, Anuradha, and Meghna Virick. "Silicon Valley's Indian Diaspora: Networking and Entrepreneurial Success." *South Asian Journal of Global Business Research* 4, no. 2 (2015): 190–208.

Basu, Aparna. *The Growth of Education and Political Development in India, 1898–1920.* Delhi: Oxford University Press, 1974.

Baviskar, Amita, and Raka Ray. *Elite and Everyman: The Cultural Politics of the Indian Middle Classes.* New York: Routledge, 2011.

Bendix, Aria. "Immigrant Arrests Are Up, but Deportation Is Down. *Atlantic*, May 17, 2017. www.theatlantic.com/news/archive/2017/05/under-trump-immigrants-arrests -are-up-but-deportation-is-down/527103.

Benhabib, Seyla, and Judith Resnik. *Migrations and Mobilities: Citizenship, Borders, and Gender.* New York: New York University Press, 2009.

Benjamin, Solomon. "Occupancy Urbanism: Radicalizing Politics and Economy beyond Policy and Programs." *International Journal of Urban and Regional Research* 32, no. 3 (2008): 719–29.

Berger, Lawrence M., and Jane Waldfogel. "Maternity Leave and the Employment of New Mothers in the United States." *Journal of Population Economics* 17, no. 2 (2004): 331–49.

Bergeron, Claire. *Going to the Back of the Line: A Primer on Lines, Visa Categories and Wait Times.* Washington, DC: Migration Policy Institute, 2013. Accessed July 25, 2017. www.migrationpolicy.org/research/going-back-line-primer-lines-visa-categories-and-wait-times.

Bevis, Teresa Brawner, and Christopher J. Lucas. *International Students in American Colleges and Universities: A History.* New York: Palgrave Macmillan, 2007.

Bhatnagar, Rashi. H-4 Visa: A Curse. Accessed August 1, 2017. www.facebook.com/H4 visaacurse/info/?entry_point=page_nav_about_item&tab=page_info.

Bhatt, Amy. "Resident 'Non-Resident' Indians: Gender, Labor and the Return to India." In *Transnational Migration and Asia: The Question of Return*, edited by Michel Baas, 55–72. Amsterdam: Amsterdam University Press, 2015.

Bhatt, Amy, and Nalini Iyer. *Roots and Reflections: South Asians in the Pacific Northwest.* Seattle: University of Washington Press, 2013.

Bhatt, Amy, Madhavi Murty, and Priti Ramamurthy. "Hegemonic Developments: New Indian Middle Class, Gendered Subalterns, and Diasporic Returnees in the Event of Neoliberalism." *Signs: Journal of Women in Culture and Society* 36, no. 1 (2010): 127–52.

Bhattacharjee, Anannya. "Immigrant Dreams and Nightmares: South Asian Domestic Workers in North America in a Time of Global Mobility." In *Trans-Status Subjects: Gender in the Globalization of South and Southeast Asia*, edited by Sonita Sarker and Esha Niyogi De, 289–308. Durham, NC: Duke University Press, 2002.

Bhattacharyya, Asmita, and Bhola Nath Ghosh. "Women in Indian Information Technology (IT) Sector: A Sociological Analysis." *Journal of Humanities and Social Science* 3, no. 6 (2012): 45–52.

Bhowmick, Nilanjana. "India's Opposition Leader Takes on Congress and Corruption." *Time Magazine*, January 20, 2014. http://world.time.com/2014/01/20/indias-opposition-leader-takes-on-congress-and-corruption.

Bhuyan, Rupaleem. "Navigating Immigration, Gender, and Domestic Violence: Domestic Violence Advocacy with Work Visa Holders." In *Body Evidence: Intimate Violence against South Asian Women in America*, edited by Shamita Das Dasgupta, 229–42. New Brunswick, NJ: Rutgers University Press, 2007.

———. "Reconstructing Citizenship in a Global Economy: How Restricting Immigrants from Welfare Undermines Social Rights for U.S. Citizens." *Journal of Sociology and Social Welfare* 37, no. 2 (2010): 63–85.

Biao, Xiang. "Gender, Dowry and the Migration System of Indian Information Technology Professionals." *Indian Journal of Gender Studies* 12, no. 2/3 (2005): 357–80.

———. *Global "Body Shopping": An Indian Labor System in the Information Technology Industry.* Princeton, NJ: Princeton University Press, 2007.

Billingham, Chase M., and Shelley McDonough Kimelberg. "Middle-Class Parents, Urban Schooling, and the Shift from Consumption to Production of Urban Space." *Sociological Forum* 28, no. 1 (2013): 85–108.

Biradavolu, Monica Rao. *Indian Entrepreneurs in Silicon Valley: The Making of a Transnational Techno-capitalist Class*. Amherst, NY: Cambria Press, 2008.

Bledsoe, Caroline. "Reproduction at the Margins: Migration and Legitimacy in the New Europe." *Demographic Research* Special Collection 3, no. 4 (2004): 85–116.

Boehm, Deborah A. *Intimate Migrations: Gender, Family, and Illegality among Transnational Mexicans*. New York: New York University Press, 2012.

———. "'Now I Am a Man and a Woman!' Gendered Moves and Migrations in a Transnational Mexican Community." *Latin American Perspectives* 35, no. 1 (2008): 16–30.

Bolaria, B. Singh, and Rosemary von Elling Bolaria. *International Labour Migrations*. Oxford: Oxford University Press, 1997.

Bragun, Magdalena. "The Golden Cage: How Immigration Law Turns Foreign Women into Involuntary Housewives." *Seattle University Law Review* 31, no. 4 (2008): 937–72.

Brenick, Alaina, and Rainer K. Silbereisen. "Leaving (for) Home: Understanding Return Migration from the Diaspora." *European Psychologist* 17, no. 2 (2012): 85–92.

Brosius, Christiane. "The Gated Romance of 'India Shining': Visualizing Urban Lifestyle in Advertisement of Residential Housing Development." In *Popular Culture in a Globalised India*, edited by K. Moti Gokulsing and Wimal Dissanayake, 174–91. New York: Routledge, 2009.

Cassen, Robert. *India: Population, Economy, Society*. London: Palgrave Macmillan, 1978.

Cattacin, Sandro, and Dagmar Domenig. "Why Do Transnationally Mobile People Volunteer? Insights from a Swiss Case Study." *Voluntas: International Journal of Voluntary and Nonprofit Organizations* 25, no. 3 (2014): 707–29.

Center for Studies of Developing Societies–Konrad Adeneur Stiftung. "Key Highlights from the CSDS-KAS Report 'Attitudes, Anxieties and Aspirations of India's Youth: Changing Patterns.'" New Delhi: CSDS-KAS, April 3, 2017. Accessed July 24, 2017, www.kas.de/wf/en/33.48472.

Chacko, Elizabeth. "From Brain Drain to Brain Gain: Reverse Migration to Bangalore and Hyderabad, India's Globalizing High Tech Cities." *GeoJournal* 68, no. 2/3 (2007): 131–40.

———. "Hybrid Sensibilities: Highly Skilled Asian Indians Negotiating Identity in Private and Public Spaces of Washington, DC." *Journal of Cultural Geography* 32, no. 1 (2015): 115–28.

Chacko, Elizabeth, and Paul Varghese. "Identity and Representations of Gated Communities in Bangalore, India." *Open House International* 34, no. 3 (2009): 57–64.

Chakravartty, Paula. "Flexible Citizens and the Internet: The Global Politics of Local High-Tech Development in India." *Emergences: Journal for the Study of Media and Composite Cultures* 11, no. 1 (2001): 69–88.

———. "Symbolic Analysts or Indentured Servants? Indian High-Tech Migrants in America's Information Economy." *Knowledge, Technology, and Policy* 19 no. 3 (2006): 27–43.

———. "Weak Winners of Globalization: Indian H-1B Workers in the American Information Economy." *AAPI Nexus* 3, no. 2 (2005): 59–84.

———. "White-Collar Nationalisms." *Social Semiotics* 16 no. 1 (2006): 39–55.

Chang, Stewart. "Dreams of My Father, Prison for My Mother: The H-4 Nonimmigrant Visa Dilemma and the Need for an 'Immigration-Status Spousal Support.'" *Asian Pacific American Law Journal* 19, no. 1 (2013): 1–28.

Charusheela, S. "'Empowering Work'? Bargaining Models Reconsidered." In *Toward a Feminist Philosophy of Economics*, edited by Drucilla K. Barker and Edith Kuiper, 287–303. New York: Routledge, 2009.

Chatterjee, Nilanjana, and Nancy Riley. "Planning an Indian Modernity: The Gendered Politics of Fertility Control." *Signs* 26, no. 3 (2001): 811–46.

Chatterji, Miabi. "Putting 'the Family' to Work: Managerial Discourses of Control in the Immigrant Service Sector." In *The Sun Never Sets: South Asian Migrants in an Age of US Power*, edited by Vivek Bald, Miabi Chatterji, Sujani Reddy, and Manu Vimalassery, 127–55. New York: New York University Press, 2013.

Chaudhury, Sudata Deb. "The American Dream: An Indian Version in the Age of Globalization." *Global Studies Journal* 5, no. 3 (2013): 122–38.

Cheng, Yuching Julia. "Bridging Immigration Research and Racial Formation Theory to Examine Contemporary Immigrant Identities." *Sociology Compass* 8, no. 6 (2014): 745–54.

Cherng, Hua-Yu Sebastian. "Social Isolation among Racial/Ethnic Minority Immigrant Youth." *Sociology Compass* 9, no. 6 (2015): 509–18.

Chettiar, Cicilia. "A Study of Need Satisfaction in Joint and Nuclear Families in Mumbai." *Journal of Psychosocial Research* 10, no. 1 (2015): 83–88.

Children's Rights and You. "About CRY Seattle." Accessed June 15, 2017. http://cryseattle.org.

Children's Rights and You Cry America. "About Child's Rights and You CRY America." Accessed June 15, 2017. http://america.cry.org/site/about-cry.html.

Chishti, Muzaffar and Stephen Yale-Loehr. "The Immigration Act of 1990: Unfinished Business a Quarter-Century Later." Washington, DC: Migration Policy Institute, 2016.

Chopra, Radhika. *Militant and Migrant: The Politics and Social History of Punjab*. New York: Routledge, 2011.

Chopra, Rohit. "Global Primordialities: Virtual Identity Politics in Online Hindutva and Online Dalit Discourse." *New Media and Society* 8, no. 2 (2006): 187–206.

Chu, Julie Y. *Cosmologies of Credit: Transnational Mobility and the Politics of Destination in China*. Durham, NC: Duke University Press, 2010.

Cline, Melanie. "Equal Rights? Not for 100,000+ American H-4 Visa Holders." *Equal Opportunities International* 22, no. 1 (2003): 46–49.

Conradson, David, and Alan Latham. "Transnational Urbanism: Attending to Everyday Practices and Mobilities." *Journal of Ethnic and Migration Studies* 31, no. 2 (2005): 227–33.

Cornia, Giovanni Andrea, and World Institute for Development Economics Research. *Inequality, Growth, and Poverty in an Era of Liberalization and Globalization*. New York: Oxford University Press, 2004.

Craig, Richard B. *The Bracero Program: Interest Groups and Foreign Policy*. Austin: University of Texas Press, 1971.

Culliton-González, Katherine. "Born in the Americas: Birthright Citizenship and Human Rights." *Harvard Human Rights Journal* 25, no. 1 (2012): 127–82.

Damani, Meghna. *Hearts Suspended.* Directed by Meghna Damani. Jersey City, NJ: Treasure Tower Films, 2007.

Das, Rupsayar. "Representation of Violence against Women in Indian Print Media: A Comparative Analysis." *Global Media Journal* 3, no. 1 (2012): 1–24.

Das Dasgupta, Shamita. "Women's Realities: Defining Violence against Women by Immigration, Race, and Class." In *Domestic Violence at the Margins: Readings on Race, Class, Gender, and Culture,* edited by Natalie J. Sokoloff and Christina Pratt, 56–70. New Brunswick, NJ: Rutgers University Press, 2005.

Dasgupta, Simanti. "Success, Market, Ethics." *Cultural Dynamics* 20, no. 3 (2008): 213–44.

Dasgupta, Swapan. "How the Non-Resident Indian Has Fallen from Grace." *Times of India,* August 16, 2009.

Davis, Theodore. "High-Skill Return Migration in the Technology, Medical, and Academic Sectors: The Case of India and the USA." *Diaspora Studies* 9, no. 1 (2016): 15–27.

D'Costa, Anthony P. *A New India: Critical Reflections in the Long Twentieth Century.* New York: Anthem Press, 2010.

Deb, Sandipan. *The IITians: The Story of a Remarkable Indian Institution and How Its Alumni Are Reshaping the World.* New Delhi: Viking, 2004.

De Henau, Jerome, and Susan Himmelweit. "Unpacking Within-Household Gender Differences in Partners' Subjective Benefits from Household Income." *Journal of Marriage and Family* 75, no. 3 (2013): 611–24.

Dhattiwala, Raheel. "Housewives on H-4 Visa Get Desperate on Chat Sites." *Times of India,* October 2, 2006.

Dittrich, Christoph. "Bangalore: Divided City under the Impact of Globalization." *Asian Journal of Water, Environment and Pollution* 2, no. 2 (2005): 23–30.

———. "Bangalore: Globalisation and Fragmentation in India's Hightech-Capital." *Asien* 103 (2007): 45–48.

———. "The Changing Food Scenario and the Middle Classes in the Emerging Mega City of Hyderabad/India." In *The New Middle Classes: Globalizing Lifestyles, Consumerism, and Environmental Concern,* edited by Hellmut Lange and Lars Meier, 289–303. Dordrecht: Springer, 2009.

D'Mello, Marisa. "Gendered Selves and Identities of Information Technology Professionals in Global Software Organizations in India." *Information Technology for Development* 12, no. 2 (2006): 131–58.

Dustmann, Christian. "Children and Return Migration." *Journal of Population Economics* 16, no. 4 (2003): 815–30.

Dutta, Debalina. "Negotiations of Cultural Identities by Indian Women Engineering Students in US Engineering Programmes." *Journal of Intercultural Communication Research* 45, no. 3 (2016): 177–95.

Economic Development Council of Seattle and King County. "King County Economy." Accessed July 20, 2017. www.edc-seaking.org/service/economic-data/economic-basics.

Ehrenreich, Barbara, and Arlie Russell Hochschild. *Global Woman: Nannies, Maids, and Sex Workers in the New Economy.* New York: Metropolitan Books, 2003.

Enchautegui, María E., and Cecilia Menjívar. "Paradoxes of Family Immigration Policy: Separation, Reorganization, and Reunification of Families under Current Immigration Laws." *Law and Policy* 37, no. 1/2 (2015): 32–60.

Engels, Friedrich. "The Origin of the Family, Private Property and the State." In *The Marx-Engels Reader,* edited by Robert C. Tucker, 734–59. New York: Norton, 1978.

Espiritu, Yen Le, and Diane L. Wolf. "The Paradox of Assimilation: Children of Filipino Immigrants in San Diego." In *Ethnicities: Children of Immigrants in America,* edited by Rubén G. Rumbaut and Alejandro Portes, 157–86. Berkeley: University of California Press, 2001.

"Expat Indian Men's Marriage Prospects Hit by Global Slowdown." *Economic Times,* January 20, 2009.

Fernandes, Leela. *India's New Middle Class: Democratic Politics in an Era of Economic Reform.* Minneapolis: University of Minnesota Press, 2006.

Folbre, Nancy, and Michael Bittman. *Family Time: The Social Organization of Care.* New York: Routledge, 2004.

Foley, Elise. "Deportation Separated Thousands of U.S.-Born Children from Parents in 2013." *Huffington Post.* June 25, 2014. www.huffingtonpost.com/2014/06/25/parents -deportation_n_5531552.html.

Fraad, Harriet, Stephen A. Resnick, and Richard D. Wolff. *Bringing It All Back Home: Class, Gender, and Power in the Modern Household: New Directions/Rethinking Marxism.* Boulder, CO: Pluto Press, 1994.

Franz, Margaret. "Will to Love, Will to Fear: The Emotional Politics of Illegality and Citizenship in the Campaign against Birthright Citizenship in the US." *Social Identities* 21, no. 2 (2015): 184–98.

Fuller, Christopher, and Haripriya Narasimhan. "Companionate Marriage in India: The Changing Marriage System in a Middle-Class Brahman Subcaste." *Journal of the Royal Anthropological Institute* 14, no. 4 (2008): 736–54.

———. "Marriage, Education, and Employment among Tamil Brahman Women in South India, 1891–2010." *Modern Asian Studies* 47, no. 1 (2013): 53–84.

———. *Tamil Brahmans: The Making of a Middle-Class Caste*: Chicago: University of Chicago Press, 2014.

Gabor, Elena. "Career as Sensemaking for Immigrant Women Engineers." *Journal of Ethnographic and Qualitative Research* 8, no. 2 (2014): 113–28.

Garcia-Rodriguez, Yolanda, Antonio Mihi-Ramirez, and Margarita Navarro-Pabsdorf. "Highly-Skilled Migration, Migrant Networks and the Prestige of Academic Institutions." *Engineering Economics* 26, no. 5 (2015): 500–506.

George, Sheba Mariam. *When Women Come First: Gender and Class in Transnational Migration.* Berkeley: University of California Press, 2005.

Glenn, Evelyn Nakano. *Unequal Freedom: How Race and Gender Shaped American Citizenship and Labor.* Cambridge, MA: Harvard University Press, 2005.

González-Ferrer, Amparo, Pau Baizán, Cris Beauchemin, Elisabeth Kraus, Bruno Schoumaker, and Richard Black. "Distance, Transnational Arrangements, and

Return Decisions of Senegalese, Ghanaian, and Congolese Migrants." *International Migration Review* 48, no. 4 (2014): 939–71.

Gopinath, Deepak. "Characterizing Indian Students Pursuing Global Higher Education: A Conceptual Framework of Pathways to Internationalization." *Journal of Studies in International Education* 19, no. 3 (2015): 283–305.

Greene, Jay. "India Draws Tech Dreamers Back Home." *Seattle Times*, November 28, 2015.

Grillo, Gina. *Between Cultures: Children of Immigrants in America*. Chicago: University of Chicago Press, 2004.

Gu, Chien-Juh. "Women's Status in the Context of International Migration." *Sociology Compass* 6, no. 6 (2012): 458–71.

Guo, Shibao. "Immigrants as Active Citizens: Exploring the Volunteering Experience of Chinese Immigrants in Vancouver." *Globalisation, Societies and Education* 12, no. 1 (2014): 51–70.

Gupta, Bishnupriya. "Where Have All the Brides Gone? Son Preference and Marriage in India over the Twentieth Century." *Economic History Review* 67, no. 1 (2014): 1–24.

Gupta, Namrata. "Indian Women in Doctoral Education in Science and Engineering: A Study of Informal Milieu at the Reputed Indian Institutes of Technology." *Science, Technology and Human Values* 32, no. 5 (2007): 507–33.

H-1B and L-1 Visa Fraud and Abuse Prevention Act of 2007. 110th U.S. Congress, 1st Session, S.1035.

H-1B and L-1 Visa Reform Act of 2009. 111th Congress, S. 887.

H-1B and L-1 Visa Reform Act of 2013. 113th Congress, 1st Session, S.600.

H-1B and L-1 Visa Reform Act of 2015. 114th Congress, S.2266.

Hairong, Yan. *New Masters, New Servants: Migration, Development, and Women Workers in China*. Durham, NC: Duke University Press, 2008.

Harding, Sandra G. *Sciences from Below: Feminisms, Postcolonialities, and Modernities*. Durham, NC: Duke University Press, 2008.

Harlow, Summer, and Dustin Harp. "Collective Action on the Web: A Cross-Cultural Study of Social Networking Sites and Online and Offline Activism in the United States and Latin America." *Information, Communication and Society* 15, no. 2 (2012): 196–216.

Hartmann, Heidi I. "The Family as the Locus of Gender, Class, and Political Struggle: The Example of Housework." *Signs* 6, no. 3 (1981): 366–94.

Harvey, David. "Globalization in Question." *Rethinking Marxism* 8, no. 4 (1995): 1–17.

Harvey, William S. "British and Indian Scientists in Boston Considering Returning to Their Home Countries." *Population, Space and Place* 15, no. 6 (2009): 493–508.

Hays, Sharon. *The Cultural Contradictions of Motherhood*. New Haven, CT: Yale University Press, 1996.

Hegde, Radha. "Food Blogs and the Digital Reimagination of South Asian Diasporic Publics." *South Asian Diaspora* 6, no. 1 (2014): 89–103.

Heinemann, Torsten, Ursula Naue, and Anna-Maria Tapaninen. "Verifying the Family? A Comparison of DNA Analysis for Family Reunification in Three European Countries (Austria, Finland and Germany)." *European Journal of Migration and Law* 15, no. 2 (2013): 183–202.

Hennessy, Rosemary. *Profit and Pleasure: Sexual Identities in Late Capitalism*. New York: Routledge, 2000.

Hewamanne, Sandya. "Threading Meaningful Lives: Respectability, Home Businesses and Identity Negotiations among Newly Immigrant South Asian Women." *Identities* 19, no. 3 (2012): 320–38.

Hewitson, Gillian. "Domestic Labor and Gender Identity: Are All Women Careers?" In *Toward a Feminist Philosophy of Economics*, edited by Drucilla K. Barker and Edith Kuiper, 266–84. New York: Routledge, 2003.

Himmelweit, Susan. "An Evolutionary Approach to Feminist Economics: Two Different Models of Caring." In *Toward a Feminist Philosophy of Economics*, edited by Drucilla K. Barker and Edith Kuiper, 247–65. New York: Routledge, 2003.

Ho, Elaine Lynn-Ee. "Identity Politics and Cultural Asymmetries: Singaporean Transmigrants 'Fashioning' Cosmopolitanism." *Journal of Ethnic and Migration Studies* 37, no. 5 (2011): 729–46.

Hochschild, Arlie. "Global Care Chains and Emotional Surplus Value." In *Global Capitalism*, edited by Will Hutton and Anthony Giddens, 130–46. New York: New Press, 2000.

Hoeffel, Elizabeth, Sonya Rastogi, Myoung Ouk Kim, and Hasan Shahid. "The Asian Population: 2010." U.S. Bureau of the Census. 2012. www.census.gov/library/publications/2012/dec/c2010br-11.html.

Hondagneu-Sotelo, Pierrette. *Doméstica: Immigrant Workers Cleaning and Caring in the Shadows of Affluence*. Berkeley: University of California Press, 2001.

——. *Gender and U.S. Immigration: Contemporary Trends*. Berkeley: University of California Press, 2003.

Honnutagi, Abdul Razak, Rajendra Sonar, and Subash Babu. "Quality Accreditation System for Indian Engineering Education Using Knowledge Management and System Dynamics." *International Journal of Quality Assurance in Engineering and Technology Education* 2, no. 3 (2012): 47–61.

Hsu, Madeline Y., and Ellen D. Wu. "'Smoke and Mirrors': Conditional Inclusion, Model Minorities, and the Pre-1965 Dismantling of Asian Exclusion." *Journal of American Ethnic History* 34, no. 4 (2015): 43–65.

Hookway, Nicholas. "'Entering the Blogosphere': Some Strategies for Using Blogs in Social Research." *Qualitative Research* 8, no. 1 (2008): 91–113.

Hurtado-de-Mendoza, Alejandra, Felisa Gonzales, Adriana Serrano, and Stacey Kaltman. "Social Isolation and Perceived Barriers to Establishing Social Networks among Latina Immigrants." *American Journal of Community Psychology* 53, no. 1/2 (2014): 73–82.

Immigration Act of 1990, Public Law 101–649, *U.S. Statutes at Large* 104 (1992): 4978.

Indo-Asian News Service. "Manmohan Singh's Address at Pravasi Bharatiya Divas." *India Forums*, January 8, 2008.

The Involuntary Housewife: Trapped!! Accessed July 20, 2017. https://trappedinh4mess.wordpress.com.

Iredale, Robyn. "Gender, Immigration Policies and Accreditation: Valuing the Skills of Professional Women Migrants." *Geoforum* 36 (2005): 155–66.

Ivanova, Vanya. "The Return Migration of Highly-Qualified Workers in Bulgaria and in Bosnia and Herzegovina: Policies and Returnees' Responses." *South East Europe Review* 18, no. 1 (2015): 93–111.

Jain, Anita N. "Imaginary Diasporas." *South Asian Diaspora* 8, no. 1 (2016): 1–14.

Jain, Shobhita. "Transmigrant Women's Agency and Indian Diaspora." *South Asian Diaspora* 2, no. 2 (2010): 185–200.

Jain, Sonali. "For Love and Money: Second-Generation Indian-Americans 'Return' to India." *Ethnic and Racial Studies* 36, no. 5 (2013): 896–914.

Jaiswal, Nimisha. "After Kansas, Indians Fear for the Safety of Their Loved Ones in Trump's America." *Public Radio International*, March 3, 2017. Accessed March 20, 2017. www.pri.org/stories/2017-03-03/after-kansas-indians-fear-safety-their-loved -ones-trumps-america.

Jensen, Joan. *Passage from India: Asian Indian Immigrants in North America*. New Haven, CT: Yale University Press, 1988.

Joseph, Manu. "Fighting to Shut out the Real India." *New York Times*, April 6, 2011.

Kalavar, Jyotsna, and J. Duvvuru. "Retirement Communities in Urban India." *Gerontologist* 48 (2008): 618.

Kalavar, Jyotsna, and D. Jamuna. "Aging of Indian Women in India: The Experience of Older Women in Formal Care Homes." *Journal of Women and Aging* 23, no. 3 (2011): 203–15.

Kamat, Sangeeta, Ali Mir, and Biju Mathew. "Producing Hi-Tech: Globalization, the State and Migrant Subjects." *Globalisation, Societies and Education* 2, no. 1 (2004): 5–23.

Kanungo, Sona. "Growth of Higher Education in India: Problems and Solutions." *Global Management Review* 9, no. 3 (2015): 53–60.

Kaplan, Sigal, Luise Grünwald, and Georg Hirte. "The Effect of Social Networks and Norms on the Inter-Regional Migration Intentions of Knowledge-Workers: The Case of Saxony, Germany." *Cities* 55 (2016): 61–69.

Kapur, Devesh, and John McHale. *Give Us Your Best and Brightest: The Global Hunt for Talent and Its Impact on the Developing World*. Washington, DC: Center for Global Development, 2005.

Kelkar, Govind, Girija Shrestha, and N. Veena N. "IT Industry and Women's Agency: Explorations in Bangalore and Delhi, India." *Gender, Technology and Development* 6, no. 1 (2002): 63–84.

———. "Women's Agency and the IT Industry in India." In *Gender and the Digital Economy: Perspectives from the Developing World*, edited by Cecilia Ng and Swasti Mitter, 110–31. Thousand Oaks, CA: Sage, 2005.

Khadria, Binod. *India Migration Report, 2010–2011: The Americas*. Cambridge: Cambridge University Press, 2012.

Khanal, Prakash. "Diasporic Shrines: Transnational Networks Linking South Asia through Pilgrimage and Welfare Development." In *Diaspora Engagement and Development in South Asia*, edited by Tan Tai Yong and Mizanur Rahman, 176–93. Hampshire: Palgrave Macmillan, 2013.

Khoo, Siew-Ean. "Attracting and Retaining Globally Mobile Skilled Migrants: Policy Challenges Based on Australian Research." *International Migration* 52, no. 2 (2014): 20–30.

Kim, Bum, Kristen Linton, and Wesley Lum. "Social Capital and Life Satisfaction among Chinese and Korean Elderly Immigrants." *Journal of Social Work* 15, no. 1 (2015): 87–100.

Kim, Minjeong. "'Forced' into Unpaid Carework: International Students' Wives in the United States." In *Global Dimensions of Gender and Carework*, edited by Mary K. Zimmerman, Jacquelyn S. Litt, and Christine E. Bose, 162–75. Stanford, CA: Stanford Social Sciences, 2006.

King, Anthony D. "Speaking from the Margins: 'Postmodernism,' Transnationalism, and the Imagining of Contemporary Indian Urbanity." In *Globalization and the Margins*, edited by Richard Grant and John R. Short, 72–90. London: Palgrave Macmillan, 2002.

King, Russell, and Anastasia Christou. "Second-Generation 'Return' to Greece: New Dynamics of Transnationalism and Integration." *International Migration* 52, no. 6 (2014): 85–99.

Kisselburgh, Lorraine G., Brenda L. Berkelaar, and Patrice M. Buzzanell. "Discourse, Gender, and the Meaning of Work: Rearticulating Science, Technology, and Engineering Careers through Communicative Lenses." *Communication Yearbook* 33 (2009): 259–300.

Kofman, Eleonore, and Parvati Raghuram. "Gender and Skilled Migrants: Into and beyond the Work Place." *Geoforum* 36, no. 2 (2005): 149–54.

———. "Women, Migration, and Care: Explorations of Diversity and Dynamism in the Global South." *Social Politics: International Studies in Gender* 19, no. 3 (2012): 408–32.

Konzett-Smoliner, Stefanie. "Return Migration as a 'Family Project': Exploring the Relationship between Family Life and the Readjustment Experiences of Highly Skilled Austrians." *Journal of Ethnic and Migration Studies* 42, no. 7 (2016): 1094–1114.

Koshy, Susan, and Rajagopala Radhakrishnan. *Transnational South Asians: The Making of a Neo-Diaspora*. New York: Oxford University Press, 2008.

Kōu, Anu, and Ajay Bailey. "'Movement Is a Constant Feature in My Life': Contextualising Migration Processes of Highly Skilled Indians." *Geoforum* 52 (2014): 113–22.

Kreisberg, Nicole. "H-1B Jobs: Filling the Skills Gap." Research brief. Great Barrington, MA: American Institute for Economic Research, 2014. www.aier.org/research/h1b -jobs-filling-skill-gap.

Kulkarni, Veena S. "Her Earnings: Exploring Variation in Wives' Earning Contributions across Six Major Asian Groups and Whites." *Social Science Research* 52 (2015): 539–55.

Kumar, B. Venkatesh, David L. Finegold, Anne-Laure Winkler, and Vikas Argod. "Will They Return? The Willingness of Potential Faculty to Return to India and the Key Factors Affecting Their Decision." Paper, Institute of Social Sciences, Penn State, and Rutgers School of Management and Labor Relations, 2011.

Kumar, Perveen, Uttam Bhattacharya, and Jayanta K. Nayek. "Return Migration and Development: Evidence from India's Skilled Professionals." In *Indian Skilled Migration and Development: To Europe and Back*, edited by Gabriela Tejada, Uttam Bhattacharya, Binod Khadria, and Christiane Kuptsch, 263–84. New York: Springer, 2014.

Kuşçu, Işık. "Ethnic Return Migration and Public Debate: The Case of Kazakhstan." *International Migration* 52, no. 2 (2014): 178–97.

Lal, Brij V., Peter Reeves, and Rajesh Rai. *The Encyclopedia of the Indian Diaspora*. Honolulu: University of Hawaii Press, 2006.

Lee, Catherine. "Family Reunification and the Limits of Immigration Reform: Impact and Legacy of the 1965 Immigration Act." *Sociological Forum* 30 (2015): 528–48.

Lee, Erika. *The Making of Asian America: A History.* New York: Simon and Schuster, 2015.

Lee, Young-joo, and Seong-Gin Moon. "Mainstream and Ethnic Volunteering by Korean Immigrants in the United States." *Voluntas: International Journal of Voluntary and Nonprofit Organizations* 22, no. 4 (2011): 811–30.

Leonard, Karen Isaksen. *Making Ethnic Choices: California's Punjabi Mexican Americans.* Philadelphia: Temple University Press, 1992.

Li, Wei. *Ethnoburb: The New Ethnic Community in Urban America.* Honolulu: University of Hawaii Press, 2009.

Li, Wei, and Lucia Lo. "New Geographies of Migration: A Canada-U.S. Comparison of Highly Skilled Chinese and Indian Migration." *Journal of Asian American Studies* 15, no. 1 (2012): 1–34.

Liu, Lisong. *Chinese Student Migration and Selective Citizenship: Mobility, Community and Identity between China and the United States.* New York: Routledge, 2015.

———. "Return Migration and Selective Citizenship: A Study of Returning Chinese Professional Migrants from the United States." *Journal of Asian American Studies* 15, no. 1 (2012): 35–68.

Liu, Mao-Mei. "Migrant Networks and International Migration: Testing Weak Ties." *Demography* 50, no. 4 (2013): 1243–77.

Lodhia, Sharmila. "Brides without Borders: New Topographies of Violence and the Future of Law in an Era of Transnational Citizen-Subjects." *Columbia Journal of Gender and Law* 19, no. 3 (2010): 703–46.

———. "Constructing an Imperfect Citizen-Subject: Globalization, National 'Security,' and Violence against South Asian Women." *Women's Studies Quarterly* 38, no. 1/2 (2010): 161–76.

———. "From 'Living Corpse' to India's Daughter: Exploring the Social, Political and Legal Landscape of the 2012 Delhi Gang Rape." *Women's Studies International Forum* 50 (2015): 89–101.

Lopez, Lori Kido. "The Radical Act of 'Mommy Blogging': Redefining Motherhood through the Blogosphere." *New Media and Society* 11, no. 5 (2009): 729–47.

Lowe, Lisa. *Immigrant Acts: On Asian American Cultural Politics.* Durham, NC: Duke University Press, 1996.

Luibhéid, Eithne. *Entry Denied: Controlling Sexuality at the Border.* Minneapolis: University of Minnesota Press, 2002.

Lung-Amam, Willow. "Malls of Meaning: Building Asian America in Silicon Valley Suburbia," *Journal of American Ethnic History* 34, no. 2 (2015): 18–53.

Luthra, Renee Reichl. "Temporary Immigrants in a High-Skilled Labour Market: A Study of H-1Bs." *Journal of Ethnic and Migration Studies* 35, no. 2 (2009): 227–50.

Maira, Sunaina. *Desis in the House: Indian American Youth Culture in New York City.* Philadelphia: Temple University Press, 2002.

Mallapragada, Madhavi. *Virtual Homelands: Indian Immigrants and Online Cultures in the United States.* Urbana: University of Illinois Press, 2014.

Man, Guida C. "Gender, Work and Migration: Deskilling Chinese Immigrant Women in Canada." *Women's Studies International Forum* 27, no. 2 (2004): 135–48.

Manohar, Namita N. "Mothering for Class and Ethnicity: The Case of Indian Professional Immigrants in the United States." *Advances in Gender Research* 17 (2013): 159–85.

Manohar, Namita N., and Erika Busse-Cárdenas. "Valuing 'Good' Motherhood in Migration." *Journal of the Motherhood Initiative for Research and Community Involvement* 2, no. 2 (2011): 175–95.

Masferrer, Claudia, and Bryan Roberts. "Going Back Home? Changing Demography and Geography of Mexican Return Migration." *Population Research and Policy Review* 31, no. 4 (2012): 465–96.

Mathews, Elsa. "Life's a Full Stop for Women with H-4 US Visas." *NewsBlaze,* June 24, 2009. Accessed July 20, 2017. http://newsblaze.com/world/south-asia/lifes-a-full-stop -for-women-with-h-4-us-visas_9686.

McEvoy, Jamie, Peggy Petrzelka, Claudia Radel, and Birgit Schmook. "Gendered Mobility and Morality in a South-Eastern Mexican Community: Impacts of Male Labour Migration on the Women Left Behind." *Mobilities* 7, no. 3 (2012): 369–88.

McKay, Ramah. "Migration Information Source: Family Reunification." Last modified May 1, 2003. Washington, DC: Migration Policy Institute. www.migrationpolicy.org /article/family-reunification.

Meares, Carina. "A Fine Balance: Women, Work and Skilled Migration." *Women's Studies International Forum* 33, no. 5 (2010): 473–81.

Mehrotra, Meeta, and Toni M. Calasanti. "The Family as a Site for Gendered Ethnic Identity Work among Asian Indian Immigrants." *Journal of Family Issues* 31, no. 6 (2010): 778–807.

Microsoft Corporation. "Facts about Microsoft | News Center." Accessed August 1, 2017. http://news.microsoft.com/facts-about-microsoft/#sm.0001accybzkz7eq2r9j254pfn 28s7.

———. Microsoft Family Immigration Network. Accessed March 1, 2010. http://msim migrationfamily.com/Home/tabid/36/%20Default.aspx.

Mies, Maria. *Patriarchy and Accumulation on a World Scale: Women in the International Division of Labour.* Atlantic Highlands, NJ: Zed Books, 1986.

Mirchandani, Kiran. "Pockets of the West: The Engagement of the Virtual Diaspora in India." In *Diaspora Engagement and Development in South Asia*, edited by Mizanur Rahman and Tai Yong Tan 231–45. Hampshire: Palgrave Macmillan, 2013.

Mithas, Sunil, and Henry C. Lucas. "Are Foreign IT Workers Cheaper? U.S. Visa Policies and Compensation of Information Technology Professionals." *Management Science* 56, no. 5 (2010): 745–65.

Mitra, Ananda. "Creating Immigrant Identities in Cybernetic Space: Examples from a Non-Resident Indian Website." *Media, Culture and Society* 27, no. 3 (2005): 371–90.

Mitra, Kalita S. "Immigrant Wives' Visa Status Keeps Them out of Workplace." *Washington Post*, October 3, 2005.

———. *Suburban Sahibs: Three Immigrant Families and Their Passage from India to America.* New Brunswick, NJ: Rutgers University Press, 2003.

Monger, Randall, and James Yankay. "U.S. Legal Permanent Residents: 2011." Washington, DC: US Department of Homeland Security, Office of Immigration Statistics, 2012. www.dhs.gov/xlibrary/assets/statistics/publications/lpr_fr_2011.pdf.

Moskal, Marta. "Transnationalism and the Role of Family and Children in Intra-European Labour Migration." *European Societies* 13, no. 1 (2011): 29–50.

Murthy, Dhiraj. "Digital Ethnography: An Examination of the Use of New Technologies for Social Research." *Sociology* 42, no. 5 (2008): 837–55.

Nandi, Ravi, Wolfgang Bokelmann, Nithya Vishwanath Gowdru, and Gustavo Dias. "Consumer Motives and Purchase Preferences for Organic Food Products: Empirical Evidence from a Consumer Survey in Bangalore, South India." *Journal of International Food and Agribusiness Marketing* 28, no. 1 (2016): 74–99.

Narayana, M. R. "Globalization and Urban Economic Growth: Evidence for Bangalore, India." *International Journal of Urban and Regional Research* 35, no. 6 (2011): 1284–1301.

National Association of Software and Service Companies. "India IT-BPM Overview." Accessed June 30, 2017. www.nasscom.in/indian-itbpo-industry.

Naujoks, Daniel. *Migration, Citizenship, and Development: Diasporic Membership Policies and Overseas Indians in the United States.* London: Oxford University Press, 2013.

Nehru, Jawaharlal, Sarvepalli Gopal, and Uma Iyengar. *The Essential Writings of Jawaharlal Nehru.* New Delhi: Oxford University Press, 2003.

Ng, Cheuk Fan, and Herbert C. Northcott. "The Ethnic and National Identity of South Asian Immigrant Seniors Living in Edmonton, Canada." *Canadian Ethnic Studies* 41, no. 3 (2010): 131–56.

Ng, Tina Kin, Tina Rochelle, Steven Shardlow, and Sik Hung Ng. "A Transnational Bicultural Place Model of Cultural Selves and Psychological Citizenship: The Case of Chinese Immigrants in Britain." *Journal of Environmental Psychology* 40 (2014): 440–50.

Oh, Christine J., and Nadia Y. Kim. "Success is Relative." *Sociological Perspectives* 59, no. 2 (2016): 270–95.

Okin, Susan Moller. *Justice, Gender, and the Family.* New York: Basic Books, 1989.

Ong, Aihwa. "Boundary Crossings: Neoliberalism as a Mobile Technology." *Transactions of the Institute of British Geographers* 32, no. 1 (2007): 3–8.

———. "Cultural Citizenship as Subject-Making: Immigrants Negotiate Racial and Cultural Boundaries in the United States." *Current Anthropology* 37, no. 5 (1996): 737–62.

———. *Flexible Citizenship: The Cultural Logics of Transnationality.* Durham, NC: Duke University Press, 1999.

Pal, Joyojeet, Priyank Chandra, and V. G. Vinod Vidyaswaran. "Twitter and the Rebranding of Narendra Modi." *Economic and Political Weekly* 51, no. 8 (2016): 52–60.

Palriwala, Rajni, and Patricia Uberoi, eds. *Marriage, Migration and Gender.* New Delhi: Sage, 2008.

Panagariya, Arvind. 2008. *India: The Emerging Giant:* New York: Oxford University Press, 2008.

Parreñas, Rhacel Salazar. *The Force of Domesticity: Filipina Migrants and Globalization.* New York: New York University Press, 2008.

———. *Servants of Globalization: Women, Migration and Domestic Work.* Stanford, CA: Stanford University Press, 2001.

Passel, Jeffrey, and Paul Taylor. *Unauthorized Immigrants and Their U.S.-Born Children.* Pew Hispanic Center, August 11, 2010. Accessed July 24, 2017. www.pewhispanic.org /2010/08/11/unauthorized-immigrants-and-their-us-born-children.

Percival, John. *Return Migration in Later Life.* Chicago: University of Chicago Press, 2013.

Pickert, Kate. "Dispelling 'Anchor Baby' Myths." *Time Magazine,* August 11, 2010. http:// swampland.time.com/2010/08/11/dispelling-anchor-baby-myths.

Pido, Eric J. "The Performance of Property: Suburban Homeownership as a Claim to Citizenship for Filipinos in Daly City." *Journal of Asian American Studies* 15, no. 1 (2012): 69–104.

Piper, Nicola, and Mina Roces. *Wife or Worker? Asian Women and Migration, Asia/ Pacific/Perspectives.* Lanham, MD: Rowman and Littlefield, 2003.

Prashad, Vijay. *The Karma of Brown Folk.* Minneapolis: University of Minnesota Press, 2000.

Puri, Jyoti. *Woman, Body, Desire in Post-colonial India: Narratives of Gender and Sexuality.* New York: Routledge, 1999.

Purkayastha, Bandana. *Negotiating Ethnicity: Second-Generation South Asian Americans Traverse a Transnational World.* New Brunswick, NJ: Rutgers University Press, 2005.

———. "Skilled Migration and Cumulative Disadvantage: The Case of Highly Qualified Asian Indian Immigrant Women in the US." *Geoforum* 36, no. 2 (2005): 181–96.

R2I-ed Blogger. "Dirty, Sexy, Wealthy India." 2009. http://r2i-thestorysofar.blogspot.com /2009/09/dirty-sexy-wealthy-india.html.

Radhakrishnan, Smitha. *Appropriately Indian: Gender and Culture in a New Transnational Class.* Durham, NC: Duke University Press, 2011.

———. "Examining the 'Global' Indian Middle Class: Gender and Culture in the Silicon Valley/Bangalore Circuit." *Journal of Intercultural Studies* 29, no. 1 (2008): 7–20.

———. "Professional Women, Good Families: Respectable Femininity and the Cultural Politics of a 'New' India." *Qualitative Sociology* 32, no. 2 (2009): 195–212.

Raghuram, Parvati. "The Difference That Skills Make: Gender, Family Migration Strategies and Regulated Labour Markets." *Journal of Ethnic and Migration Studies* 30, no. 2 (2004): 303–21.

———. "Migration, Gender, and the IT Sector: Intersecting Debates." *Women's Studies International Forum* 27, no. 2 (2004): 163–76.

Raghuram, Parvati, Ajaya Kumar Sahoo, Brij Maharaj, and Dave Sangha. *Tracing an Indian Diaspora: Contexts, Memories, Representations.* New York: Sage, 2008.

Rajan, Gita, and Shailja Sharma, eds. *New Cosmopolitanisms: South Asians in the US.* Stanford, CA: Stanford University Press, 2006.

Rajan, Rajeswari Sunder. *Real and Imagined Women: Gender, Culture, and Postcolonialism.* New York: Routledge, 1993.

Ravuri, Evelyn D. "Return Migration Predictors for Undocumented Mexican Immigrants Living in Dallas." *Social Science Journal* 51 (2014): 35–43.

Ray, Manashi. "The Global Circulation of Skill and Capital: Pathways of Return Migration of Indian Entrepreneurs from the United States to India." In *Diaspora*

Engagement and Development in South Asia, edited by Mizanur Rahman and Tai Yong Tan, 75–102. Hampshire: Palgrave Macmillan, 2013.

Ray, Raka, and Seemin Qayum. *Cultures of Servitude: Modernity, Domesticity, and Class in India*. Stanford, CA: Stanford University Press, 2009.

Rayaprol, Aparna. *Negotiating Identities: Women in the Indian Diaspora*. New York: Oxford University Press, 1997.

Razack, Sherene. *Looking White People in the Eye: Gender, Race, and Culture in Courtrooms and Classrooms*. Toronto: University of Toronto Press, 1998.

Reddy, Chandan. "Asian Diasporas, Neoliberalism, and Family: Reviewing the Case for Homosexual Asylum in the Context of Family Rights." *Social Text* 23, no. 3/4 (2005): 101–20.

Reddy, Sujani. *Nursing and Empire: Gendered Labor and Migration from India to the United States*. Chapel Hill: University of North Carolina, 2015.

Rouse, Roger. "Making Sense of Settlement: Class Transformation, Cultural Struggle, and Transnationalism among Mexican Migrants in the United States." In *Towards a Transnational Perspective on Migration: Race, Class, Ethnicity, and Nationalism Reconsidered*, edited by Nina Glick Schiller, Linda G. Basch, and Cristina Szanton Blanc, 25–52. New York: New York Academy of Sciences, 1992.

Roy, Srirupa. "'A Symbol of Freedom': The Indian Flag and the Transformations of Nationalism, 1906–2002." *Journal of Asian Studies* 65, no. 3 (2006): 495–527.

Rubenstein, Edwin. "Legal Immigration: The Bigger Problem." *Social Contract* 17, no. 4 (2007): 258–59.

Rudrappa, Sharmila. "Braceros and Techno-braceros: Guest Workers in the United States and the Commodification of Low-Wage and High-Wage Labour." In *Transnational South Asians: The Making of a Neo-Diaspora*, edited by Susan Koshy and R. Radhakrishnan, 291–324. New York: Oxford University Press, 2008.

———. "Law's Culture and Cultural Difference." In *Body Evidence: Intimate Violence against South Asian Women in America*, edited by Shamita Das Dasgupta, 181–94. New Brunswick, NJ: Rutgers University Press, 2007.

Rumbaut, Rubén G., and Alejandro Portes, eds. *Ethnicities: Children of Immigrants in America*. Berkeley: University of California Press, 2001.

Sagebiel, Julian, and Kai Rommel. "Preferences for Electricity Supply Attributes in Emerging Megacities: Policy Implications from a Discrete Choice Experiment of Private Households in Hyderabad, India." *Energy for Sustainable Development* 21 (2014): 89–99.

Sanchez-Mazas, Margarita, and Olivier Klein. "Social Identity and Citizenship: Introduction to the Special Issue." *Psychologica Belgica* 43, no. 1/2 (2003): 1–8.

Sargent, Lydia. *Women and Revolution: A Discussion of the Unhappy Marriage of Marxism and Feminism*. Boston: South End Press, 1981.

Sassen, Saskia. "The Repositioning of Citizenship: Emergent Subjects and Spaces for Politics." *CR: The New Centennial Review* 3, no. 2 (2003): 41–66.

Sastry, Chandrashekhar. *The Non-resident Indian: From Non-being to Being*. Bangalore: Panther Publishers, 1991.

Satzewich, Vic. "Canadian Visa Officers and the Social Construction of 'Real' Spousal Relationships." *Canadian Review of Sociology* 51, no. 1 (2014): 1–21.

Saxenian, AnnaLee. *The New Argonauts: Regional Advantage in a Global Economy.* Cambridge, MA: Harvard University Press, 2006.

———. *Silicon Valley's New Immigrant Entrepreneurs.* San Francisco: Public Policy Institute of California, 1999.

———. "Silicon Valley's New Immigrant High-Growth Entrepreneurs." *Economic Development Quarterly* 16, no. 1 (2002): 20–31.

Schiller, Nina Glick, Linda G. Basch, and Cristina Blanc-Szanton. *Nations Unbound: Transnational Projects, Postcolonial Predicaments, and Deterritorialized Nation-States.* New York: Routledge, 1994.

Schiller, Nina Glick, and Georges Fouron. "Long-distance Nationalism Defined." In *The Anthropology of Politics: A Reader in Ethnography, Theory, and Critique,* edited by Joan Vincent, 356–64. Malden, MA: Blackwell, 2002.

Seol, Dong-Hoon, and John D. Skrentny. "Why Is There So Little Migrant Settlement in East Asia?" *International Migration Review* 43, no. 3 (2009): 578–620.

Shade, Leslie Regan, and Jenna Jacobson. "Hungry for the Job: Gender, Unpaid Internships, and the Creative Industries." *Sociological Review* 63, no. 1 (2015): 188–205.

Shah, Shivali. "Middle Class, Documented, and Helpless: The H-4 Visa Bind." In *Body Evidence: Intimate Violence against South Asian Women in America,* edited by Shamita Das Dasgupta, 195–210. New Brunswick, NJ: Rutgers University Press, 2007.

Sharma, Aradhana. *Logics of Empowerment: Development, Gender, and Governance in Neoliberal India.* Minneapolis: University of Minnesota Press, 2008.

Singh, Shalini. "Reverse Marriage Drain." *Hindustan Times,* January 23, 2012.

Skrentny, John D., Stephanie Chan, Jon Fox, and Denis Kim. "Defining Nations in Asia and Europe: A Comparative Analysis of Ethnic Return Migration Policy." *International Migration Review* 41, no. 4 (2007): 793–825.

Sneed, Tierney. "Why Ending Birthright Citizenship Would Be Terrible for Silicon Valley." *Talking Points Memo.* August 25, 2015. Accessed August 5, 2016. http://talking pointsmemo.com/dc/birthright-citizenship-techcommunity.

Society for Human Resources Management. "Internships." November 6, 2013. www .shrm.org/hr-today/trends-and-forecasting/research-and-surveys/pages/shrm-2013 -internships.aspx.

Sohoni, Deenesh. "Unsuitable Suitors: Anti-Miscegenation Laws, Naturalization Laws, and the Construction of Asian Identities." *Law and Society Review* 41 no. 3 (2007): 587–618.

Spitzer, Denise, Anne Neufeld, Margaret Harrison, Karen Hughes, and Miriam Stewart. "Caregiving in Transnational Context: 'My Wings Have Been Cut; Where Can I Fly?'" In *Global Dimensions of Gender and Carework,* edited by Mary K. Zimmerman, Jacquelyn S. Litt, and Christine E. Bose, 176–94. Stanford, CA: Stanford University Press, 2006.

Sreeleakha, P. "Managing Culture Shock and Reverse Culture Shock of Indian Citizenship Employees." *International Journal of Management Practice* 7, no. 3 (2014): 250–74.

Stepick, Alex, Carol Dutton Stepick, Emmanuel Eugene, Deborah Teed, and Yves Labissiere. "Shifting Identities and Intergenerational Conflict: Growing up Haitian in Miami." In *Ethnicities: Children of Immigrants in America*, edited by Rubén G. Rumbaut and Alejandro Portes, 229–66. Berkeley: University of California Press, 2001.

Stevens, Harry. "Indian Women Are Rapidly Leaving the Workplace." *Hindustan Times*, June 29, 2016.

Stone, Pamela. *Opting Out? Why Women Really Quit Careers and Head Home*. Berkeley: University of California Press, 2007.

Sun, Ken Chih-Yan. "Transnational Kinscription: A Case of Parachute Kids in the USA and Their Parents in Taiwan." *Journal of Ethnic and Migration Studies* 40, no. 9 (2013): 1431–49.

Takaki, Ronald T. *Strangers from a Different Shore: A History of Asian Americans*. Boston: Little, Brown, 1989.

Tejaswi, Mini Joseph. "Bangalore Third Richest City in Country." *Times of India*. January 4, 2007.

Thapan, Meenakshi. *Transnational Migration and the Politics of Identity, Women and Migration in Asia*. Thousand Oaks, CA: Sage, 2005.

Tharu, Susie, and Tejaswini Niranjana. "Problems for a Contemporary Theory of Gender." *Subaltern Studies* 9 (1996): 232–60.

Thomas, Jayan Jose. "An Uneasy Coexistence: The New and the Old in Indian Industry and Services." In *A New India? Critical Reflections in the Long Twentieth Century*, edited by Anthony P. D'Costa, 71–98. New York: Anthem Press, 2010.

Thompson, Lynn. "Bellevue Schools Engage Influx of Tech-Sector Immigrants' Children." *Seattle Times*, February 16, 2015.

———. "Identity Crisis: Wives of Immigrant Tech Workers Struggle to Find Purpose." *Seattle Times Pacific NW Magazine*. August 28, 2015. www.seattletimes.com/pacific-nw-magazine/while-their-husbands-work-immigrant-wives-often-struggle-in-this-new-land.

Torres, Rebecca M., and Lindsey Carte. "Migration and Development? The Gendered Costs of Migration on Mexico's Rural 'Left Behind.'" *Geographical Review* 106, no. 3 (2016): 399–420.

The Ugly Indian (2010). Accessed July 8, 2017. www.theuglyindian.com/intro1.html.

United Nations. "International Migration Report 2013." New York: Department of Economic and Social Affairs, Population Division, 2013. www.un.org/en/development/desa/population/publications/migration/migration-report-2013.shtml.

United Nations General Assembly. "International Covenant on Economic, Social and Cultural Rights." December 16, 1966. www.ohchr.org/EN/ProfessionalInterest/Pages/CESCR.aspx.

Upadhya, Carol. "Controlling Offshore Knowledge Workers: Power and Agency in India's Software Outsourcing Industry." *NTW New Technology, Work, and Employment* 24, no. 1 (2009): 2–18.

———. "Software and the 'New' Middle Class in the 'New India.'" In *Elite and Everyman: The Cultural Politics of the Indian Middle Class*, edited by Amita Baviskar and Raka Ray, 167–92. New Delhi: Routledge, 2011.

Upadhya, Carol, and Aninhalli R. Vasavi. "Work, Culture, and Sociality in the Indian IT Industry: A Sociological Study." Bangalore: National Institute of Advanced Studies, August 2006. Accessed June 24, 2015. http://eprints.nias.res.in/107.

US Citizenship and Immigration Services. "DHS Extends Eligibility for Employment Authorization to Certain H-4 Dependent Spouses of H-1B Nonimmigrants Seeking Employment Based Lawful Permanent Residence." US Department of Homeland Security. Accessed July 21, 2017. www.uscis.gov/working-united-states/temporary -workers/employment-authorization-certain-h-4-dependent-spouses.

———. "H-1B Specialty Occupations, DOD Cooperative Research and Development Project Workers, and Fashion Models." US Department of Homeland Security, April 3, 2017. Accessed July 20, 2017. www.uscis.gov/working-united-states/temporary -workers/h-1b-specialty-occupations-dod-cooperative-research-and-development -project-workers-and-fashion-models.

———. "Number of H-1B Filings." 2017. Accessed October 13, 2017. www.uscis.gov/sites/ default/files/USCIS/Resources/Reports%20and%20Studies/Immigration%20Forms %20Data/BAHA/h-1b-2007-2017-trend-tables.pdf.

US Consulate General Chennai. "Child and Family Matters." Accessed May 2, 2010. http://chennai.usconsulate.gov/childfamily.html.

US Congress. Senate. Committee on the Judiciary United States Senate. *Testimony of Karen Panetta on How Comprehensive Immigration Reform Should Address the Needs of Women and Families*. 113th Cong, 1st sess., March 18, 2013.

Usdansky, Margaret L., and Thomas J. Espenshade. "The H-1B Visa Debate in Historical Perspective: The Evolution of U.S. Policy toward Foreign-Born Workers." Working Paper 11, Center for Comparative Immigration Studies, San Diego, May 2000. http:// escholarship.org/uc/item/8qf435d5#page-1.

US Department of State. "Report of the Visa Office 2016." Washington, DC: US Department of State, Bureau of Security and Consular Affairs, 2016. https://travel.state.gov /content/visas/en/law-and-policy/statistics/annual-reports/report-of-the-visa-office -2016.html.

Ustinova, Anastasia. "Indian Women Isolated in Silicon Valley." *San Francisco Chronicle*, March 9, 2008.

Van Laer, Koen, and Maddy Janssens. "Between the Devil and the Deep Blue Sea: Exploring the Hybrid Identity Narratives of Ethnic Minority Professionals." *Scandinavian Journal of Management* 30 (2014): 186–96.

Varadarajan, Latha. *The Domestic Abroad: Diasporas in International Relations*. New York: Oxford University Press, 2010.

Varma, Roli. "Exposure, Training, and Environment: Women's Participation in Computing Education in the United States and India." *Journal of Women and Minorities in Science and Engineering* 15, no. 3 (2009): 205–22.

———. *Harbingers of Global Change: India's Techno-Immigrants in the United States*. Lanham, MD: Lexington Books, 2006.

———. "Why So Few Women Enroll in Computing? Gender and Ethnic Differences in Students' Perception." *Computer Science Education* 20, no. 4 (2010): 301–16.

Varma, Roli, and Deepak Kapur. "Comparative Analysis of Brain Drain, Brain Circulation and Brain Retain: A Case Study of Indian Institutes of Technology." *Journal of Comparative Policy Analysis* 15, no. 4 (2013): 315–30.

Varshney, Deepanjana. "The Return of the Natives: Asian Diaspora Issues and Dilemmas; The Case of India." *African and Asian Studies* 12, no. 3 (2013): 290–321.

Verma, Ashish, T. M. Rahul, and Malvika Dixit. "Sustainability Impact Assessment of Transportation Policies: A Case Study for Bangalore City." *Case Studies on Transport Policy* 3, no. 3 (2015): 321–30.

Vogel, Ann, and Iain Lang. "Working in the Age of Flexibility: The 'Crisis of Work' and the Meaning of Volunteering." Paper presented at the American Sociological Association 101th Annual Conference, Montreal, Canada, 2006.

Wadhwa, Vivek. "An Outflow of Talent: Nativism and the US Reverse Brain Drain." *Harvard International Review* 31, no. 1 (2009): 76–80.

———. "A Reverse Brain Drain." *Issues in Science and Technology* 25, no. 3 (2009): 45–52.

Werbner, Pnina. "Global Pathways: Working Class Cosmopolitans and the Creation of Transnational Ethnic Worlds." *Social Anthropology* 7, no. 1 (1999): 17–35.

Wilson-Forsberg, Stacey, and Bharati Sethi. "The Volunteering Dogma and Canadian Work Experience: Do Recent Immigrants Volunteer Voluntarily?" *Canadian Ethnic Studies Journal* 47, no. 3 (2015): 91–110.

Wong, Madeleine. "Navigating Return: The Gendered Geographies of Skilled Return Migration to Ghana." *Global Networks* 14, no. 4 (2014): 438–57.

Woszczynski, Amy B., Pamila Dembla, and Humayun Zafar. "Gender-Based Differences in Culture in the Indian IT Workplace." *International Journal of Information Management* 36, no. 4 (2016): 507–19.

Yarow, Jay. "A Tour of Microsoft's Truly Gigantic, Sprawling Headquarters." *Business Insider*, Accessed July 23, 2017. www.businessinsider.com/a-tour-of-microsofts-truly -gigantic-sprawling-headquarters-2013-7.

Yeates, Nicola. 2011. "Going Global: The Transnationalization of Care." *Development and Change* 42, no. 4 (2011): 1109–30.

Yeoh, Brenda, and Katie Willis. "Singaporeans in China: Transnational Women Elites and the Negotiation of Gendered Identities." *Geoforum* 36, no. 2 (2005): 211–22.

Yong, Tan Tai, and Mizanur Rahman. *Diaspora Engagement and Development in South Asia.* Hampshire: Palgrave Macmillan, 2013.

Zanfrini, Laura. "Family Migration: Fulfilling the Gap between Law and Social Processes." *Societies* 2, no. 3 (2012): 63–74.

Zhou, Min. *Contemporary Chinese America: Immigration, Ethnicity, and Community Transformation.* Philadelphia: Temple University Press, 2009.

———. "'Parachute Kids' in Southern California: The Educational Experience of Chinese Children in Transnational Families." *Educational Administration Abstracts* 34, no. 2 (1999): 682–704.

———. "Straddling Different Worlds: The Acculturation of Vietnamese Refugee Children." In *Ethnicities: Children of Immigrants in America*, edited by Rubén G. Rumbaut and Alejandro Portes, 187–227. Berkeley: University of California Press, 2001.

Zong, Jie, and Jeanne Batalova. "Indian Immigrants in the United States." Washington, DC: Migration Policy Institute, 2015. www.migrationpolicy.org/article/indian -immigrants-united-states.

Index

Abrams, Kerry, 68
Adam, Paul, 92
American Dream, pursuit of: access to resources, 145; anti-immigrant backlash, 35–37; cultural integration, 26–33; desirability of H-1B visa, 18, 22–26. *See also* permanent residency
Amrute, Sareeta, 28
"anchor babies," 59
anti-immigrant attitudes: family reunification and, 68; return migration and, 96, 100; toward transmigrant childbearing, 59, 60; Trump administration, 21–22, 27, 145–46. *See also* stereotyping; xenophobic attacks
Argod, Vikas, 24
arranged marriages, 54–55, 77
Ascend report, 34
Asian immigration patterns, 27–28, 158n18
Asiatic Barred Zones Act, 27, 68
Association for India's Development (AID), 38, 39, 41

Baas, Michiel, 55
Bailey, Ajay, 152n16
Banerjee, Payal, 19
Bangalore, 15, 106–8, 128
banking reforms in India, 98, 170nn7,8
Bassett, Ross, 138
Batalova, Jeanne, 151n11
bhadramahila, 111, 173n35
Bhartiya Janata Party (BJP), 44, 45, 160n41
Bhattacharayya, Asmita, 78
Biao, Xiang, 25–26, 50, 64
Billingham, Chase, 88–89

birthright citizenship, 59–63, 142
BJP. *See* Bhartiya Janata Party (BJP)
Bledsoe, Caroline, 61
blogs, 92–93
body shoppers, 29–30, 32
Boehm, Deborah A., 7, 162n23
Boeing Company, 13, 155n38
Bracero Program, 150n9
bridge building, 10, 13, 19, 37–43, 142, 144, 159n32. *See also* neoliberalism; volunteering activities
Busse-Cárdenas, Erika, 90
"Buy American, Hire American," 146–47

Canada's immigration policies, 24–25
capitalism, 10, 27–28, 70, 79, 143, 144. *See also* neoliberalism; unpaid labor
capitalist contradiction, 94–95
career advancement: importance of migration to, 3–4, 5, 13, 24, 25, 144; in India, 100–101, 132; stasis in, 33–35, 46
career purgatory, 4, 26. *See also* transnational housewives
caste stratification, 55, 111, 113–14, 116, 118, 138, 155n41
Cattacin, Sandro, 39
Center for Studies of Developing Societies–Konrad Adeneur Stiftung (CSDS-KAS) survey, 54
Chakravartty, Paula, 43
childrearing. *See* family formation; motherhood
children: academic success of, 137–38; social engagement, 104–5. *See also* birthright citizenship; schools in India

GLOBAL
SOUTH
ASIA

Padma Kaimal
K. Sivaramakrishnan
Anand A. Yang
SERIES EDITORS

GLOBAL SOUTH ASIA takes an interdisciplinary approach to the humanities and social sciences in its exploration of how South Asia, through its global influence, is and has been shaping the world.